Color Atlas
of
TURFGRASS DISEASES

Disease Characteristics and Control

Original Japanese Text and Photos

Author

Toshikazu Tani, Ph.D.

Professor Emeritus of Kagawa University
Kagawa, Japan

and

President
Green Environmental Research Foundation of Japan

Ann Arbor Press

CHELSEA • MICHIGAN

© 1997 by Ann Arbor Press and James B Beard

Translated by

Kazuya Akimitsu, Ph.D.

Associate Professor
Plant Pathology Laboratory
Kagawa University
Miki, Kagawa, Japan

Original Japanese Book published by

Soft Science, Inc.

Nishiyama Akasaka Building 4F
15-18, Akasaka 2-chome, Minato-ku
Tokyo, 107 Japan

Production Editor

Harriet J. Beard

Beard Books
College Station, Texas 77840

PRINTED IN CANADA

Color Atlas
of
TURFGRASS
DISEASES

Disease Characteristics and Control

Contributing Author and Editor for the Expanded English Version

James B Beard, Ph.D.

Professor Emeritus of Turfgrass Science
Texas A&M University

and

President
International Sports Turf Institute, Inc.
College Station, Texas

Japanese Preface *for the* English Version

The rationale of disease control involves, first, the correct diagnosis of disease and an understanding of the conditions favoring disease occurrences. Secondly, one must routinely practice cultural programs that are effective in maintaining a minimum level of disease proneness and also to reduce the disease potential of pathogens. The use of fungicides should be a final measure, and implemented only when necessary. In those cases, the appropriate selective and possibly systemic fungicides should be chosen based on the species of causal pathogen. Preventive application of non-selective fungicides prior to disease occurrence is an approach that should be reconsidered for most diseases. These points of view were presented in the Japanese version of the *Color Atlas of Turfgrass Diseases in Golf Courses*, published in 1991, to people who practice turf management.

Exact diagnosis by the symptoms is important in the field where rapid identification of disease is necessary, especially at an early stage of symptom development. Descriptions in the text are supplemented with many photographs of symptoms, not only typical but also those at different stages of disease development under different environmental conditions, to further aid in disease diagnosis. This unique aspect of the Japanese version of the book led to its extensive use in Japan and some other Asian countries.

In 1994, this book received the attention of Dr. James B Beard, Professor Emeritus of Texas A&M University, and Mr. R.A. DeWall, Jr., President of Ann Arbor Press Inc., Chelsea, Michigan, through Mr. S. Yoshida, President of Soft Science, Inc., Tokyo. An agreement was quickly established to supplement the Japanese version with descriptions and photographs of additional diseases and to translate it into English for international use. Diseases found in Japan since 1991 have been included, and materials concerning the added diseases, which are rare in Japan but are important in other countries, have been added through the efforts of Dr. Beard. It is hoped that this English version finds use in many regions internationally.

The author is grateful to Dr. and Mrs. J.B Beard, and to the plant pathologists in the United States who offered valuable photographs for use in this book. Appreciation is given to Dr. K. Akimitsu, Associate Professor of Kagawa University, for his work on the translation. Appreciation also is extended to Mr. S. Yoshida of Soft Science, Inc. and to Mr. R.A. DeWall of Ann Arbor Press, Inc., for their support throughout this project. Acknowledgment is expressed to my Japanese colleagues who kindly provided color photos and/or valuable information. They include Dr's. T. Aoki, T. Araki, M. Elliott, T. Hatta, M. Hyakumachi, T. Ichitani, H. Koga, H. Kunoh, N. Matsumoto, A. Ogose, S. Ohgi, A. Tajimi, M. Tsuda, O. Yamashita, and S. Yamashsita

Toshikazu Tani
May, 1996

Preface *for the* Expanded English Version

The highlight of this book is found in the extensive, quality color photographs of turfgrass diseases produced by Dr. Tani. Unlike most color photos in books that show only one classic appearance of the disease, this *Color Atlas of Turfgrass Diseases* shows multiple stages in the development of each disease including the initial symptoms, the classic symptoms stage, and the advanced stage of dead turf symptoms. In addition, close-ups of shoot lesions are shown as appropriate. The elaborate organization of color photographs in this book is designed to enhance the diagnostic capabilities of practitioners and students interested in the diseases and causal pathogens of turfgrass science.

The original 1991 Japanese edition of the *Color Atlas of Turfgrass Diseases* by Dr. Tani also was unique in its comprehensive, in-depth coverage concerning diseases of warm-season turfgrasses. In contrast, most books on turfgrass diseases have been oriented more to cool-season climatic regions. This book provides a more balanced approach.

Another unique aspect of this book is the color photographs illustrating a number of laboratory diagnostic techniques that can be used in the assessment and identification of the causal pathogen of a turfgrass disease. Included in this approach are actual color photographs of both fungal structures and mycelial mats grown in petri dishes that can be used in the identification of individual causal pathogens.

In view of the extraordinarily comprehensive nature and quality of the color photographs, a decision was made to translate this color atlas into the English language for world-wide readership. In the process of drafting the edited English translation, the text and photographs were expanded to include additional diseases that are not common in Japan, but are major diseases affecting turfgrasses in some other region of the world. Most of the additions were diseases of cool climatic regions.

It is important to indicate that Dr. Tani, author of the original Japanese version, has focused considerable attention on turfgrass cultural practices and curative fungicide approaches to disease management, especially on the patch diseases, which is in contrast to an extensive program of preventive fungicide use. These aspects certainly should be given consideration by readers of the *Color Atlas of Turfgrass Diseases*. Success in using the cultural and curative approaches depends on early diagnosis, which is emphasized in the atlas.

Acknowledgment and appreciation is expressed to key individuals who contributed technical information and color photographs for the diseases and causal pathogens that were added to the expanded English version. They include Dr's. A.H. Bruneau, L. L. Burpee, R.S. Byther, P. F. Colbaugh, P.H. Dernoeden, M.L. Elliott, T.E. Freeman, A.K. Hagan, G.E. Holcomb, R.A. Keen, P.J. Landschoot, N.R. O'Neill, D.L. Roberts, M.C. Shurtleff, J.M. Vargas, Jr., and H.T. Wilkinson. Finally, appreciation is expressed to Harriet Beard for the production of the English text.

James B Beard
May, 1996

Book Format

NOMENCLATURE

Both the common names of diseases and the scientific names of the causal pathogens vary greatly around the world. Unfortunately, there is no international organization that is actively involved in developing a standardized set of names.

One of the first plant pathology organizations to develop a standardized procedure, including documentation by Koch's postulates and subsequent naming of the disease as well as a scientific name of the causal organism, was the Phytopathological Society of Japan. In the United States, a more recent effort in terms of standardization has been made through the American Phytopathological Society publication. Still there are a number of books on turfgrass diseases recently published in the United States that vary considerably in the nomenclature used.

The nomenclature followed in this book is based on officially documented research involving Koch's postulates. This nomenclature generally conforms to the Phytopathological Society of Japan, and is similar to that proposed in the United States, with the exception of species within the *Rhizoctonia* and *Pythium* genera. In the United States these species are included in two general groupings with each under a common name. In Japan, however, individual casual pathogens within the *Rhizoctonia* genus have been identified and documented by Koch's Postulates, and specific names for the causal pathogens at the species level have been subsequently assigned. In addition to the specific common names for diseases caused by different species, names descriptive of the symptoms characterizing the diseases caused by different anastomosis groups and culture types of each species have been used for convenience. Names descriptive of diseases symptoms also have been developed for the Pythium diseases of zoysiagrasses. For the Pythium diseases of cool-season grasses, however, the general common name "Pythium Blight" is proposed, with the exception of Pythium red blight. The nomenclature used in this book for the *Rhizoctonia* and *Pythium* genera is that of the Japenese system.

The description of each disease in the book is organized within six subheadings. The criteria and utilization of the information provided in each of the subsections will now be described.

DISEASE CHARACTERISTICS

Each disease has certain specific symptoms that are important in disease diagnosis. They may include (a) various types, shapes, and colors of leaf lesions, (b) various shapes, sizes, and colors of turf injury, and (c) lateral stem and root necrosis symptoms. These symptoms may change during the chronological development of the disease. Furthermore, the symptoms for a specific disease may vary among the host turfgrass species.

The descriptive characteristics of the individual diseases are of two general types.

I. One is a foliar blighting causal pathogen in which considerable descriptive information is provided as to the individual symptoms that develop on leaves and shoots, and which may eventually form some sort of shape or pattern in the turf.

II. The second grouping involves soil-borne, root-rotting organisms which generally cause symptoms that appear as patches of varying sizes. In the case of these patch diseases, a browning and loss of the root system is typical. Then as a result of water stress the shoots may die, with the symptoms involving desiccation and tanning of individual leaves starting at the leaf tip and progressing downward. These soil-borne, patch diseases may not exhibit distinct foliar leaf lesion symptoms.

ENVIRONMENTAL EFFECTS

Climate, microenvironment, soil physical and chemical conditions, and turfgrass cultural practices affect the severity of each disease. By understanding the environmental conditions under which each disease is most likely to occur, a more timely effort in monitoring the potential development of disease symptoms can be achieved. Also, knowing the environmental conditions under which a disease has developed will aid in correct diagnosis.

CAUSAL PATHOGEN

Description of the causal pathogen, especially in terms of specific colors and types of mycelium growth, spores, or fruiting bodies, can be important in the diagnosis of certain diseases, whereas for other diseases it is not a realistic field approach. An understanding of where and how the causal organism overwinters and how it is disseminated is important in terms of developing turfgrass cultural strategies that will minimize the severity with which a disease may occur.

HOST TURFGRASSES

Most diseases typically have certain major turfgrass hosts, and possibly some minor occasional turfgrass hosts, while for other turfgrass species the disease does not occur at all. During a diagnosis, an assessment of the specific turfgrass species on which the disease occurred or did not occur may aid in diagnosis.

OCCURRENCE DOCUMENTED

A further aid in disease diagnosis is a knowledge of whether a particular disease has in fact been found in the specific country of concern. Accordingly, the particular continents or portions of continents where each disease has been documented as occurring are listed. Please note that this does not imply there are not other countries in which the disease also occurs.

CULTURAL CONTROL

The timing, extent, and severity with which an individual disease occurs can be influenced significantly by the cultural practices being utilized. Water management, plant nutritional levels, and thatch/mat control are particularly important dimensions in the cultural control of diseases. These cultural controls are the first line of defense against a potential disease problem. If the appropriate strategies are followed, they will minimize the amount of pesticide that may be required to ensure proper disease control.

CHEMICAL CONTROL

There are a number of diseases, which under particularly favorable conditions for occurrence of a specific causal pathogen, will result in the necessity for fungicide use. The fungicides and their use are discussed in the chemical control subsection. The fungicide listings are not intended to be all-inclusive. In addition, there are fungicides listed which may be available in one country, but not in others. Seek advice from the appropriate legal governing authorities in your specific country regarding the fungicides which have been officially registered and labeled for use on turfgrasses.

Table *of* Contents

Part III
DISEASES OF COOL-SEASON TURFGRASSES   81

Part IV
DISEASES COMMON TO BOTH WARM- AND COOL-SEASON TURFGRASSES   167

Part V
SIMPLE METHODS FOR DISEASE DIAGNOSIS   197

APPENDIX   227

GLOSSARY OF TERMS   236

INDEX   243

Part I
TURFGRASS DISEASE OVERVIEW

CHAPTER 1

Types *of* Turfgrass Diseases

The causal agents of turfgrass diseases typically are classified as infectious or biotic agents, including the pathogenic organisms (Fig. 1-1). Pathogenic fungi are the major infectious agents of turfgrass diseases. Viruses and mycoplasma-like organisms (MLO) or phytoplasma are other causes of turfgrass diseases, while bacteria are rarely known as causal agents of turfgrass diseases. No diseases caused by viroids have been known for turfgrasses, so far.

About 50 pathogenic fungi are known to be turfgrass pathogens, including more than 20 for zoysiagrasses (*Zoysia* spp.) and another 20 for bentgrasses (*Agrostis* spp.). But only 8 among the 50 pathogenic fungi cause severe damage as the major pathogens on zoysiagrasses and 15 pathogenic fungi on the bentgrasses. (Tables 1-1, 1-2, and 1-3).

Noninfectious or abiotic agents, including physical and chemical disorders (Fig.1-1), can be easily misdiagnosed as infectious diseases by an untrained or inexperienced person. A common symptom on many kinds of turf caused by noninfectious (abiotic) agents is leaf yellowing. Damage to turfs caused by traffic stress, hydrophobic dry spot, and phytotoxic chemicals also are noninfectious problems.

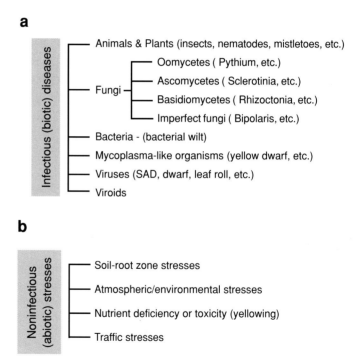

Figure 1-1. Major causal agents of (a) infectious turfgrass diseases and (b) noninfectious stress problems that can be misdiagnosed as diseases.

Table 1-1. Summary Characterizations of the Major Diseases that Occur Primarily on *Warm-Season Turfgrasses*

Disease	Causal pathogen(s)	Location(s) where disease commonly occurs **	Major host turfgrass(es)	Minor host turfgrass(es)
Curvularia leaf blight (dog footprint)	*Curvularia geniculata, C. lunata, C. lunata* var. *aeria,* & *C. verruculosa* *	all turf areas, mainly greens	zoysiagrasses	bermudagrasses
dollar spot	(not clarified)	all turf areas	bermudagrasses	zoysiagrasses, centipedegrass, & St. Augustinegrass
large patch	*Rhizoctonia solani* AG-2-2(LP) *	all turf areas, mainly fairways	St. Augustinegrass & zoysiagrasses	bermudagrasses
Bipolaris leaf blotch	*Bipolaris cynodontis*	all turf areas	bermudagrasses	zoysiagrasses, kikuyugrass, & St. Augustinegrass
Leptosphaeria spring dead spot	*Leptosphaeria korrae* & *Leptosphaeria narmari*	greens, tees, & fairways	bermudagrasses	common carpetgrass, kikuyugrass, St. Augustinegrass, & zoysiagrasses
Pythium spring dead spot	*Pythium graminicola, Pythium vanterpoolii, Microdochium nivale,* & *Fusarium acuminatum* *	greens	manila zoysiagrass	(none known)
Rhizoctonia spring dead spot	binucleate *Rhizoctonia* AG-D(I) *	all turf areas	zoysiagrasses	(none known)
zoysia decline	*Gaeumannomyces graminis* var. *graminis* *	all turf areas	zoysiagrasses & bermudagrasses	(none known)
zoysia rust	*Puccinia zoysia* *	all turf areas, mainly fairways	zoysiagrasses	(none known)

*Koch's postulates successfully completed by Japanese turfgrass research pathologists.

**"all turf areas" includes golf courses, sport fields, and lawns.

Table 1-2. Summary Characterizations of the Major Diseases that Occur Primarily on *Cool-Season Turfgrasses*

Disease	Causal pathogen(s)	Location(s) where disease commonly occurs **	Major host turfgrass(es)	Minor host turfgrass(es) including warm-season turfgrasses
anthracnose	*Colletotrichum graminicola*	greens, tees, & fairways	annual bluegrasses	bentgrasses, fescues, & perennial ryegrass
brown blight	*Drechslera siccans*	all turf areas	ryegrasses	annual ryegrass & tall fescue
dollar spot	(not clarified)	all turf areas	bentgrasses & fine-leaf fescues	bluegrasses & tall fescue
Bipolaris leaf spot	*Bipolaris sorokiniana*	all turf areas	bentgrasses, fine-leaf fescues	annual bluegrasses, ryegrasses, & Kentucky bluegrass
melting-out	*Drechslera poae*	fairways, roughs, sport fields, & lawns	Kentucky bluegrass	other bluegrasses
Microdochium patch (pink snow mold)	*Microdochium nivale*	all turf areas	annual bluegrasses & bentgrasses	fescues, Kentucky bluegrass, rough bluegrass, & ryegrasses
necrotic ring spot	*Leptosphaeria korrae*	fairways, roughs, sport fields, & lawns	Kentucky bluegrass, annual bluegrasses, & rough bluegrass	fine-leaf fescues
net blotch	*Drechslera dictyoides*	fairways, roughs, sport fields & lawns	fescues & perennial ryegrass	Kentucky bluegrass
powdery mildew	*Erysiphe graminis*	fairways, roughs, sport fields, & lawns	Kentucky bluegrass & fine-leaf fescues	bentgrasses & ryegrasses
Pythium blights (I) & (II)	*Pythium graminicola, P. vanterpoolii, P. ultimum, & P. aristosporum* *	all turf areas	bentgrasses & ryegrasses	annual bluegrasses

Table 1-2. Summary Characterizations of the Major Diseases that Occur Primarily on *Cool-Season Turfgrasses* (*continued*)

Disease	Causal pathogen(s)	Location(s) where disease commonly occurs **	Major host turfgrass(es)	Minor host turfgrass(es) including warm-season turfgrasses
Pythium red blight	*Pythium aphanidermatum*	all turf areas	bentgrasses & ryegrasses	bluegrasses & fescues
Pythium snow blight	*Pythium iwayamai* & *Pythium paddicum*	all turf areas	annual bluegrasses & bentgrasses	fine-leaf fescues
red thread	*Laetisaria fuciformis*	fairways, roughs, sport fields, & lawns	fine-leaf fescues & ryegrasses	bentgrasses & bluegrasses
Rhizoctonia brown patch	*Rhizoctonia solani* AG-2-2 (III B) and AG-1	all turf areas	annual bluegrasses, bentgrasses, & perennial ryegrass	fine-leaf fescues, Kentucky bluegrass, & tall fescue
rusts—crown, leaf, stem, & stripe,	*Puccinia coronata, Uromyces dactylidis, P. graminis, P. striiformis,* etc.	fairways, roughs, sport fields, & lawns	bluegrasses & ryegrasses	bentgrasses & fescues
snow scald	*Myriosclerotinia borealis*	all turf areas	bentgrasses, fine-leaf fescues, & ryegrasses	most other cool-season turfgrasses
summer patch	*Magnaporthe poae*	all turf areas	bluegrasses & fine-leaf fescues	creeping bentgrass & perennial ryegrass
take-all patch	*Gaeumannomyces graminis* var. *avenae*	greens; especially new, high-sand ones	bentgrasses	bluegrasses & fescues
Typhula blights (gray snow mold)	*Typhula incarnata* & *Typhula ishikariensis*	all turf areas	annual bluegrasses, bentgrasses, & ryegrasses	fescues & Kentucky bluegrass
yellow patch (winter patch)	binucleate *Rhizoctonia* AG-D(I)*	greens	annual bluegrasses & bentgrasses	Kentucky bluegrass & ryegrasses

*Koch's postulates successfully completed by Japanese turfgrass research pathologists.
**"all turf areas" includes golf courses, sport fields, and lawns.

Table 1-3. Summary Characterizations of the Minor Diseases of Turfgrasses in Most Regions

Disease	Causal pathogen(s)	Location(s) where disease commonly occurs **	Remarks	Host turfgrass(es)
bacterial wilt	*Xanthomonas campestris* pathovar	greens	limited occurrence, but with severe damage	certain vegetatively propagated bentgrass cultivars
bermudagrass decline	*Gaeumannomyces graminis* var. *graminis*	greens	limited occurrence, but with major damage	bermudagrasses & manila zoysiagrass
downy mildew (yellow tuft)	*Sclerophthora macrospora*	tees, fairways, roughs, & lawns	limited occurrence, but with major damage	bentgrasses, bluegrasses, St. Augustinegrass, fescues, perennial ryegrass, & rough bluegrass
fairy rings	*Agaricus campestris, Lepiota sordida, Lycoperdon perlatum, Marasmius oreades, Tricholoma sordidum, etc.*	all turf areas	random-like occurrence, with varying damage	all turfgrasses
Fusarium blight diseases	*Fusarium acuminatum, F. avenaceum, F. oxysporum,* & *F. tricinctum* *	all turf areas	disease occurs, usually with varying damage	bentgrasses, Kentucky bluegrass, fescues, manila zoysiagrass, & ryegrasses
gray leaf spot	*Pyricularia grisea*	tees, fairways, & lawns	disease occurs, usually with varying damage	St. Augustinegrass & perennial ryegrass
irregular Pythium patch	*Pythium graminicola* & *Pythium vanterpoolii* *	greens	disease occurs in discrete spots, with severe damage	manila zoysiagrass
Leptosphaerulina leaf blight	*Leptosphaerulina australis* & *Leptosphaerulina Trifolii*	all turf areas	disease occurs, but with minor damage	bentgrasses, bluegrasses, fescues, & ryegrasses
pink patch	*Limonomyces roseipellis*	greens, tees, fairways, & lawns	limited occurrence, but with severe damage	bentgrasses, fescues, ryegrasses, & bluegrasses
pseudo-Rhizoctonia brown patch***	*Rhizoctonia circinata* var. *circinata* *	greens	disease occurs, but with minor damage	bentgrasses

Table 1-3. Summary Characterizations of the Minor Diseases of Turfgrasses in Most Regions (*continued*)

Disease	Casual pathogen(s)	Location(s) where disease commonly occurs **	Remarks	Host turfgrass(es)
Pythium yellow spot***	*Pythium torulosum**	greens	disease occurs, but with minor damage	bentgrasses
Rhizoctonia patch (elephant footprint)	binucleate *Rhizoctonia* AG-D (II)*	tees, fairways, & roughs	severity of disease depends on the site	zoysiagrasses
slime molds	*Mucilago spongiosa* & *Physarum cinereum*	all turf areas	limited occurrence, but with minor damage	all turfgrasses
stripe smut	*Ustilago striiformis*	fairways, roughs, sport fields, & lawns	disease occurs, with varying damage	Kentucky bluegrass, bentgrasses, & annual bluegrasses
St. Augustine decline (SAD)	Panicum mosaic virus strain-group (CMMV)	roughs & lawns	disease occurs, but with minor damage	St. Augustinegrass centepedegrass
Stripe leaf roll	(not identified)	roughs	disease occurs, but with minor damage	Japanese zoysiagrass
superficial fairy ring	many species	all turf areas	disease occurs, but with minor damage	all turfgrasses
yellow dwarf & white leaf	mycoplasma-like organisms (MLOs) or phytoplasma	greens	disease occurs, but with minor damage	bentgrasses, bermudagrasses, & manila zoysiagrass
zoysia dwarf virus	wheat mottle dwarf virus (WMDV)*	roughs and roadsides	disease occurs, but with minor damage	Japanese zoysiagrass
zoysia mosaic virus	zoysia mosaic virus (ZMV)*	roughs and roadsides	disease occurs, but with minor damage	Japanese zoysiagrass
zoysia Pythium blight	*Pythium periplocum**	greens	limited occurrence, but with severe damage	manila zoysiagrass

*Koch's postulates successfully completed by Japanese turfgrass research pathologists. ***Tentative name.
**"all turf areas" includes golf courses, sport fields, and lawns.

CHAPTER 2

Favorable Conditions *for* Disease Occurrence

The climatic conditions of high humidity and high temperatures are especially suitable to allow the growth of many pathogenic fungi. Some diseases, such as Rhizoctonia brown patch, Pythium diseases, and fairy ring are common and major diseases. But in fact some disease causal pathogens exhibit climatic-regional preferences in terms of the severity of their occurrences.

For example:

- Large patch disease on zoysiagrasses can rarely be seen in some climatic regions.
- Rhizoctonia spring dead spot occurs on zoysiagrasses in temperate areas, but not in subtropical areas that have a warm climate during the winter.
- Pythium red blight occurs in areas with night temperatures above 77°F (25°C) and high humidities in midsummer.
- Most snow molds tend to occur in regions with more than forty days of snow cover.

The intensities of diseases are regulated by climatic and microenvironmental conditions. For example, the severity of large patch disease in the fall may be suppressed by a shortage of rain in early fall, while Pythium red blight tends to occur after intense rains during periods of continuous hot nights.

Factors other than climatic conditions also are important for disease occurrence. The features of disease appearance may be changed depending on soil and drainage differences among turf facilities, and even on each hole of a single golf course. It is not uncommon to see one golf hole with severe damage from large patch disease, while a nearby golf hole has essentially no disease. The severity of Pythium spring dead spot, Pythium red blight, and Pythium blights tend to be affected more by these factors.

Most of the known turfgrass diseases do not occur regularly in the same places of a particular region, and the occurrences of diseases are not easy to predict. The accumulation of knowledge on the environmental and weather conditions associated with the occurrence of disease is most important for disease protection and prevention. The unnecessary use of fungicides, especially repeated preventive treatments, leads to inappropriate management of turfs when these factors are not considered.

CHAPTER 3
Characteristics *of* Turfgrass Diseases

The process of disease development is outlined in Figure 3-1. Note that a simple encounter between plants and microorganisms is not enough to establish disease. Plants are controlled by genetic factors and environmental factors that affect the conditions that render them suitable to serve as the hosts of pathogens, termed **susceptibility**. Microorganisms also must acquire the ability to act as pathogens, termed **pathogenicity**. Disease occurs only when these two coincide.

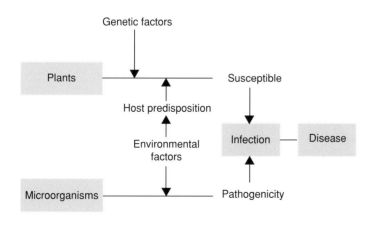

Figure 3-1. Factors that affect the development of disease.

CHARACTERISTICS OF TURFGRASSES

The major turfgrasses grown on golf courses and sports fields are the bermudagrasses (*Cynodon* species) and zoysiagrasses (*Zoysia* species) among the C$_4$, perennial, warm-season turfgrasses; and the bluegrasses (*Poa* species) and perennial ryegrass (*Lolium perenne*) among the C$_3$, perennial, cool-season turfgrasses, plus the bentgrasses (*Agrostis* species) which are used primarily on greens. Winter overseeding with perennial ryegrass and rough bluegrass (*Poa trivialis*) is used to maintain ever-green or winter-green turfs. Centipedegrass (*Eremochloa ophiuroides*) among the warm-season turfgrasses, and fine-leaf fescues (*Festuca* species) among the cool-season turfgrasses also are used to a lesser extent. This book mainly addresses the major diseases that occur on bentgrasses, bermudagrasses, fescues, bluegrasses, ryegrasses, and zoysiagrasses.

Most cultivars of turfgrasses have been mainly derived by natural selection, rather than by genetic breeding programs. Therefore, the disease-resistance genes, particularly the horizontal-resistance genes, may be retained for longer periods than those genes in vegetables or fruit trees. These polygenes of horizontal resistance may contribute stronger resistance similar to that possessed by wild plants. These horizontal resistances often are influenced by various environmental condi-

Table 3-1. Classification of Fungal Pathogens on Turfgrasses Based on Their Life Habits

Parasitism type	Host specificity	Infection site	Pathogen genera
Obligate parasites	high	foliage**	*Erysiphe, Puccinia, Sclerophthora,* * *Urocystis,* & *Ustilago*
Facultative saprophytes	relatively high	roots foliage foliage and roots	*Gaeumannomyces,* * *Leptosphaeria,* * & *Magnaporthe* * *Mastigosporium* & *Pyricularia* *Drechslera* *
Facultative parasites	relatively low	foliage mainly foliage mainly roots	*Laetisaria, Leptosphaerulina, Limonomyces,* & *Myriosclerotinia* *Bipolaris, Colletotrichum,* & *Curvularia* *Fusarium* * & *Microdochium* *
	low	mainly roots	*Pythium,* * *Rhizoctonia,* * *Sclerotinia,* * & *Typhula* *
Obligate saprophytes	none	roots foliage	*Agaricus,* * *Lepiota,* * *Lycoperdon,* * *Marasmius,* * & *Tricholoma* * *Mucilago* & *Physarum*

*Soil inhabitant pathogens.

** Includes leaves, shoots, and lateral stems.

tions. Thus, the practical use of these potentials by appropriate cultural practices can be a key for turfgrass disease control.

CHARACTERISTICS OF PATHOGENS

An understanding of the life habit characteristics for each pathogen is important in decision-making involved in maximizing the cultural control of specific diseases. Fungal pathogens that cause turfgrass diseases are classified depending on their life habits as shown in Table 3-1.

An **obligate parasite** is highly specialized in its parasitism. These pathogens grow and multiply in the field only on live host tissues. The specificity of parasitism is strictly defined at the species-species level, while only smut fungi are less specific. Genetic analyses of rusts and powdery mildews reveal that specificity is well established at the host variety-pathogen race level. The inoculum potential of obligate parasites is high so these pathogens have the ability to attack host tissues with a minimal amount of fungal organs, for example with a single spore. No soil inhabitants are found in this group.

A **facultative saprophyte** is less specific in parasitism as compared with an obligate parasite. In general, the host range of these pathogens is specific at the species-species level, and in certain cases at the host species-pathogen subspecies (variety) or host cultivar-pathogen species levels. These pathogens are able to survive as parasites, but they also are capable of surviving saprophytically by taking nutrients from dead plant tissues, such as thatch. Their inoculum potential to invade host tissues is relatively moderate.

A **facultative parasite** has a wide host range. These pathogens survive mainly saprophytically on plant debris. They attack living plants that are growing under unfavorable cultural conditions. Since their inoculum potential is generally weak, a massing of fungal bodies that have multiplied under conditions favorable to the pathogen is required to invade host tissues.

An **obligate saprophyte** has no ability to attack living plants, but the fungi belonging to this group can cause diseases indirectly. For example, in the case of fairy rings, the pathogens develop hydrophobic mycelial mats around the rhizospheres of grasses which interrupt the soil water supply to the roots that results in water stressed-wilted turfgrasses.

Based on the descriptions in this section plus in Table 3-1, the characteristic behaviors of turfgrass pathogens can be summarized as follows:

1. Most important pathogens are capable of surviving saprophytically; thus, the presence of plant debris in the turf canopy is advantageous to their growth.

2. The inoculum potentials of many major pathogens are relatively moderate to low; thus the pathogens are required to multiply to a certain extent in order to acquire the ability to invade plant tissues.

3. Pathogens causing serious diseases are mostly soil-borne. The aerial transmission or dispersal by rain droplets, such as with Curvularia leaf blight and the rusts, is rather rare. Thus, soil conditions strongly affect the growth of such pathogens.

CHAPTER 4
Fundamental Concepts *in* Disease Control

FUNDAMENTALS OF DISEASE CONTROL

Disease control consists of a complexity of practices (Fig. 4-1). The practices of plant protection include:

a. selection of disease-resistant turfgrass species and/or cultivars.
b. turfgrass breeding.
c. enhancement of plant resistance mechanisms by use of the appropriate cultural practices (cultural control).
d. induction of plant resistance systems by using avirulent strains of pathogens (cross protection).
e. induction and enhancement of resistance mechanisms by using physiologically active compounds (internal treatment).

On the other hand, disease protection by the control of pathogens is achieved by:

a. treatment with chemicals (sterilization).
b. control of pathogens infected into plant tissues (internal treatment).
c. preventing introduction of pathogens to the fields (prevention).
d. control of the populations of pathogens in the field by cultural practices (cultural control).
e. elimination of diseased parts of infected plants (surgical treatment).

f. restricting the increase of a pathogen population by using antagonists of the pathogens (biological control).

Among these methods, cultural management can be the preferred way to control the pathogens of turfgrass diseases. As mentioned before, many pathogens of turfgrass have relatively weak aggressiveness, and the horizontal and polygenic resistances of turfgrasses usually are effective against such

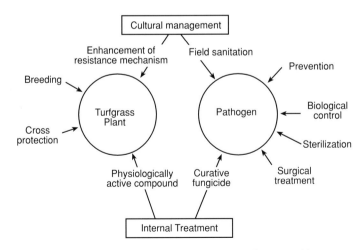

Figure 4-1. Complex interactions of the practices used in disease control.

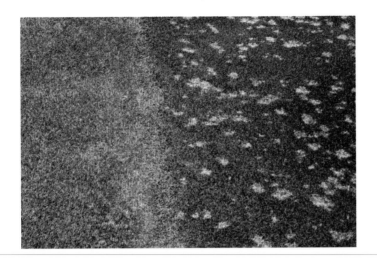

Photo 4-1. Select a cultivar of creeping bentgrass that is resistant to dollar spot: (left) resistant cultivar; (right) susceptible cultivar.

Photo 4-2. Control of Pythium patch in the winter season on a creeping bentgrass green by a plant growth regulator complex: (left) treated and (right) untreated.

pathogens (Photo 4-1). The effective use of resistance genes in a breeding program is considered to be important, but selection of disease resistant cultivars has only succeeded for some diseases, such as dollar spot of bentgrasses, while it is still progressing but not satisfactorily completed for all the major diseases. Biological protection using antagonist agents has been recently reported, but additional data are necessary before becoming a commonly used protection practice. The use of physiologically active compounds isolated from natural sources also is being studied, but this may require more development before being used as a common protection method (Photo 4-2). Sanitary prevention of pathogen transport in the field is very effective for some turfgrass diseases, such as certain patch diseases, but does not work effectively for many other diseases.

CULTURAL CONTROL

There are numerous methods of cultural disease control that are widely used. The combination of methods selected will depend on the conditions on each golf course and even each hole in order to protect them from an outbreak of a particular disease. The following are common practices used for cultural disease management:

Turf cultivation and vertical cutting during the optimal growth periods of turfgrasses. The initial minor injury to turfgrasses caused by turf cultivation and vertical cutting is of minimal significance compared to the long-term resultant benefits such as the activation of defense mechanisms and prevention against the over-growth of turf, and these can be disadvantageous for the infection and increase of pathogen mass (Photo 4-3). Also vertical cutting and turf cultivation control thatch formation in turfs, and therefore putting quality tends to be improved.

Photo 4-3. Turf becomes less prone to stresses and disease proneness is decreased after turf cultivation by coring:
  A: more resistant to traffic stress (*Japanese zoysiagrass; late spring*).
  B: healthy grass plants are scattered within a Pythium blight infected turf (*creeping bentgrass green; early summer*).

Increase the permeability of the root zone and maintain appropriate water-retention capacity. A water-saturated root zone reduces the growth of turfgrass roots, and also increases the population of some pathogenic microorganisms. But if the water-retention capacity is too low, root growth can be reduced by over-drying. Dryness of turf also may reduce the amount of biological agents that are antagonistic to the pathogens.

Appropriate irrigation. The prevention of internal plant water deficits is an important concept of irrigation. Since roots, even those of warm-season grasses, are still active even in periods of dormancy, timely watering through all dry seasons is important (Photos 4-4 and 4-5).

Air movement. Stagnation of air leads to an increase in atmospheric humidity and temperature near the surface of turfs. These conditions are favorable for mycelium growth and infection by pathogens. Proper air movement should be considered in the design stage of a golf course. The installation of mechanical fans can be an alternate way to increase air movement that is beneficial, especially on bentgrass greens with surround designs and plantings that impair air movement.

Remove plant residues, such as thatch. Most pathogens inhabit plant residues saprophytically, including the thatch and mat. The cultural prevention or removal by vertical cutting of the relatively undecomposed organic materials may contribute to a reduction in the inoculum mass of some pathogens. The frequent use of sweepers also may be an effective approach. The use of undecomposed organic root zone amendments is not desired. Physical or chemical improvements in the soil, plus appropriate fertilization (Photo 4-6) and cutting height (Photo 4-7) of the turfgrass are other important cultural practices. But the advantages gained in disease prevention by these cultural practices are not fully understood yet.

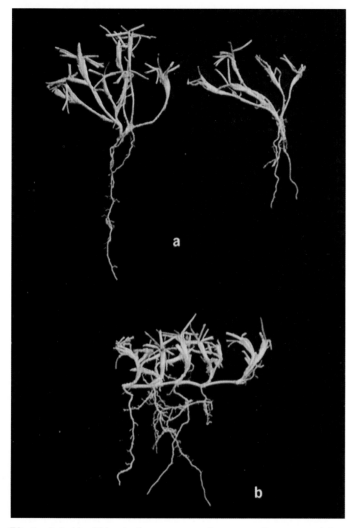

Photo 4-4. Healthier turfgrasses can be grown by appropriate irrigation and turf cultivation. Thatch formation also can be controlled by these treatments:

    a: weak grasses.   **b:** healthier grasses (*manila zoysiagrass green; late summer*).

Photo 4-5. Dryness of the turf-soil is correlated with the severity of Rhizoctonia spring dead spot:

    A: elevated berms tend to become too dry, and the disease often occurs on the site (*zoysiagrass fairway; early spring*).

    B: sites possessing proper moisture (arrow) are much less prone to the disease (*zoysiagrass fairway; early spring*).

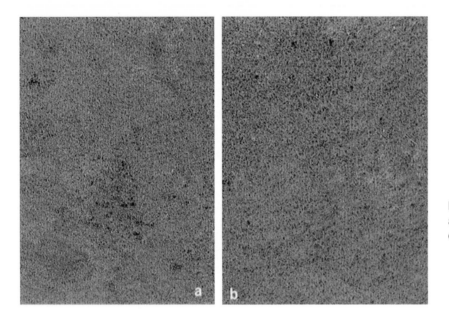

Photo 4-6. Symptoms of Rhizoctonia brown patch in a nutrient deficient turf are reduced by a small amount of nitrogen (N) fertilizer:

a: untreated control.

b: nitrogen (N) fertilizer at 0.2 lb/1,000 ft^2 (0.1 kg/ 100 m^2) was applied in early summer (*creeping bentgrass green; midsummer*).

Photo 4-7. Pythium blight tends to be more severe in areas where the turf has been mowed excessively short: left, higher cut collar and right, putting green cutting height (*creeping bentgrass; late summer*).

CHAPTER 5

Basic Considerations *in the* Selection *and* Use *of* Fungicides

Preventive treatment with fungicides is not necessary for most of the major turf diseases. Spraying of fungicides at the initial stage of disease development may be enough to control the pathogens. Repeated applications of **nonselective or wide-spectrum** fungicides without detailed examination and identification of the diseases or the pathogens is ill advised. Usually, nonselective fungicides need to be applied repeatedly to obtain sufficient effect. Because of the nonselective feature of these chemicals, they disturb the microbial balance in the soil and many beneficial microbes may be killed.

A reduction in the use of nonselective fungicides and the choice of the proper specific pathogen-selective fungicides for curative control of disease are very important not only for the effective control of disease, but also for environmental protection. The following are some important features concerning selection of the proper fungicide(s).

SELECTION OF FUNGICIDES BASED ON EFFECTIVENESS

Fungicidal activity. Use of a fungicide that has anti-fungal activity for control of the causal pathogen at low concentrations is important in order to reduce the amount of chemical needed for disease control. The EC_{50} of the older fungicides previously used frequently was low, at about 5.0 to 10.0 ppm. On the other hand, many of the newer registered fungicides have a very high EC_{50} of 0.1 to 1.0 ppm (Table 5-1). Also, the older fungicides were applied at rates of about 0.9 to 1.35 lb/1,000 ft^2 (200 to 300 g/100 m^2), while the newer ones need rates of only 0.09 to 0.45 lb/1,000 ft^2 (20 to 100 g/100 m^2) to control the diseases.

Selection of fungicides based on residual effectiveness. Many of the newer fungicides have a longer residual effectiveness. Once the population of a pathogen has been reduced to a large extent by an active fungicide, the recovery of that population will take a long time. During this period, the disease does not reappear (Fig. 5-1).

Selection of fungicides based on absorption and translocation into turfgrass tissues. The absorption and translocation of fungicides are important factors in their selection. Many of the older preventive fungicides are neither absorbed nor translocated into tissues, and thus must remain on the surface of the turfgrasses to achieve control. They are termed **nonsystemic** or **contact fungicides.** These fungicides have no effect unless they are applied just before infection by the

Table 5-1. Characteristics of Selected Systemic Fungicides, Each in a Single Formulation, Based on Inhibitory Tests on PDA Plates in Which the Fungicides Were Dissolved or Suspended

Fungicide generic name	Anti-fungal activity (ppm)*			Absorption/ translocation	Mammalian-fish toxicity
	Pythium	*Rhizoctonia*	*Helminthosporium*		
I hymexazol[†]	0.5 - 6.0	< 100	< 100	+	o.s.****/A
metalaxyl	0.4 - 1.2	< 100	< 100	+	o.s./A
propamocarb	2.0 - 12.0	< 100	< 100	+	o.s./A
II flutolanil	< 100 **	< 1.0**	< 100 **	+	o.s./B
mepronil[†]	< 100	0.1	< 100	+	o.s./B
pencycuron[†]	< 100	0.2***	< 100	(+)[††]	o.s./B
III fenarimol	< 100 **	< 100 **	1.0 - 10**	+	o.s./B
IV iprodione	< 100 **	< 3.0**	< 2.0**	(+)[††]	o.s./A
benomyl	< 100 **	< 1.0**	< 1.0**	+	o.s./B
triflumizole[†]	50	1.6	< 0.1	+	o.s./B
tolclofos-methyl	< 100	0.1	0.5	±	o.s./A

*EC_{50} — 50% effective concentration.

** EC_{95} or MIC—minimum inhibitory concentration.

*** Only to *Rhizoctonia solani.*

****o.s. = ordinary substance.

[†] Not registered for turfgrass use in the United States.

[††] Possibly positive.

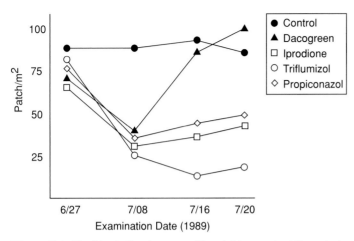

Figure 5-1. Residual effectiveness of fungicides against Curvularia leaf blight on a manila zoysiagrass green.

pathogens, and they also are easily washed off the surface by rain. Multiple applications may be necessary to obtain sufficient disease control because of these reasons.

Most of the fungicides developed recently have been improved on these points, and require a lower quantity of application for satisfactory disease control. This is because many are **systemic fungicides** that are absorbed into the grass plant wherein they provide a sustained, longer period of control compared to the contact fungicides. A list of systemic fungicides and their characteristics is shown in Table 5-1.

SELECTION OF FUNGICIDES BASED ON SAFETY

Selection of fungicides based on low toxicity. Many effective fungicides are categorized for mamalian toxicity as ordi-

nary substances (o.s.), and these fungicides also are rated with a fish toxicity of A or B (Table 5-1). Use of fungicides rated B-s or C for fish toxicity is not necessary.

Selection of fungicides based on selective activity. The selection of fungicides should depend on the kinds of pathogens. The major pathogens can be classified into three groups (Fig. 1-1). The fungicides that are selectively active against one group of pathogens are less effective against other groups of pathogens and also against various saprophytically inhabiting microbes (Fig. 4-1). The use of pathogen specific, selective fungicides is important to protect the beneficial microbes that are naturally present (Photo 5-1). Nonselective, broad spectrum fungicides may kill most microbes, including the antagonistic agents of the pathogens.

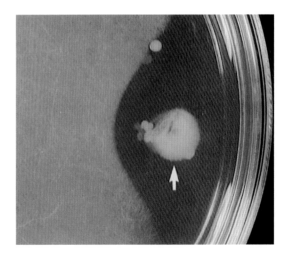

Photo 5-1. Certain microbes (arrow) living on the surface of the turfgrass are antagonistic to the pathogen *Pythium graminicola*, represented by the gray mycelium to the left.

Selection of fungicides based on the rapidity of degradation. Fungicides with higher persistence have a greater chance of spreading unless they are absorbed onto the soil and/or thatch. Rapid decomposition of the compounds after their application is desired to prevent environmental contamination.

The fungicides may be decomposed by ultraviolet rays, hydrolysis, or various microorganisms. The **half-life** of the fungicides, which is the period necessary for half the applied compound to decompose, should be standardized to less than 30 days if applied widely on the turf. With spot applications, however, a fungicide with a half-life as long as 150 days may be used without resulting in efflux of the chemical outside of the golf course.

Residual effectiveness and persistence usually are correlated, but are not to be considered equivalent. Triflumizole has a high residual effectiveness, as previously shown (Fig. 5-1), but the half-life of the compound is 4 to 7 days. In contrast, the half-lives of iprodione and propiconazole are about 30 days and 100 to 150 days, respectively.

Selection of fungicides based on soil adsorption. Most of the registered fungicides used for the control of turfgrass diseases exhibit high adsorption or binding on soils, such as clays and organic matter. Thus, their movement in soil may be limited to a depth of less than 4 inches (100 mm). But if the adsorption ability is less, an intense rain of more than 0.8 inch (20 mm) may have the potential to move the fungicides with the surface runoff water.

The adsorption of fungicides depends on the types of compounds and the dominant soil components. The use of fungicides with a higher adsorption level is recommended. Improving adsorption by adding a soil amendment to the root zone or by including the amendment with the topdressing mix also is beneficial.

Selection of fungicides based on a low volatility. Some fungicides have a high vapor pressure, and easily diffuse to the air. Limited actual data exist regarding the measurement of diffusion of fungicides on turfs, and the potential problem(s) posed is not completely known. But considering the potential of the problem, fungicides with lower vapor pressures should be selected.

Summary. Eight considerations regarding the selection of fungicides have just been described. Satisfactory information is available regarding the first five subjects, but information is lacking concerning the residual effectiveness and for the last three subjects. The complete availability of all necessary data concerning individual fungicides is desired.

CONSIDERATIONS REGARDING THE APPLICATION OF FUNGICIDES

Application of fungicides must be recognized as a last-resort effort to control diseases. A minimal application of fungicides to a limited diseased area at the initial stage of disease development is fundamental. Detection of the initial development of a disease and accurate diagnosis are essential to achieve these principles.

Prevention of the appearances of fungicide-resistant strains of pathogens is the other principle of fungicide application. Repeated applications of a single type of fungicide often lead to the appearances of strains resistant to the fungicide. For example, iprodione which offers superior control of Curvularia leaf blight on manila zoysiagrass greens, has been

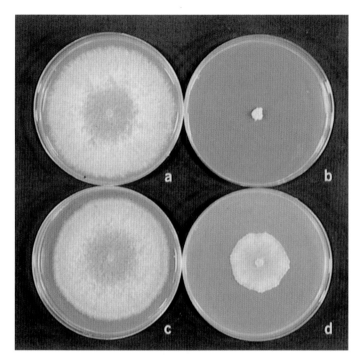

Photo 5-2. The iprodione-resistant strain of the pathogen causing dollar spot is about 10,000 times less sensitive to iprodione than the wild type:

   a.   wild-type strain (untreated control).
   b.   wild-type strain (0.1 ppm iprodione).
   c.   resistant strain (untreated control).
   d.   resistant strain (800 ppm iprodione).

repeatedly used in certain areas for about ten years. As a result, the fungicide is reported to have become less effective in controlling this disease, and at least 3 to 4 applications at 1- to 2-week intervals are necessary now. Over-application of iprodione also leads to the appearances of resistant strains of the dollar spot pathogen (Photo 5-2). The strains resistant to iprodione also are resistant to similar compounds, such as procymidone, vinclozolin, and PCNB (Photo 5-3).

A strain of *Pythium vanterpoolii,* the pathogen causing Pythium blight, that is resistant to metalaxyl also has been reported recently.

Such examples regarding the development of fungicide-resistant strains will increase in number. The reciprocal use of different chemical groups of fungicide compounds is suggested to minimize further development of resistant strains.

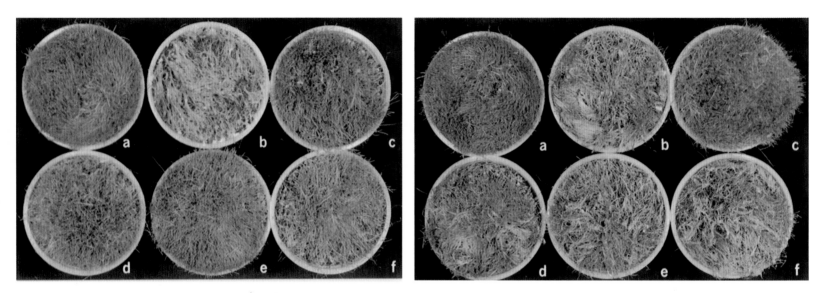

Photo 5-3. The iprodione-resistant strains of the pathogen causing dollar spot also are resistant to other dicarboximide compounds in this creeping bentgrass seedling test: Left side shows the wild-type pathogen, and the right side shows the iprodione-resistant strain of the pathogen.

    a. no treatment, no inoculation, **b.** no treatment, pathogen inoculated, **c.** propiconazole* treated, pathogen inoculated,

    d. vinclozolin treated, pathogen inoculated, **e.** procymidone treated, pathogen inoculated, and **f.** iprodione treated, pathogen inoculated.

*Propiconazole belongs to the demethylation inhibitor (DMI) or sterol inhibitor group, and the other three belong to the dicarboximide group.

CHAPTER 6

Turfgrass Culture *with* Minimal Use *of* Fungicides, *and* Control *of* Environmental Pollution

We have been monitoring the turfgrass cultural practices that have allowed the minimum use of fungicides on golf courses in several locations in Japan. Spot treatment of fungicides was practiced on limited areas during the very initial stage of disease development, except for the control of Rhizoctonia spring dead spot. The results of one example are shown in Figure 6-1. The total quantity of fungicides used in a year was 1/5 to 1/8 the historical average use of fungicides in Japan.

Also analyzed in 1990 were the effluxes of fungicide residues in the runoff water from golf courses. The examinations were repeated after every rainfall or twice in each month. The results showed less than the detection limit (0.2 to 1.0 ppb) of fungicide efflux in all examinations. Golf course management without any fungicide treatment is still not possible, but fortunately turfgrass cultural systems, including disease scouting, proper cultural practices, and judicious fungicide usage, can be practiced without environmental pollution.

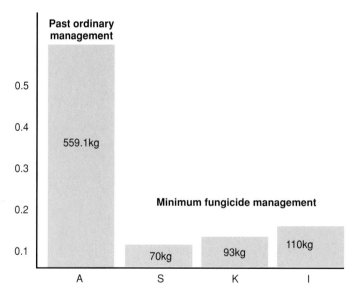

Figure 6-1. The amount of fungicide application on an 18-hole golf course (1989-1990).
  A -   The average of 156 courses in Japan.
  S & K - manila zoysiagrass putting greens.
  I -   manila zoysiagrass and creeping bentgrass putting greens.

Part II
DISEASES OF WARM-SEASON TURFGRASSES

CHAPTER 7
Rhizoctonia Diseases

INTRODUCTION

In many parts of the world, including the United States, the diseases caused by *Rhizoctonia* are included in two principal groups: Rhizoctonia brown patch (*Rhizoctonia solani*) and yellow patch (*Rhizoctonia cerealis*). However, herein are presented three specific Rhizoctonia diseases of C_4, perennial, warm-season turfgrasses as officially named and/or documented in Japan.

The causal pathogens of the *Rhizoctonia* genus attack a broad range of turfgrass species, and can be especially severe on St. Augustinegrass, zoysiagrasses, annual bluegrasses, bentgrasses, and ryegrasses. The *Rhizoctonia* causal pathogens exhibit some species specialization. The symptoms can vary greatly among the Rhizoctonia diseases. Also, the height of cut can affect the resultant symptoms substantially.

Rhizoctonia species are capable of saprophytic growth on plant debris. Infection of turfgrasses occurs primarily through wetted leaf blades and sheaths. Extensive turf damage can occur very rapidly during rainy, humid, hot weather. High to excessive nitrogen (N) fertilization and irrigation are cultural practices that favor severe Rhizoctonia disease development. The *Rhizoctonia* causal pathogens survive unfavorable periods for growth by structures such as bulbils, monilioid cells, and/or thick-walled mycelium in plant debris.

Table 7-1. A Summary of the Rhizoctonia Diseases, Causal Pathogens, and Host Turfgrasses

Common name	*Rhizoctonia* causal pathogen	Major host turfgrasses	Chapter
large patch*	*Rhizoctonia solani* AG-2-2 (LP)	St. Augustinegrass zoysiagrasses	7B
Rhizoctonia patch* (elephant footprint)	binucleate *Rhizoctonia* AG-D (II)	zoysiagrasses	7C
Rhizoctonia spring dead spot*	binucleate *Rhizoctonia* AG-D (I)	zoysiagrasses	7A
pseudo- Rhizoctonia brown patch*†	*Rhizoctonia circinata* var. *circinata*	bentgrasses	17C
Rhizoctonia brown patch	*Rhizoctonia solani* AG-1 &AG-2-2 (III B)	annual bluegrasses bentgrasses perennial ryegrass	17A
yellow patch	binucleate *Rhizoctonia* AG-D (I)	annual bluegrasses bentgrasses	17B

* Japanese descriptive name.

† Tentative name, as it is not yet approved by the Phytopathological Society of Japan.

Note. The Rhizoctonia diseases of C_3, cool-season turfgrasses are discussed in Chapters 17, 17A, 17B, and 17C.

CHAPTER 7A
Rhizoctonia Spring Dead Spot

Disease Characteristics. Rhizoctonia spring dead spot causes brown patches of 12 to 20 inches (300 to 500 mm) in diameter on greens and tees, while more irregularly-shaped patches appear to a great extent on fairways, sport fields, and lawns. Leaves in the patch are uniformly browned and no lesions are formed on the leaves.

Environmental Effects. The disease symptoms typically start to appear during the initial tillering period of the zoysiagrass in early spring when the day temperature rises to 59°F (15°C). Patches do not enlarge in the spring and subsequently disappear in late spring when grass growth becomes more active. Occurrence of the patch symptoms is more pronounced on droughty, sandy soils. Also, Rhizoctonia spring dead spot is more severe under a high nitrogen level and excessive thatch.

Causal Pathogen. Binucleate *Rhizoctonia* AG-D (I).
teleomorph *Ceratobasidium cereale*.
(syn. *Rhizoctonia cerealis*)

Optimum growth of the pathogen is at 73°F (23°C), but infection into turfgrass plants occurs at a lower temperature of around 50° F (10°C). The pathogen survives the winter as mycelium in plant tissues. Local spread is by plant-to-plant contact. Dissemination is by mechanical means such as turf cultivation and vertical cutting.

Host Warm-Season Turfgrasses:
> Major - zoysiagrasses (*Zoysia* species).
> Minor - (none known).

Occurrence Documented: Japan.

Cultural Controls:

1. Timely irrigation should be practiced to avoid plant water stress in the spring.
2. Control excessive thatch when it occurs, as by vertical cutting.
3. Excessive nitrogen (N) fertilization should be avoided in the fall. Apply only sufficient N as needed to sustain moderately low shoot growth.
4. The application of topdressing in the fall may be withheld to reduce this disease, unless the topdressing is very necessary.

Chemical Control. This disease may be successfully controlled by a single application of the appropriate fungicide. A preventive application of a fungicide, such as flutolanil or tolclofos-methyl, in midfall is the most effective control. Fungicide applications in the spring when the patches start appearing have no effect in controlling Rhizoctonia spring dead spot. Note that while pencycuron is effective on large patch, it is not effective on Rhizoctonia spring dead spot.

Note: This pathogen also causes yellow patch on C_3, cool-season turfgrasses, which is addressed in Chapter 17B.

Photo 7A-1. Typical patches of Rhizoctonia spring dead spot on a green of manila zoysiagrass *(midspring)*.

Photo 7A-2. Severe turf damage from coalesced Rhizoctonia spring dead spot patches on the apron of a manila zoysiagrass putting green *(midspring)*.

Photo 7A-3. Severe patches of Rhizoctonia spring dead spot on a fairway of zoysiagrass *(early spring)*.

Photo 7A-4. Severe patches of Rhizoctonia spring dead spot on a primary rough near a bunker *(midspring)*.

Photo 7A-5. Fungicide test A for the control of Rhizoctonia spring dead spot on a tee of manila zoysiagrass in Japan. Fungicide was sprayed twice in midfall:

a: tolclofos-methyl wettable powder (1,000 times dilution, 24.5 gal/1,000 ft^2 or 100 liters/100 m^2).

b: control or untreated area where no fungicide was sprayed.

Other areas: other types of fungicides were sprayed.

Photo was taken in midspring of the next year after the fungicide application.

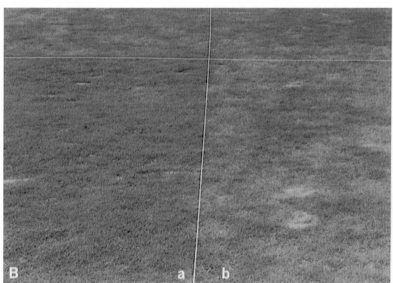

Photo 7A-6. Fungicide test B for the control of Rhizoctonia spring dead spot on a fairway of Japanese zoysiagrass in Japan. Fungicide was sprayed once in midfall:

a: flutolanil + isoprothiolane wettable powder (500 times dilution, 24.5 gal/1,000 ft^2 or 100 liters/100 m^2).

b: control or untreated area where no fungicide was sprayed.

Other areas: other types of fungicide were sprayed.

Photo was taken in midspring of the next year after the fungicide application.

CHAPTER 7B
Large Patch

Disease Characteristics. Small patches of 2 to 3 inches (50 to 75 mm) in diameter appear first, and then develop rapidly to as large as 200 to 400 inches (5 to 10 meters) in diameter within several months. Grasses in the patch turn brown with a light- to reddish-brown fringe. Occasionally, large patches of 40 inches (1 meter) or more in diameter appear suddenly in the spring and fall, probably due to a latent infection during the cold and hot seasons.

Large patch disease usually appears on Japanese zoysiagrass and manila zoysiagrass in fairways, roughs, sport fields, and lawns, and rarely on the more closely mowed tees and putting greens. Severe disease symptoms have appeared on St. Augustinegrass in the fall. Dactylon bermudagrass usually is tolerant to large patch, while there are a few reports of this disease on hybrid bermudagrasses. This disease has not been reported on cool-season turfgrasses, such as the bentgrasses and ryegrasses.

Environmental Effects. Large patch disease development is favored by air temperatures around 68°F (20°C). It usually appears twice a year in early spring and in early fall, coupled with prolonged periods of a moisture-saturated atmosphere associated with rains. Dryness in late summer and early fall substantially reduces the development of large patch in the fall. Wetness caused by poor soil drainage promotes disease severity.

Large patch disease that appears in the spring may develop continuously until early summer, when the symptoms begin to disappear at temperatures above 82°F (28°C). Enlargement of the patches in the fall may continue until turfgrass winter dormancy occurs, and sometimes enlargement begins again the next spring. In cooler areas, such as in the mountains, large patch may be observed continuously from late spring until a period of winter dormancy, while in subtropical areas it may be observed from late fall until mid- to late spring.

Causal Pathogen. *Rhizoctonia solani* AG-2-2 (LP).
teleomorph *Thanatephorus cucumeris*.
Formerly named *Rhizoctonia* AG-2-2(IV).

This pathogen attacks the shoots of grasses. Optimum growth of the pathogen is observed in the range of 77 to 82°F (25 to 28°C), but a rapid increase in the mycelium population occurs at soil temperatures of 50 to 59°F (10 to 15°C), when infection of turfgrasses begins. The fungal mycelium is able to survive either (a) as a saprophyte in the plant residues, such as thatch, or (b) in infected plant tissues, especially in stolons. Local spread is by plant-to-plant contact. Dissemination is by mechanical means, such as turf cultivation and vertical cutting.

Host Warm-Season Turfgrasses:

Major - St. Augustinegrass (*Stenotaphrum secundatum*).
- zoysiagrasses (*Zoysia* species).

Minor - hybrid bermudagrasses (*Cynodon dactylon* x *C. transvaalensis*).

Occurrence Documented: Japan and southern North America.

Cultural Controls:

1. Successful control of large patch disease requires proper sanitary practices during vegetative turfgrass introduction. In many cases, newly introduced turfgrass sods infected with the large patch pathogen serve as the major reservoir of inoculum. Immediate quarantine of the infected turfgrass around the disease symptoms, and disinfection of the infected area by treatment with the appropriate fungicide are necessary.

2. Injury to turfgrasses by vertical cutting during periods when the large patch pathogen is active increases the severity of large patch. Thus, vertical cutting should be completed during high temperatures, usually in early to midsummer, after the activity of the pathogen ceases and while the growth of the turfgrass is very active.

3. Minimize the duration of leaf surface wetness, such as by (a) the removal of dew and exudates in early morning and (b) judicious, timely irrigation.

4. Install a subsurface drainage system on poorly drained soils.

5. Maintain moderate to low nitrogen (N) fertility levels during periods favorable for large patch disease.

Chemical Control. Successful control of large patch depends on early diagnosis, coupled with immediate application of the appropriate fungicide. Effective control can be judged by disappearance of the light- to reddish-brown ring around the perimeter of the patches.

Satisfactory control by curative treatment of large patch diseased areas with a fungicide, such as flutolanil, pencycuron, propiconazole or tolclofos-methyl, is obtained in the spring, but not in the fall. In the fall, however, patches remain until the next spring if the fungicide is applied after disease appearance, because recovery of the turf is weak.

In a situation where large patch disease appears severely over the entire golf course, or sports field, control is best achieved by a program of preventive fungicide applications over the whole area, rather than spot treatments once in the spring and again in the fall. Since this disease appears first in the roughs in the fall, and then on fairways after the next rain, observations of the disease on a rough is an indication that fungicides need to be applied. A granular fungicide, such as flutolanil, is suggested for treatment of a whole golf course, since less time is required for application when compared with aqueous solutions.

Photo 7B-1. Severe damage from typical patches of large patch disease on a fairway of zoysiagrass *(early spring)*.

Photo 7B-2. Coalesced, large patches of large patch disease on a fairway of zoysiagrass *(late fall)*.

Photo 7B-3. Faint symptom of a patch of large patch disease on a fairway of zoysiagrass *(midfall)*.

Photo 7B-4. Unusual appearance of a patch of large patch disease on a fairway of Japanese zoysiagrass *(late spring)*.

Photo 7B-5. Dispersed appearance of a large patch of diseased Japanese zoysiagrass on a fairway. Note reddish-brown color *(midspring)*.

Photo 7B-6. Faint symptoms of a patch of large patch disease on a fairway of zoysiagrass *(midfall)*.

Photo 7B-7. Irregularly-shaped patches of large patch disease around the edge and on a green of manila zoysiagrass *(early fall)*.

Photo 7B-9. Loss of turfgrass on a fairway of Japanese zoysiagrass in the winter, caused by patches of large patch disease that developed the previous fall *(early winter)*.

Photo 7B-8. Patch symptoms of large patch disease during the winter, with patches remaining on the Japanese zoysiagrass during warm weather in the winter:

   A: tee *(midwinter)*.

   B: fairway *(midwinter)*.

Photo 7B-10. A large-sized patch of large patch disease on a primary rough of Japanese zoysiagrass *(early fall)*.

Photo 7B-11. Large-sized patch of large patch disease on a rough of Japanese zoysiagrass. Patches appear earlier on a rough than on a fairway *(early fall)*.

Photo 7B-12. Patches of large patch disease on a putting green of manila zoysiagrass *(midfall)*.

Photo 7B-13. Recovery and loss of turfgrass from large patch disease:

A: satisfactory control by fungicide spot treatment on a fairway of Japanese zoysiagrass in the spring. Patches disappear by recovery of grass in late June. Dotted lines indicate traces of patches *(early summer)*.

B: loss of turf due to development of patches on a fairway of Japanese zoysiagrass in the spring, without early diagnosis and failure to make an immediate application of a fungicide in the fall *(early spring)*.

Photo 7B-14. Double appearance of patches of large patch disease on a fairway of Japanese zoysiagrass, probably caused by inadequate application of a fungicide *(very early summer)*.

Photo 7B-15. Light-brown ring (arrow) at the edge of developing patches of large patch disease on a fairway of Japanese zoysiagrass *(midspring)*.

Photo 7B-16. Reactivation of patches of large patch disease that have persisted through the winter appears as a light-brown ring at the edge of patches in the spring. Active patches (arrow) possess the light-brown ring at the edge of patches, and are easily distinguished from inactive ones *(fairway of Japanese zoysiagrass; midspring)*.

Photo 7B-17. Transplanted sod possessing the causal fungus of large patch becomes the reservoir of inoculum. Patches on a primary rough of Japanese zoysiagrass in midspring spread from infected turfgrass sods (arrow) that were introduced in late winter. Proper sanitary practices to exclude those pathogen carriers is essential *(midspring)*.

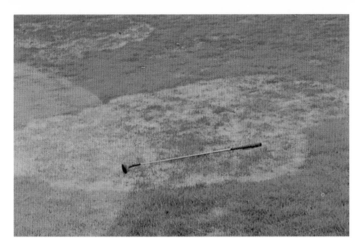

Photo 7B-18. Newly transplanted manila zoysiagrass sods infected with the causal pathogen of large patch disease were transplanted in the summer, with severe, large-sized patches appearing the next spring *(midspring)*.

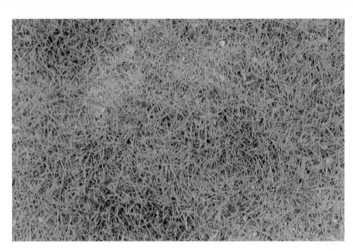

Photo 7B-19. Initial stage of patch development of large patch disease on a resodded rough of manila zoysiagrass. Immediate quarantine of the infected turfgrass at the initial stage, and disinfection by fungicide of soil on the excluded area are essential. Careful observation of symptoms after sodding of the turfgrass is recommended *(midspring)*.

Photo 7B-20. Severe patch of large patch disease on zoysiagrass located around a drain box where the turf is continually wet. Control by a fungicide is not effective in such microenvironments *(late spring)*.

Photo 7B-21. A large patch of large patch disease on a golf course rough of St. Augustinegrass *(late fall in subtropical climate)*.

Photo 7B-22. Patches of large patch disease on a fairway of St. Augustinegrass *(late fall in subtropical area)*:

A: large patches with circular forms.

B: patches with irregular forms. Inside the dotted line is Japanese zoysiagrass which has less severe symptoms than those found on St. Augustinegrass. St. Augustinegrass is more susceptible to this disease.

Photo 7B-23. Soft-rotted and dark-brown symptoms on St. Augustinegrass stems infected with the causal pathogen of large patch disease. *(arrow; late fall.)*

Photo 7B-24. A test of fungicides for the control of large patch disease in Japan. Fungicides were sprayed once at 24.5 gal/1,000 ft² (100 liters/100 m²) on a fairway of Japanese zoysiagrass in midspring, just before the patches appeared:

  a: iprodione wettable powder (1,000 times dilution).

  b: tolclofos-methyl wettable powder (1,000 times dilution).

  c: untreated control.

  d: thiram + chlorothalonil wettable powder (750 times dilution).

Photo was taken two weeks after application (midspring).

Photo 7B-25. The large patch pathogen does not attack bentgrass and bermudagrass:

  A: patch cannot develop into a bentgrass turf at the putting green edge *(late spring)*.

  B: bermudagrass remains free of infection in the center of a patch *(late spring)*.

Photo 7B-26. Preventive test of granular fungicides for the control of large patch disease in Japan:

A: effective application on an 18-hole golf course within 1 to 2 days is possible by using a centrifugal spreader.

B: drift condition by an application of granular fungicide at 3.0 lb/1,000 ft^2 (1.5 kg/100 m^2).

Photo 7B-27. Preventive test for the control of large patch disease in Japan. Application of granular flutolanil + isoprothiolane with a centrifugal spreader at 3.0 lb/1,000 ft^2 (1.5 kg/100 m^2) prevented the disease completely on a Japanese zoysiagrass fairway severely infected during previous season *(late spring)* :

a: untreated control.

b: fungicide treated.

CHAPTER 7C
Rhizoctonia Patch
(Elephant Footprint)

Disease Characteristics. Rhizoctonia patch usually occurs on taller turfgrasses around bunkers or in high-cut roughs, and has been observed frequently on primary roughs and fairways. The disease occasionally is observed on the closely mowed turfs of tees, especially in shaded areas. No occurrence has been observed on closely-mowed putting greens. It is known by the name of elephant footprint in Japan.

The large-sized, pale brown patches reach a diameter of 20 inches (500 mm) or more on turfgrasses in high-cut roughs, lawns, and roadsides. On fairways and sport fields, patches with smaller diameters of about 12 to 20 inches (300 to 500 mm), sometimes with a smoky-ring shape, are observed. Partially infected leaves exhibit ash-colored lesions with dark-brown edges. Fully infected leaves often turn pale brown.

Environmental Effects. Rhizoctonia patch usually appears from very early fall to the onset of turf winter dormancy. On some occasions, this disease occurs in midspring. The optimum temperature for disease development on leaves is between 59 and 68°F (15 and 20°C). The severity is increased by plant water stress, high levels of nitrogen fertilization, and the presence of thatch.

Causal Pathogen. Binucleate *Rhizoctonia* AG-D (II).
perfect stage *Ceratobasidium cereale*.
(syn. *Rhizoctonia cerealis*)

The optimum growth temperature for the pathogen is 77°F (25°C), but the disease usually appears at temperatures between 50 and 68°F (10 and 20°C) on Japanese zoysiagrass and manila zoysiagrass. Survival during periods unfavorable for growth is by bulbils, monilioid cells, and/or thick-walled mycelium in plant debris. Local spread is by plant-to-plant contact. Dissemination of the pathogen is thought to occur by mechanical means such as turf cultivation and vertical cutting.

Host Warm-Season Turfgrasses:

Major - Japanese zoysiagrass (*Zoysia japonica*).

Minor - manila zoysiagrass (*Zoysia matrella*).

Occurrence Documented: Japan.

Cultural Controls:

1. Timely irrigation should be practiced as needed to prevent plant water stress.

2. Control excessive thatch when it occurs, as by vertical cutting.

3. Avoid excessive nitrogen (N) fertilization, especially in the fall.

4. The application of topdressing in the fall may be withheld to reduce this disease, unless very necessary.

Chemical Control. Flutolanil, mepronil, or tolclofos-methyl is effective on Rhizoctonia patch. The fungicide should be applied at the early stage of disease development. Once the disease has developed, the patches are slow to recover because this disease occurs primarily during the fall period of slow growth for warm-season turfgrasses.

Note: No satisfactory cultural control measures have been found for Rhizoctonia patch on high-cut turfs.

Photo 7C-1. Large-sized patches of Rhizoctonia patch on a tall rough of Japanese zoysiagrass with no mowing *(early fall)*.

Photo 7C-2. Medium-sized patches of Rhizoctonia patch. These types of patches were observed on an intermediate rough **(A)** and a fairway **(B)** of zoysiagrasses *(early fall)*.

Photo 7C-3. Small-sized patches of Rhizoctonia patch on a tee of manila zoysiagrass *(midfall)*.

Photo 7C-4. Medium-sized patches of Rhizoctonia patch on a shaded tee of manila zoysiagrass *(midfall)*.

Photo 7C-5. Shapes of patches of Rhizoctonia patch. Many patches are circular forms of 8 to 20 inches (200 to 500 mm) diameter, with a smoky-ring form *(fairway of Japanese zoysiagrass; early fall)*.

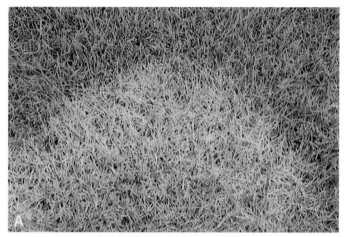

Photo 7C-6. Color of patches of Rhizoctonia patch:

A: a dark-brown ring usually appears around the perimeter of the patch.

B: some patches consist of decolonized symptoms on infected leaves *(fairway of Japanese zoysiagrass; early fall)*.

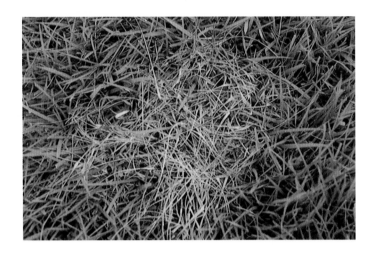

Photo 7C-7. Small patch of Rhizoctonia patch disease observed on a high-cut rough. Some small patches have only decolonized leaves *(Japanese zoysiagrass; early fall)*.

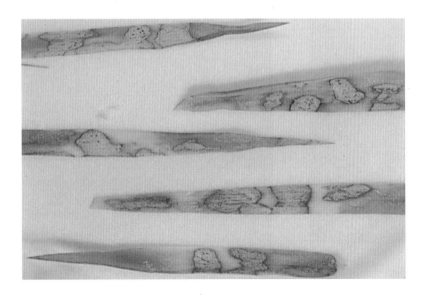

Photo 7C-8. Leaves partially infected with Rhizoctonia patch exhibit ash-colored lesions with dark brown edges *(Japanese zoysiagrass; early fall)*.

CHAPTER 8
Pythium Diseases

INTRODUCTION

In many parts of the world most of the diseases caused by *Pythium* species tend to be called Pythium blight. But herein are discussed three specific Pythium diseases of C_4, warm-season turfgrasses as officially named and recognized in Japan.

The Pythium diseases are feared because of the rapidity with which severe damage can occur, such as in less than one day. All turfgrasses can be attacked by *Pythium* species. Pythium blight is commonly thought to be a disease of humid, hot weather. However, the environmental-seasonal occurrence can vary greatly among the various Pythium diseases.

The causal *Pythium* pathogen is transmitted rapidly by moving water through such structures as mycelium, oospores, and sporangia. The fungus also can spread from leaf-to-leaf by the rapid growth of a cottony mycelium, especially on closely-mowed turfgrasses.

Note: The Pythium diseases of C_3, cool-season turfgrasses are discussed in Chapters 18, 18A, 18B, and 18C, and 18D. Also, Pythium snow blight of C_3, cool-season turfgrasses is discussed in Chapter 23C under the snow mold disease group.

Table 8-1. A Summary of the Pythium Diseases, Causal Pathogens, and Host Turfgrasses

Common name	*Pythium* causal pathogen(s)	Major host turfgrasses	Chapter
Irregular Pythium patch*	*P. graminicola* *P. vanterpoolii*	manila zoysiagrass	8B
Pythium spring dead spot*†	*P. graminicola* *P. vanterpoolii*	manila zoysiagrass	8A
Zoysia Pythium blight*	*P. periplocum*	manila zoysiagrass	8C
Pythium blight (I)*	*P. aristosporum* *P. graminicola* *P. ultimum* *P. vanterpoolii*	bentgrasses ryegrasses	18B
Pythium blight (II)*	*P. graminicola*	bentgrasses ryegrasses	18C
Pythium red blight*	*P. aphanidermatum*	bentgrasses ryegrasses	18A
Pythium yellow spot*††	*P. torulosum*	bentgrasses	18D
Pythium snow blight	*P. iwayamai* *P. paddicum*	annual bluegrasses bentgrasses	23C

* Japanese descriptive name.

† Occurs by double seasonal infection with *Microdochium nivale* and *Fusarium acuminatum*.

†† Tentative name, as it is not yet approved by the Phytopathological Society of Japan.

CHAPTER 8A
Pythium Spring Dead Spot

Disease Characteristics. Pythium spring dead spot is observed primarily on putting greens with certain genotypes of manila zoysiagrass. Once the disease occurs on the green, the patches reappear every year with the same shapes and at the same locations on the green. Patterns of faint dark-brown, caused by the deposition of anthocyanin, are the typical symptoms of this disease in late fall, while light-brown patches start to appear the following spring. Usually there are no leaf lesions. Turfgrasses in the patches gradually turn brown, blight, and sometimes become bare from traffic stress. Turf recovery in the patches can be expected in early summer, but replacement of the turf by sodding often is necessary for those patches that do not show satisfactory turf recovery.

Shapes of the patches vary. Some are circular with diameters of 8 to 12 inches (200 to 300 mm), while others may have irregular, doughnut, or belt shapes. In rare cases, the disease is observed on the apron of putting greens, with the patches usually resembling a divot mark.

Environmental Effects. The dual mechanism for occurrence of this disease is based on the frequency of fungal isolations and control by chemicals. The primary infection by *Fusarium* species occurs onto the grass roots which have reduced physiological activity due to decreasing temperatures in late fall. A second infection by *Pythium* species occurs on the grass tissues because the resistance potential has been decreased by the primary infection. Poor soil drainage favors the occurrence of Pythium spring dead spot.

Causal Pathogens. This disease occurs by double infection in the same location. The multiple infection involves (**a**) *Pythium graminicola* or *Pythium vanterpoolii* in the spring, and (**b**) *Microdochium nivale* or *Fusarium acuminatum* in the fall.

It is called Pythium spring dead spot, because *Pythium* species are frequently isolated from infected leaves of patches in the spring. The disease caused only by *Pythium* species and appearing only in the spring is called irregular Pythium patch.

All of these pathogens attack the roots, lateral stems, and crowns of zosiagrass. All these fungi can cause the disease at 50 to 59°F (10-15°C) in inoculation tests. Both the *Pythium* species and *Fusarium* species survive periods unfavorable for growth in plant debris via oospores and chlamydospores, respectively. Under favorable conditions, these structures produce mycelium which invade plant tissues. Local spread is by plant-to-plant contact. Dissemination is by mechanical means such as mowing, turf cultivation, and vertical cutting.

Host Warm-Season Turfgrasses:

Major - manila zoysiagrass (*Zoysia matrella*), certain genotypes.

Minor - (none known).

Occurrence Documented: Japan.

Cultural Controls:

1. Use a Pythium spring dead spot resistant turfgrass cultivar, if possible.
2. Multiple turf cultivation, as by coring.
3. Control excess thatch when it forms, as by vertical cutting.
4. Avoid the use of compost that is not fully decomposed.
5. Avoid introducing the pathogens into healthy turf areas via infected sod.

Chemical Control. Application of two different types of fungicides in different seasons is essential: one should be effective on *Fusarium* species when applied in fall, such as benomyl, and another should be effective on *Pythium* species when applied in the spring, such as metalaxyl + hymexazol or fosetyl-Al + chloroneb. Targeting applications of these fungicides only to infected turf areas should be sufficient.

Photo 8A-1. Irregular patches of Pythium spring dead spot after the spring grass tillering period. Smaller patches also are scattered around the irregular patch *(manila zoysiagrass putting green; midspring).*

Photo 8A-2. The coalescing of small patches of Pythium spring dead spot results in bigger, irregular patches *(manila zoysiagrass putting green; early spring).*

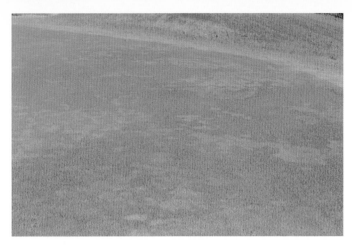

Photo 8A-3. Many small patches of Pythium spring dead spot, plus coalesced small patches showing irregular shapes *(manila zoysiagrass putting green; midspring).*

Photo 8A-4. Small patches of Pythium spring dead spot during the spring grass tillering period. Some patches form a smoky ring *(arrow; manila zoysiagrass putting green; midspring).*

Photo 8A-5. Symptoms of Pythium spring dead spot as they appear after removal of dead leaves inside small patches *(manila zoysiagrass putting green; late spring).*

Photo 8A-6. Patches of Pythium spring dead spot appear as belt shapes from sodding with infected turf after an irrigation system installation. Arrows indicate irregular patches that spread from the infected turfs on a green *(manila zoysiagrass; midspring).*

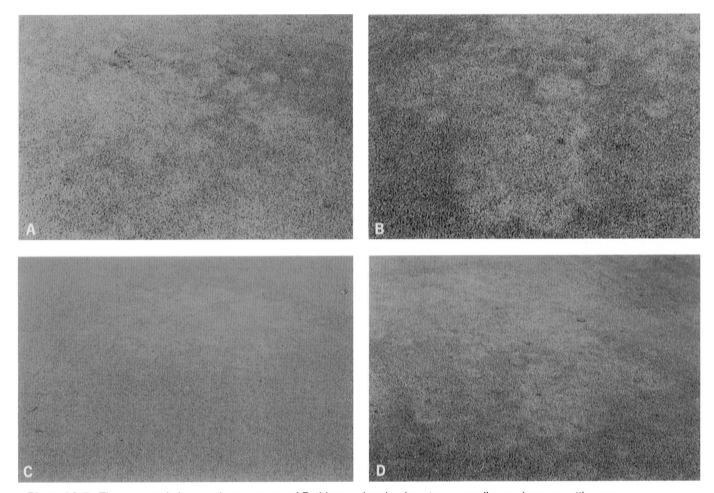

Photo 8A-7. The seasonal changes in symptoms of Pythium spring dead spot on a manila zoysiagrass putting green:

    A: pattern of patches starts to appear before turf dormancy *(midfall)*.

    B: patches reappear when grass tillering begins *(very early spring)*.

    C: color of leaves of healthy turfgrasses surrounding the patches is darker than normal grass *(midspring)*.

    D: development of withering on turfgrass leaves inside the patches *(late spring)*.

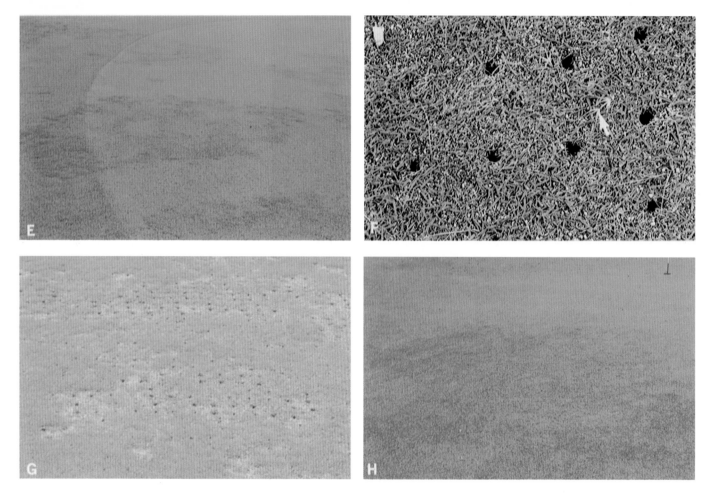

E: failure of natural turf recovery leads to loss of grasses at the sites of withering, and the turf in the patch area becomes thin *(early summer)*.

F: a new lateral stem (arrow) is observed at the site of grass shoot withering, and turf in the patch becomes thin *(early summer)*.

G: severe disease causes a continuous progression of grass shoot withering in early summer, and recovery of the turfgrass is necessary at this point *(early spring)*.

H: recovery of turfgrasses is not expected throughout the year on turf that is severely diseased and not treated *(late fall)*.

Photo 8A-9. Introduction of a Pythium spring dead spot resistant genotype of manila zoysiagrass by sodding can prevent the disease; the newly introduced genotype is inside the white dotted line *(manila zoysiagrass putting green; midspring).*

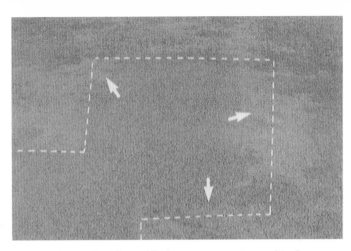

Photo 8A-10. Sodding with the same genotype of turfgrass as the diseased one leads to reappearance of the Pythium spring dead spot disease within 2 to 3 years. Inside the white dotted line: the sodded turfgrass. Arrows: infected areas *(manila zoysiagrass putting green; midspring).*

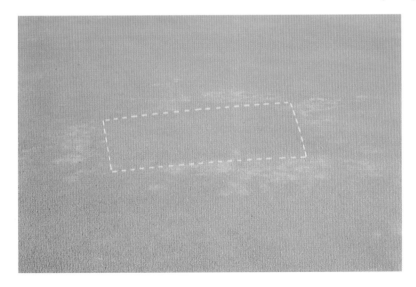

Photo 8A-11. A wide area of damaged turf caused by Pythium spring dead spot around transplanted sod composed of a resistant genotype. The green turf inside the dotted rectangle represents sod of a resistant genotype *(manila zoysiagrass putting green; midspring).*

Photo 8A-12.　Application of fungicides effective on *Pythium* species in early spring can reduce Pythium spring dead spot disease symptoms in Japan, but cannot control this disease completely:

a: thiram + chlorothalonil wettable powder (750 times dilution, 24.5 gal/1,000 ft^2 or 100 liters/100 m^2) applied twice.

b: hymexazol + metalaxyl liquid formulation (750 times dilution, 24.5 gal/1,000 ft^2 or 100 liters/100 m^2) applied twice.

c: untreated control.

(Photo was taken in late spring.)

Photo 8A-13.　Applications of two different types of fungicides provide complete control of Pythium spring dead spot in Japan. One should be applied in the fall for *Fusarium* species, and another in early spring for *Pythium* species.

The second block from front:

Benomyl wettable powder (750 times dilution, 49.0 gal/1,000 ft^2 or 200 liters/ 100 m^2) applied twice in mid- and late fall; hymexazol + metalaxyl liquid formulation (750 times dilution, 24.5 gal/1,000 ft^2 or 100 liters/100 m^2) applied twice in early spring.

Other blocks:

Different combinations of other fungicide treatments.

(Photo was taken in late spring.)

CHAPTER 8B
Irregular Pythium Patch

Disease Characteristics. Irregular Pythium patch is observed only on putting greens with certain genotypes of manila zoysiagrass, which is different from the genotype that is susceptible to Pythium spring dead spot. A reduction in the shoot density and faint browning of the leaves is first observed in limited areas after the spring tillering period. Irregular-shaped patches of 2 to 3 inches (50 to 75 mm) in diameter appear later. The irregular patches have no well-defined borders between the healthy and infected areas. Turf recovery usually starts in midspring, and complete turf recovery can be expected in early summer. Severely diseased areas are slow to recover, and the damaged turf areas may persist as divot mark-like symptoms without browning.

Environmental Effects. Poor soil drainage and an excessive thatch accumulation favor activation of this causal pathogen. These conditions also weaken the host plant tissues and reduce resistance against the invasion of the causal pathogens, especially during the early-spring tillering phase.

Causal Pathogens:

- *Pythium graminicola.*
- *Pythium vanterpoolii.*

These pathogens attack the roots and shoots. Optimum pathogenicity of the former is observed at 50 to 77°F (10-25°C), and for the latter at 50 to 59°F (10-15°C). The causal pathogens survive periods unfavorable for growth as oospores. Under favorable conditions the oospores produce mycelium that infect the root tissues of grasses. Local spread is by plant-to-plant contact. Dissemination is by mechanical means such as mowing, turf cultivation, and vertical cutting.

Host Warm-Season Turfgrass:

    Major - manila zoysiagrass (*Zoysia matrella*), certain genotypes.

    Minor - (none known).

Occurrence Documented: Japan.

Cultural Control:

1. When replanting the infected turfgrass, eliminate the same genotype of turfgrass as the diseased one by fumigation and then replant another resistant genotype or cultivar.

2. Practice multiple turf cultivations, as by coring.

3. Increase shoot carbohydrate reserves by moderate fertilization in the fall.

Chemical Control. One or two applications of a fungicide(s) effective on *Pythium* species, such as hymexazol + metalaxyl or fosetyl-Al + chloroneb, made in late winter just before the spring grass tillering period, are sufficient to control irregular Pythium patch.

Note: These two pathogens also cause Pythium spring dead spot of zoysiagrasses as described in Chapter 8A and Pythium blight (I) of bentgrasses as described in Chapter 18B.

Photo 8B-1. The initial symptoms of irregular Pythium patch. Browning of grasses in irregular shapes begins just after grass tillering starts in the spring *(manila zoysiagrass putting green; early spring)*.

Photo 8B-2. Close-up of patches of irregular Pythium patch. The border between the healthy and infected areas is not well defined *(manila zoysiagrass putting green; early spring)*.

Photo 8B-3. Symptoms of irregular Pythium patch in the late stage. Browning disappears gradually during initiation of turfgrass growth, but damage symptoms persist in appearance similar to divot marks *(manila zoysiagrass putting green; late spring)*.

Photo 8B-4. Cultural control of irregular Pythium patch by reestablishment of turf with another resistant genotype of grass (inside the dotted line) prevents further expansion of the disease *(manila zoysiagrass putting green; late spring).*

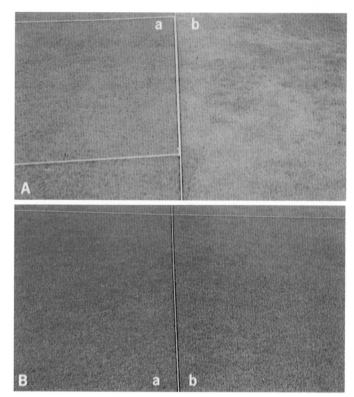

Photo 8B-5. Application of fungicides containing metalaxyl just before a grass tillering period effectively controls irregular Pythium patch in Japan:

A a: hymexazol + metalaxyl liquid formulation (1,000 times dilution, 24.5 gal/1,000 ft² or 100 liters/100 m²; single application).

    b: untreated control.

B a: etridiazole emulsifiable concentrate (1,000 times dilution, 24.5 gal/1,000 ft² or 100 liters/100 m²; four applications).

    b: metalaxyl granular (6.75 lb/1,000 ft² or 3.3 kg/100 m²; single application).

(Photos were taken in midspring.)

CHAPTER 8C
Zoysia Pythium Blight

Disease Characteristics. Pale-green or faint-brown, irregular patches of 20 square feet (~ 2 sq m) with ill-defined borders are the typical symptoms of zoysia Pythium blight. These patches sometimes coalesce with each other to eventually cover large areas of a green. The pathogen causes necrosis on the leaf blades, browning of the infected shoots, and root rot. Turf areas infected with the patches sometimes become bare by traffic stress. Turf recovery usually can be expected in early fall, but the number of lateral stems is reduced and the turf quality becomes poor.

Environmental Effects. Zoysia Pythium blight is most severe at high atmospheric and canopy humidities, and on poorly-drained putting green sites in the hot summer season.

Causal Pathogen. *Pythium periplocum.*

This fungus has weak pathogenicity to turfgrasses, and can only infect weakened turfs under unfavorable growth conditions, such as poor soil drainage. It survives periods unfavorable for growth as oospores in plant debris. Under favorable conditions the oospores produce mycelium which invade the young tissues of grasses. Local spread is by plant-to-plant contact. Dissemination is by mechanical means such as mowing, turf cultivation, and vertical cutting.

Host Warm-Season Turfgrass:

Major - manila zoysiagrass (*Zoysia matrella*).

Minor - (none known).

Occurrence Documented: Japan.

Cultural Control:

Improve soil water drainage by modification of the root zone mix and/or by coring.

Chemical Control. Temporary control by using fungicides effective on *Pythium* species, such as hymexazol + metalaxyl or fosetyl-Al + chloroneb, is possible. But since the major contributing factors for this disease are a high humidity and a poorly drained site, improvement of the root zone drainage is essential.

Photo 8C-1. Irregularly-shaped patches of zoysia Pythium blight on a very humid, poorly drained putting green site (*manila zoysiagrass putting green; midsummer*).

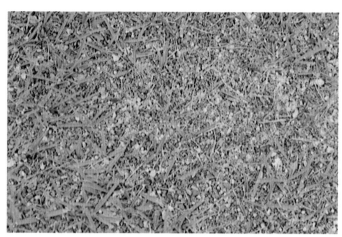

Photo 8C-2. Browning and blighting of infected leaves in a patch caused by zoysia Pythium blight (*manila zoysiagrass putting green; midsummer*).

Photo 8C-3. Turf reestablishment of diseased areas caused by zoysia Pythium blight is not enough to control the disease. The pale-green diseased areas reappear during the next summer (*manila zoysiagrass putting green; midsummer*).

CHAPTER 9
Fusarium Blight

Disease Characteristics. Pale-brown patches of Fusarium blight appear on greens in a circular shape with a diameter of 8 to 20 inches (200 to 500 mm). The leaf lesions are not distinct. The patches may coalesce together to form larger, irregular shapes. Irregular patches of 20 square feet (2 m²) in area may occur on fairways. This disease causes much more severe damage on turfs of a specific manila zoysiagrass genotype than does Rhizoctonia spring dead spot. No occurrence of this disease has been reported on Japanese zoysiagrass.

Environmental Effects. Fusarium blight typically appears in mid- to late fall. Turfed patches exhibiting poor tillering may persist in early to midspring in the infected area after a winter dormancy period. Turf recovery in the patches can be expected in late spring, but slow turf growth persists even after the patches disappear which causes the turf on greens to be inferior in shoot density.

Causal Pathogen. *Fusarium acuminatum.*

A single infection of *Fusarium* species had been thought to cause negligible damage on manila zoysiagrass. However, recent studies indicate that a disease found on a specific manila zoysiagrass genotype is caused by a single infection of *Fusarium* species, with the turf suffering severe damage. *Fusarium* species are isolated at a high frequency from in-fected tissues of manila zoysiagrasses. They are identified as *Fusarium acuminatum* and *Fusarium equiseti*. The pathogenicity of *Fusarium equiseti* is known to be very weak.

The role of *Fusarium* species as a cause of diseases on zoysiagrasses also has been described in the section on Pythium spring dead spot of manila zoysiagrass (Chapter 8A). This disease is caused by a multiple infection with *Fusarium* and *Pythium* species. *Microdochium nivale*, which is one of the pathogens causing Pythium spring dead spot, has not been isolated from infected tissues of this disease.

The *Fusarium acuminatum* pathogen attacks crowns, lateral shoots, and roots of grasses. The optimum temperature range for pathogenicity of *Fusarium acuminatum* is from 50 to 59°F (10 to 15°C), as assessed by inoculation onto zoysiagrass seedlings. The pathogen survives in plant debris as chlamydospores and/or thick-walled mycelium. Local spread is by plant-to-plant contact. Dissemination is by mechanical means such as turf cultivation and vertical cutting.

Host Warm-Season Turfgrass:

Major - manila zoysiagrass (*Zoysia matrella*), one
        genotype.
Minor - (none known).

Occurrence Documented: Japan.

Cultural Controls:

1. Replacement of Fusarium blight infected turfs with a resistant genotype of manila zoysiagrass.
2. Practice appropriate coring and vertical cutting during the active vegetative growth period of the grass.

Chemical Control. An application of a fungicide, such as benomyl or thiophanate-methyl, in midfall should be sufficient to control Fusarium blight on manila zoysiagrass.

Note: Fusarium blight diseases of C_3, cool-season turfgrasses are discussed in detail in Chapter 19.

Photo 9-1. Patches of Fusarium blight on manila zoysiagrass turfs:

A: patches on a putting green *(late fall)*.

B: numerous patches on a putting green *(midspring)*.

C: numerous patches on a fairway *(midspring)*.

Round-shaped, single patches and coalesced patches with irregular shapes are seen in B and C.

Photo 9-2. Close-up of a single patch of Fusarium blight on a fairway of manila zoysiagrass:

A: *(midfall)*.

B: *(early spring)*.

Photo 9-3. The appearance of Fusarium blight disease is different depending on the genotype of manila zoysiagrass. The disease can be controlled by the introduction of resistant genotypes in both the fall and spring:

A: a susceptible (right) and a resistant genotype (left) *(late fall)*.

B: a susceptible (left) and a resistant genotype (right) *(midspring)*.

CHAPTER 10
Zoysia Decline

Disease Characteristics. The diameter of circular patches of zoysia decline ranges from 2 to 20 inches (50 to 500 mm), while coalesced patches will form larger, irregular shapes. The growth of turfgrasses in the patches is poor and this causes severe turf thinning. The typical color of zoysia decline patches is pale green to light-brown, and it is without a defined border between the healthy and the infected areas. The patches gradually turn brown under dry conditions, when a relatively defined border can be observed. The turf area usually does not become bare when attacked by this disease.

Zoysia decline typically occurs on greens, tees, and fairways of manila zoysiagrass.

Environmental Effects. Typical symptoms of zoysia decline appear from mid- to late spring and also from early to late fall, while minor symptoms also may be observed during other periods. This disease is more severe under alkaline, and droughty soil conditions and under excessive thatch accumulations.

Causal Pathogen. *Gaeumannomyces graminis* var. *graminis*.

The pathogen attacks the roots of grasses. The causal pathogen of zoysia decline forms dark-brown to black, ectotrophic runner mycelium on the leaf sheath surface of grasses near the soil surface. The optimum growth temperature of the pathogen is 86°F (30°C), and it does not grow below 59°F (15°C) or above 95°F (35°C). The pathogen survives on grass tissue surfaces and in plant debris around the rhizosphere as mycelial strands. Local spread is by plant-to-plant contact. Dissemination is by mechanical means such as turf cultivation and vertical cutting.

Host Warm-Season Turfgrasses:

Major - manila zoysiagrasses (*Zoysia* matrella).
　　　　- bermudagrasses (*Cynodon* species).

Minor - (none known).

Gaeumannomyces graminis var. *graminis* has strong aggressiveness to attack manila zoysiagrass, but the symptoms of this disease are not as severe as take-all patches of bentgrasses.

Occurrence Documented: Japan.

Cultural Controls:

1. Practice multiple coring and vertical cutting during periods of active turfgrass growth.

2. Control any excessive thatch when it occurs, as by vertical cutting.

3. Proper irrigation is essential, since the severity of zoysia decline is much greater under dry conditions.

4. Use acidifying fertilizers, such as ammonium sulfate and sulfur-coated carriers.

Chemical Control. Benomyl, propiconazole, or thiophanate-methyl is effective in the control of this pathogen. An application of one of these fungicides when the symptoms start to appear is sufficient to control zoysia decline.

Note: This pathogen also causes bermudagrass decline in the United States as described in Chapter 11.

Photo 10-2. Patches of zoysia decline on a manila zoysiagrass tee. The patches turn brown under dry conditions, and the border between healthy and infected areas becomes well defined *(very early summer).*

A: turfgrasses in the patch become uniformly brown.

B: smoky-ringed patches also are observed.

Photo 10-1. Severe coalesced patches of zoysia decline form irregular spots on manila zoysiagrass green *(putting green, early fall).*

Photo 10-3. Severe patches of zoysia decline on a manila zoysiagrass fairway *(midspring)*.

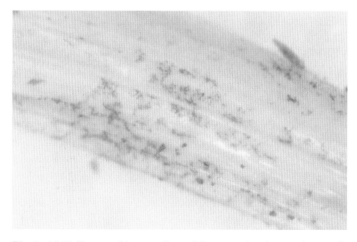

Photo 10-5. Ectotrophic mycelium of the causal pathogen for zoysia decline on the leaf sheath surface. These structures can be observed under a low-power magnifying glass (10x).

Photo 10-4. Patches of zoysia decline on a manila zoysiagrass fairway:

A: numerous appearance of patches *(midwinter)*.

B: close-up of patches *(midwinter)*.

CHAPTER 11
Bermudagrass Decline

Disease Characteristics. The initial symptom of this take-all root rot disease is a yellow patch ranging from 0.5 to 3 feet (0.15 to 1 m) in diameter. There are no visual lesions on the leaves. The lower leaves on a shoot develop yellowing first. The shoots then turn dark-brown, followed by serious thinning of the turf in the patch. Stolons and rhizomes of infected plants also become dark-colored. The roots darken and become thin and shortened. A majority of the roots under the patch are lost. The patches may become bare and coalesce to form larger, irregular-shaped areas.

Environmental Effects. Bermudagrass decline typically appears in late summer through late fall, especially in the southeastern United States. It is most severe during periods with intense rainfall, and most commonly occurs on closely mowed turfs, such as greens.

Causal Pathogen. *Gaeumannomyces graminis* var. *graminis.*

The pathogen attacks the roots of grasses, with black to dark-brown, ectotrophic runner hyphae present on the root surface. Lobed hyphopodia or appressoria can be observed on stolons and rhizomes. Dark-brown to black perithecia may be observed under the lower leaf sheaths. Survival during periods unfavorable for growth is via mycelial colonization of roots and lateral stems. Local spread is by plant-to-plant contact. Dissemination of the pathogen is via infected plant parts by mechanical means such as coring, vertical cutting, sprigging, and sodding.

Host Warm-Season Turfgrasses:

Major - bermudagrasses (*Cynodon* species).
- zoysiagrasses (*Zoysia* species).
- St. Augustinegrass (*Stenotaphrum secundatum*).
Minor - centipedegrass (*Eremochloa ophiuroides*).

Occurrence Documented: Southern United States.

Cultural Controls:

1. Enhance root growth by means of moderate nitrogen (N) fertilization and high potassium (K) levels.
2. Raise the height of cut, if possible.
3. Maintain a positive plant water balance via appropriate irrigation.
4. No bermudagrass decline resistant turfgrass cultivars are known.

Chemical Control. No fungicides have been demonstrated to be useful as preventive or curative treatments.

Note: This pathogen also causes zoysia decline in Japan as described in Chapter 10.

Photo 11-1. Close view of the initial patch symptoms of bermudagrass decline on a Tifgreen hybrid bermudagrass putting green *(Courtesy of Dr. Monica L. Elliott).*

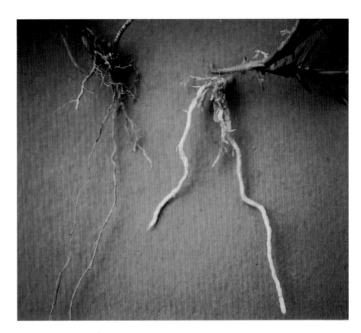

Photo 11-3. Healthy roots (right) and thin, brown roots of Tifgreen hybrid bermudagrass infected with *Gaeumannomyces graminis* var. *graminis* (left) *(Courtesy of Dr. Monica L. Elliott).*

Photo 11-2. Advanced irregular-shaped patch symptoms of bermudagrass decline on a Tifgreen hybrid bermudagrass putting green *(Courtesy of Dr. Monica L. Elliott).*

CHAPTER 12
Leptosphaeria Spring Dead Spot

Disease Characteristics. Leptosphaeria spring dead spot causes sunken, circular patches of straw-colored, dead grass ranging from 1 to 40 inches (25 to 1,000 mm) in diameter. The disease appears when the winter-dormant grass initiates new spring shoot growth. The roots and lateral stems become brown and rotted. Also, patches may coalesce to form irregular-shaped patches. It typically occurs on turfs that are more than two years old. The patches tend to reoccur annually and expand in the same spots for three or more years. The grass in the center of patches may start to regrow, resulting in a ring symptom.

Environmental Effects. Patches caused by Leptosphaeria spring dead spot typically appear in early to midspring at the time of initial grass tillering, and the turf partially recovers in late spring. The patch symptoms usually do not appear in the fall. Leptosphaeria spring dead spot is most severe in the cooler portions of the bermudagrass adaptation range. The colder and longer that low temperatures persist, the greater the disease damage. This is because death of the turfgrass in the winter is caused by low temperature kill in patchy areas where the grass has been weakened by the causal pathogen during the previous growing season. The disease tends to cause more damage on intensively managed turfs.

Causal Pathogens:
- *Leptosphaeria korrae.*
- *Leptosphaeria narmari.*

These pathogens are considered to be the principal causal pathogens in the United States and Australia, but the species in Japan is unclear.

In the United States, two additional pathogens have been associated with a spring dead spot type disease. They are *Ophiosphaerella herpotricha*, and *Gaeumannomyces graminis* var. *graminis*.

The pathogens have ectotrophic, runner hyphae and attack primarily the roots, stolons, and rhizomes of grasses. Infection of the fungi into host tissues begins in midfall. The optimum growth temperature of *Leptosphaeria korrae* is in the range of 77°F (25°C), while *Leptosphaeria narmari* is in the range of 50 to 68°F (10 to 20°C). Sclerotia and pseudothecia develop on roots, lateral stems, and lower leaf sheaths. Survival under unfavorable conditions is by ectotrophic hyphae, sclerotia, and pseudothecia on lateral stems and roots. Local spread is by plant-to-plant contact. Dissemination is by mechanical means, such as turf cultivation and vertical cuttings.

Host Warm-Season Turfgrasses:

Major - bermudagrasses (*Cynodon* species).

Minor - common carpetgrass (*Axonopus compressus*).
- kikuyugrass (*Pennisetum clandestinum*).
- St. Augustinegrass (*Stenotaphrum secundatum*).
- zoysiagrasses (*Zoysia* species).

Occurrence Documented: Australia, Japan, and southern United States.

Cultural Controls:

1. Avoid excessive shoot growth of the turfgrass.
2. Practice moderate nitrogen (N) fertilization, especially in mid- to late summer.
3. Remove any excess thatch when it occurs, as by vertical cutting.

Chemical Control. The fall application of a systemic fungicide, such as benomyl or thiophanate-methyl, is important. Apply to those turf areas that had the disease in previous years. Application to the entire turf area may not be necessary.

This disease may be mistaken for Rhizoctonia spring dead spot or large patch, and fungicides effective against Rhizoctonia are applied. But most of these fungicides are not effective in controlling Leptosphaeria spring dead spot.

Photo 12-2. A single patch of Leptosphaeria spring dead spot in a semi-winter dormant hybrid bermudagrass turf.

(Courtesy of Dr. Ray A. Keen.)

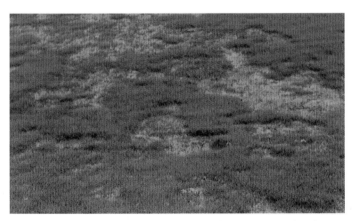

Photo 12-1. Typical patches of Leptosphaeria spring dead spot. They resemble large patch disease, but unlike large patch, these patches do not develop to a larger size and also do not appear in the fall *(hybrid bermudagrass fairway; midspring).*

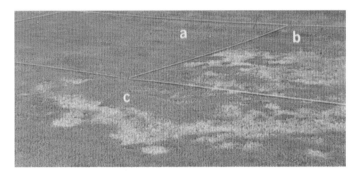

Photo 12-3. Fungicide test for the control of Leptosphaeria spring dead spot in Japan:

a: benomyl wettable powder (750 times dilution, 24.5 gal/1,000 ft^2 or 100 liters/100 m^2) applied twice in midfall.

b: flutolanil wettable powder 50 (750 times dilution, 24.5 gal/1,000 ft^2 or 100 liters/100 m^2) applied twice in midfall.

c: untreated control.

(Photo was taken in midspring.)

CHAPTER 13
Curvularia Leaf Blight *(Dog Footprint)*

Disease Characteristics. The typical symptoms of Curvularia leaf blight or leaf spot are brown, circular patches with a diameter of 2 to 8 inches (50 to 200 mm). Subsequently, irregular-shaped patches may appear due to coalescing of small patches. The patches usually appear in late fall, with a dark-brown color, that may become bare from traffic stress. It is known by the name of dog footprint in Japan.

Environmental Effects. Curvularia leaf blight patches usually appear sporadically on manila zoysiagrass greens in early spring, and spread extensively from very late spring to early summer. The disease then declines, but typically starts to reappear again in late summer to early fall. The disease develops most commonly at temperatures of 68 to 86°F (20 to 30°C). It spreads more severely after a rain, and a rainy year usually is characterized by increased occurrence of the disease. Curvularia leaf blight tends to occur on sites with poor drainage and on turfgrasses that have been weakened by temperature stress or nematodes.

Causal Pathogens:
- *Curvularia geniculata.*
- *Curvularia lunata.*
- *Curvularia lunata* var. *aeria.*
- *Curvularia verruculosa.*

Besides these four fungi, one or more mycelia sterilia fungi also seem to be pathogenic, but the details are not well defined as yet. The *Curvularia* pathogen also occurs in disease complexes with other pathogens, which may cause confusion in diagnosis.

These pathogens attack the leaves of grasses. The optimum growth temperature of the pathogenic *Curvularia* species is 82°F (28°C). They survive unfavorable growth periods saprophytically by mycelium on plant debris and thatch. Large quantities of conidia are formed during the saprophytic survival phase. Cuticular infection by the conidia tends to be associated with rain. Dissemination is by rain and by mechanical means such as mowing, turf cultivation, and vertical cutting. They also may be seed-borne.

Host Warm-Season Turfgrasses:

   Major - zoysiagrasses (*Zoysia* species).

   Minor - bermudagrasses (*Cynodon* species).

Occurrence Documented: Japan.

Cultural Controls:

1. Reduce the inoculum source by removal of excess thatch, as by vertical cutting.
2. Provide proper root zone drainage.
3. Avoid plant water stress by timely irrigation.
4. Avoid excessive nitrogen (N) fertilization that forces lush shoot growth.

5. Use acidifying fertilizers, such as ammonium sulfate and sulfur-coated carriers.

6. Avoid unnecessarily close mowing, if possible.

Chemical Control. At the initial development stage of Curvularia leaf blight, spot treatment with a fungicide on the patch areas is effective. Preventive application of a fungicide on the entire turf area is the best approach before a rainy, warm period in late spring and a longer rainy period in early fall. Repeated applications of a single group of fungicides must be avoided. Alternate the use of iprodione, iminoctadine triacetate, and a demethylation inhibitor (DMI) fungicide, such as triflumizole or fenarimol, every 1 to 2 months is effective.

Note: Certain *Curvularia* species may cause diseases on C_3, cool-season turfgrasses, and frequently occur in a complex with other diseases.

Photo 13-2. Close-up of Curvularia leaf blight patches *(manila zoysiagrass putting green; late spring)*.

Photo 13-1. Severe patches of Curvularia leaf blight that occurred during a rainy season *(manila zoysiagrass putting green; late spring)*.

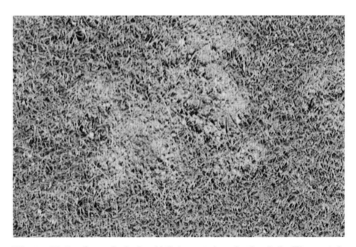

Photo 13-3. Curvularia leaf blight patches in the fall. The patch area becomes bare, and persists in appearance similar to a divot mark *(manila zoysiagrass putting green; midfall)*.

Photo 13-4. Curvularia leaf blight patches just before the turfgrass winter-dormancy period. The patches become dark-brown *(manila zoysiagrass putting green; late fall).*

Photo 13-5. Numerous Curvularia leaf blight patches on a fairway characterized by poor soil drainage *(manila zoysiagrass; very early summer).*

Photo 13-6. Curvularia leaf blight patches on a fairway of bermudagrass *(early summer).*

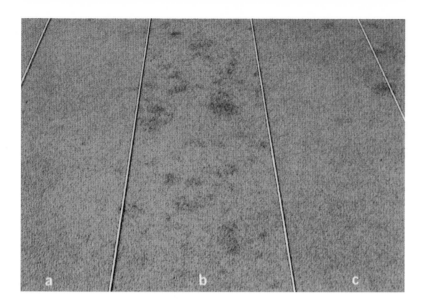

Photo 13-7. A fungicide test for the control of Curvularia leaf blight in Japan:

a: iprodione wettable powder (1,000 times dilution, 24.5 gal/1,000 ft² or 100 liters/100 m²), two applications.

b: untreated control.

c: iprodione wettable powder (1,500 times dilution, 24.5 gal/1,000 ft² or 100 liters/100 m²), two applications.

(Photo was taken two weeks after second application.)

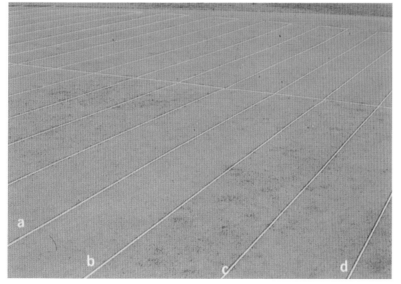

Photo 13-8. A fungicide test for the control of Curvularia leaf blight in Japan:

Fungicide applied once to all blocks in the front row, and twice to the rear row. Some fungicides are effective enough with a single application:

a: triflumizole wettable powder (1,000 times dilution, 24.5 gal/1,000 ft² or 100 liters/100 m²).

b: guazatine liquid formulation 25 (1,000 times dilution, 24.5 gal/1,000 ft² or 100 liters/100 m²).

c: benomyl wettable powder (1,000 times dilution, 24.5 gal/1,000 ft² or 100 liters/100 m²).

d: iprodione wettable powder (1,000 times dilution, 24.5 gal/1,000 ft² or 100 liters/100 m²).

(Photo was taken two weeks after second application.)

CHAPTER 14
Dollar Spot

Disease Characteristics. The typical dollar spot symptoms on a closely mowed turf are small, circular, sunken, straw-colored patches of 1 to 2 inches (25 to 50 mm) in diameter. With severe attacks, the individual spots may coalesce to form larger, irregular-shaped patches. A grayish to white, cobweb-like growth of fungal mycelium may be visible in early morning over newly formed spots on the upper leaf blades that are wetted by dew and/or leaf exudates.

Lesions may be seen on infected leaves. They initially appear as small chlorotic spots, that become water-soaked and then turn a bleached-whitish color. Typically the lesion has a reddish-brown to tan margin and will enlarge across the full width of the leaf blade. Also, multiple lesions may occur on individual blades which cause blighting of the entire leaf.

Environmental Effects. Dollar spot development is favored by temperatures between 59 and 86°F (15-30°C), plus a continuous, high humidity within the turf canopy. Conditions of warm days and cool nights, plus intense dews, are especially favorable for dollar spot. Low nitrogen nutritional levels and dry soil conditions favor severe disease development. Close mowing results in a dense leaf blade canopy that facilitates the growth of mycelium across the cut leaf-tip wounds, especially when nocturnal leaf exudation occurs.

Causal Pathogen. Not clarified, thus will continue to use the name *Sclerotinia homoeocarpa*.

This pathogen attacks the shoots of grasses. It does not form sclerotia, while stromata are formed occasionally. The causal pathogen survives unfavorable growth periods as mycelium in infected plants, and for some species as stromata on the leaf surface. Dissemination is via infected leaves and leaf debris by mechanical means such as movement on equipment, animals, people, and water.

Host Warm-Season Turfgrasses:

Major - bermudagrasses (*Cynodon* species).

Minor - zoysiagrasses (*Zoysia* species).
- bahiagrass (*Paspalum notatum*).
- centipedegrass (*Eremochloa ophiuroides*).
- St. Augustinegrass (*Stenotaphrum secundatum*).

Occurrence Documented: Australasia, Japan, and United States.

Cultural Controls:

1. Avoid nitrogen stress by maintaining an adequate nitrogen (N) nutritional level that sustains a moderate shoot growth rate.

2. Remove dew and exudate from the leaves in early morning, especially on closely mowed turfs.

3. Avoid plant water stress through irrigation as needed.

4. Raise the height of cut, if possible.

5. Select turfgrass cultivars that are less susceptible to dollar spot.

Chemical Control. Severe dollar spot attacks can be controlled by many contact-nonsystemic and by systemic fungicides, such as fenarimol, propiconazole, triadimefon, and vinclozolin. Other fungicides for which tolerant strains have developed include anilazine, the benzimidazoles, and iprodione. Suppression of mild dollar spot infections has been achieved with certain composted organic materials.

Note: Dollar spot of C_3, cool-season turfgrasses is discussed in Chapter 26.

Photo 14-1. Patches of dollar spot on a manila zoysiagrass tee *(midfall)*.

Photo 14-2. Patches of dollar spot on a Japanese zoysiagrass fairway. Dollar spot with light-brown and dark-brown spots of Curvularia leaf blight intermixed *(midfall)*.

Photo 14-3. Patches of dollar spot on a hybrid bermudagrass tee *(midfall)*.

Photo 14-4. Patch of dollar spot on a Japanese zoysiagrass turf *(Courtesy of Dr. Malcolm C. Shurtleff)*.

CHAPTER 15
Zoysia Rust

Disease Characteristics. The initial symptoms of zoysia rust appear as pale-green flecks on the leaves, that develop to orange- to yellow-colored pustules. Damage to the turf usually is limited, because the pathogen only forms uredinia on the surface of leaves without killing the grass plants. However, once severe disease occurs, it can not be ignored since orange-colored urediniospores from these uredinia stain shoes and clothes of individuals walking on the zoysia rust infected turf areas.

Environmental Effects. Zoysia rust typically appears in mid- to late spring, and also in early to midfall. Areas characterized by frequent fogs and/or a high atmospheric humidity are especially favorable for severe rust development, as are turfs in shaded sites with extended dew persistence.

Causal Pathogen. *Puccinia zoysiae* .

This pathogen attacks the leaves and shoots of grasses. The rust pathogen of zoysiagrasses is pathogenic only to *Zoysia* species, and does not infect other warm-season and cool-season turfgrasses. Theoretically, parasitism of the rust fungus on zoysiagrasses should be specific at the race-turf cultivar level, as is the case for other rust fungi. However, no genetic analysis has been made for this pathogen.

Successful infection of this fungus requires a saturated atmospheric humidity at its optimum growth temperature of 59 to 68°F (15 to 20°C). The fungus does not grow under 50°F (10°C) or above 82°F (28°C). Penetration of urediniospores is by growth of germ tubes through open stomata. The rust fungi are obligate parasites, and thus can grow and multiply only in living tissues. The rust pathogen survives in the host tissue during midsummer in shaded areas under trees, and as mycelium and urediniospores during the winter season in sunny sites. The urediniospores usually are wind disseminated to other grass leaves, but also may be disseminated by mechanical means.

Host Warm-Season Turfgrasses:

> Major - zoysiagrasses (*Zoysia* species).
>
> Minor - (none known).

Occurrence Documented: Japan, southern Asia, and southern North America.

Cultural Controls:

1. Maintain an adequate nitrogen (N) nutritional level that sustains a moderate shoot growth rate, but avoid excessive applications of nitrogen fertilizers.

2. Avoid excessively close mowing heights, if possible.

3. Reduce any excessive thatch depth when it forms, as by vertical cutting.

4. Schedule irrigations to minimize the time moisture remains on the leaf surface.

5. Irrigate judiciously.

Chemical Control. Several fungicides are very effective in controlling zoysia rust, such as carboxin, mancozeb, propiconazole, or triadimefon. The application of a fungicide over a wide area when urediniospores are produced abundantly and symptoms start to develop on the turf is sufficient to control this disease.

Note: Rust diseases of C_3, cool-season turfgrasses are discussed in Chapter 30.

Photo 15-1. Severe appearance of zoysia rust on a manila zoysiagrass putting green. Note the many red-brown urediniospores formed *(midfall)*.

Photo 15-2. Close-up of urediniosori with urediniospores of zoysia rust on the leaves of Japanese zoysiagrass *(midfall)*.

CHAPTER 16
Bipolaris Leaf Blotch

Disease Characteristics. Bipolaris leaf blotch is one of the Drechslera/Bipolaris diseases. Initial symptoms of leaf blotch are small, irregular-shaped, olive-green blotches on the leaves. The blotches enlarge, and turn black in color. With a severe infection the leaves wither and become light-tan, followed by crown and root rots. This death of individual plants may occur in irregular-shaped patches of up to 3 feet (1 m).

Environmental Effects. Typically infection occurs during cool, wet weather of the fall through spring. The crown and root rot phases usually occur during the summer period under warm, dry weather.

Causal Pathogen. *Bipolaris cynodontis.*
  teleomorph *Cochliobolus cynodontis.*
  Formerly named *Helminthosporium cynodontis* Marignoni.

  The pathogen attacks the shoots, lateral stems, and roots of grasses. It survives unfavorable periods as dormant mycelium in infected live plant tissue and saprophytically in dead tissue, such as thatch and mat. Dissemination is by spores via wind, water, machines, and animals.

Host Warm-Season Turfgrasses:

  Major - bermudagrasses (*Cynodon* species).

  Minor - zoysiagrasses (*Zoysia* species).

  - kikuyugrass (*Pennisetum clandestinum*).
  - St. Augustinegrass (*Stenotaphrum secundatum*).

Occurrence Documented: Africa, India, Middle East, southern North America, South America, and southern Europe.

Cultural Controls:

1. Use a Bipolaris leaf blotch resistant turfgrass cultivar, e.g., Ormond, Tifgreen, or Texturf 10.

2. Maintain an adequate nitrogen (N) nutritional level that sustains moderate shoot growth, especially in early fall and early spring.

3. Ensure adequate phosphorus (P) and potassium (K) levels, based on an annual chemical soil test.

4. Schedule irrigations so free water remains on the leaves as short a time as possible.

5. Raise the height of cut, if possible.

6. Remove excess thatch as it occurs, as by vertical cutting.

Chemical Control. For best fungicide control apply on a preventive basis before the disease occurs. Systemic local-penetrant fungicides, such as iprodione or vinclozolin, should be applied at a 2- to 3-week interval; while nonsystemic contact fungicides, such as maneb, should be applied every 7 to 10 days.

Zonate leaf spot caused by *Drechslera gigantea* is another Drechslera/Bipolaris disease that attacks bermudagrasses, and also less commonly the zoysiagrasses and bentgrasses, but usually is of limited significance.

Note: The Drechslera/Bipolaris diseases of C_3 cool-season turfgrasses are discussed in Chapters 28, 28A, 28B, 28C, and 28D.

Photo 16-2. Irregular-shaped blotch lesions of Bipolaris leaf blotch on the leaf of dactylon bermudagrass *(Courtesy of Dr. Austin K. Hagan).*

Photo 16-1. Lesions of Bipolaris leaf blotch on leaves of a dactylon bermudagrass lateral shoot *(Courtesy of Dr. T.E. Freeman).*

Photo 16-3. An irregular-shaped patch of thinned turf in a dactylon bermudagrass caused by Bipolaris leaf blotch *(Courtesy of Dr. Phillip F. Colbaugh).*

Photo 16-4. Severe damage to a dactylon bermudagrass turf caused by Bipolaris leaf blotch. The lower, older canopy exhibits the injury, with young, healthy shoots developing above *(Courtesy of Dr. Phillip F. Colbaugh).*

Photo 16-5. Initial small, irregular-shaped patches of Bipolaris leaf blotch on a hybrid bermudagrass putting green *(Courtesy of Dr. Monica L. Elliott).*

DISEASES OF COOL-SEASON TURFGRASSES

CHAPTER 17
Rhizoctonia Diseases

INTRODUCTION

In many parts of the world, including the United States, the diseases caused by *Rhizoctonia* are included in two principal groups: Rhizoctonia brown patch (*Rhizoctonia solani*) and yellow patch (*Rhizoctonia cerealis*). However, herein is presented one additional specific Rhizoctonia disease of C_3, perennial, cool-season turfgrasses as officially named and/or documented in Japan.

The causal pathogens of the *Rhizoctonia* genus attack a broad range of turfgrass species, and can be especially severe on annual bluegrasses, bentgrasses, ryegrasses, St. Augustinegrass, and zoysiagrasses. The *Rhizoctonia* causal pathogens exhibit some species specialization. The symptoms can vary greatly among the Rhizoctonia diseases. Also, the height of cut can affect the resultant symptoms substantially.

Rhizoctonia species are capable of saprophytic growth on plant debris. Infection of turfgrasses occurs primarily through wetted leaf blades and sheaths. Extensive turf damage can occur very rapidly during rainy, humid, hot weather. High-to-excessive nitrogen (N) fertilization and irrigation are cultural practices that favor severe Rhizoctonia disease development. The *Rhizoctonia* causal pathogens survive periods unfavorable for growth by structures such as bulbils, monilioid cells, and/or thick-walled mycelium in plant debris.

Table 17-1. A Summary of the Rhizoctonia Diseases, Causal Pathogens, and Host Turfgrasses

Common name	*Rhizoctonia* causal pathogen	Major host turfgrasses	Chapter
pseudo-Rhizoctonia brown patch*†	*Rhizoctonia circinata* var. *circinata*	bentgrasses	17C
Rhizoctonia brown patch	*Rhizoctonia solani* AG-1 & AG-2-2 (III B)	annual bluegrasses bentgrasses perennial ryegrass	17A
yellow patch	binucleate *Rhizoctonia* AG-D (I)	annual bluegrasses bentgrasses	17B
large patch*	*Rhizoctonia solani* AG-2-2 (LP)	St. Augustinegrass zoysiagrasses	7B
Rhizoctonia patch* (elephant footprint)	binucleate *Rhizoctonia* AG-D (II)	zoysiagrasses	7C
Rhizoctonia spring dead spot*	binucleate *Rhizoctonia* AG-D (I)	zoysiagrasses	7A

* Japanese descriptive name.

† Tentative name, as yet not approved by the Phytopathological Society of Japan.

Note: The Rhizoctonia diseases of C_4, warm-season turfgrasses are discussed in Chapters 7, 7A, 7B, and 7C.

CHAPTER 17A
Rhizoctonia Brown Patch

Disease Characteristics. Rhizoctonia brown patch initially appears as circular-shaped patches with a diameter of 1 to 5 inches (25 to 125 mm). The patches develop quickly up to 2 feet (600 mm) in diameter and fade to a light-brown color. A purplish to grayish-brown border or ring may appear under humid, warm conditions. The patches may coalesce within ten days to form irregular shapes of larger patches. The color of the patches is varied, depending on the condition of the turf where disease occurs, especially the moisture level. Leaves of infected grasses become brown and blighted; then the injury symptoms spread to the crown and roots.

Environmental Effects. Rhizoctonia brown patch typically starts to appear during a period of high temperature and high humidity in early summer, and may continue to develop until very late summer. It mainly occurs on turfs with a very close cutting height, such as greens, but can occur at high cutting heights. A high canopy humidity and wet surface soil conditions tend to cause more severe symptoms. An example is extended leaf wetness for ten hours per day for 2 to 3 days.

Causal Pathogens: *Rhizoctonia solani* AG-1 and AG-2-2 (IIIB). teleomorph *Thanatephorus cucumeris*.

These two strains may cause this disease, with the latter being the major pathogen in Japan. Strain AG-1 occurs more in cooler climates and exhibits a smoke ring of dark-black mycelium in early morning, while strain AG-2-2 occurs more in warmer climates and has no smoke ring.

These pathogens attack the leaves and shoots, and occasionally the roots of grasses. They grow at an optimum temperature of 95°F (35°C), with strong pathogenicity observed in the range of 77 to 95°F (25 to 35°C). The fungi are known to survive saprophytically by bulbils, monilioid cells, and/or thick-walled mycelium in thatch. Local spread is by plant-to-plant contact. Dissemination is by mechanical means such as turf cultivation and vertical cutting.

Host Cool-Season Turfgrasses: This disease has a wide host range.

Major - annual bluegrasses (*Poa annua*).
- bentgrasses (*Agrostis* species).
- perennial ryegrass (*Lolium perenne*).

Minor - Kentucky bluegrass (*Poa pratensis*).
- fescues (*Festuca* species).

Occurrence Documented: Africa, Australasia, Europe, Japan, and North America.

Cultural Controls:

1. Remove any excess thatch when it occurs, as by vertical cutting.

2. Avoid excessive watering.

3. Avoid unnecessarily close mowing, if possible.

4. Maintain a nitrogen (N) nutritional level that provides a moderate shoot growth rate.

5. Practice turf cultivation as needed, as by coring.

Chemical Control. Fungicides effective against Rhizoctonia brown patch, such as fenarimol, flutolanil, iprodione, mancozeb, propiconazole, thiophanate-methyl, or triadimefon, should be sprayed over the entire turf, especially greens, at the initial stage of disease development. Spot treatment of fungicides to diseased patch areas is not enough to control this disease. A repeat fungicide treatment may be necessary on the entire putting green should symptoms of the disease reappear.

Photo 17A-2. Rhizoctonia brown patch with dark-brown color. The patch appears to be darker-brown because of excess watering of a putting green *(creeping bentgrass putting green; midsummer)*.

Photo 17A-1. Severe patches of Rhizoctonia brown patch with a brown color. Each single patch is round in shape, but often coalesce with each other to form irregular shapes *(creeping bentgrass putting green; early summer)*.

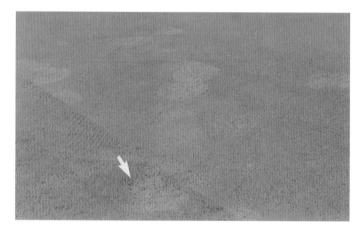

Photo 17A-3. Rhizoctonia brown patch with a light-brown color during a dry period; this type often occurs on putting greens with very close mowing. Sometimes the same symptoms may appear on the collar *(arrow)* at a higher mowing height *(creeping bentgrass putting green; midsummer)*.

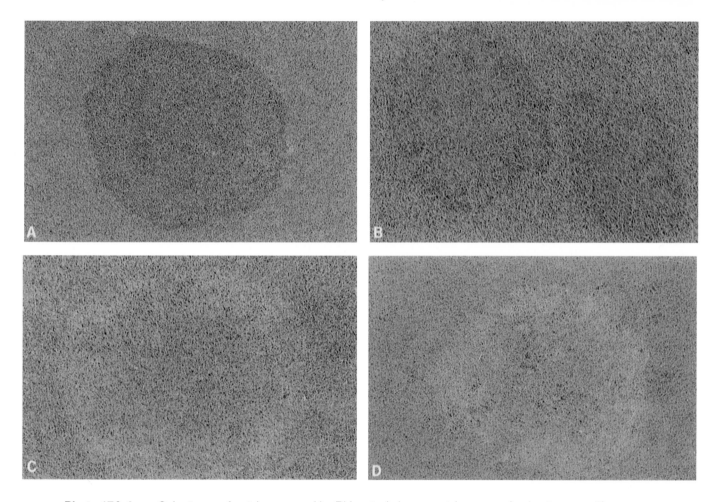

Photo 17A-4. Color tones of patches caused by Rhizoctonia brown patch on creeping bentgrass putting greens:

    A: patch at the initial stage of development *(very early summer)*.

    B: patch formed under a high humidity *(early summer)*.

    C: a light patch symptom with a smoky ring *(early summer)*.

    D: patch appeared under dry conditions *(late summer)*.

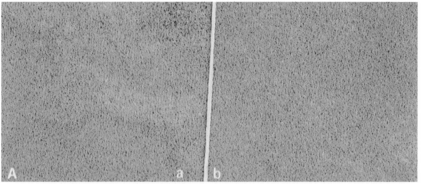

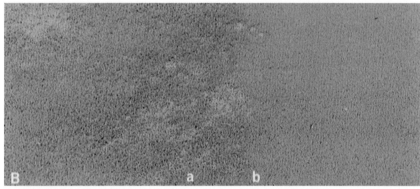

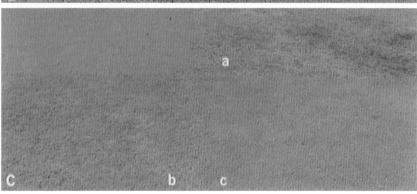

Photo 17A-5. A fungicide test for the control of Rhizoctonia brown patch in Japan:

A a: untreated control.
   b: validamycin A liquid formulation 5 (1,000 times dilution, 24.5 gal/1,000 ft² or 100 liters/100 m²) applied once.

Photo was taken two weeks after application (midsummer).

B a: untreated control.
   b: mepronil + propiconazole wettable powder (500 times dilution, 24.5 gal/1,000 ft² or 100 liters/100 m²) applied twice.

Photo was taken two weeks after the second application (midsummer).

C a: untreated control.
   b: thiram + chlorothalonil wettable powder (500 times dilution, 24.5 gal/1,000 ft² or 100 liters/100 m²) applied twice.
   c: flutolanil + propiconazole wettable powder (333 times dilution, 24.5 gal/1,000 ft² or 100 liters/100 m²) applied twice.

Photo was taken two weeks after second application (midsummer).

CHAPTER 17B
Yellow Patch
(Winter Patch)

Disease Characteristics. The disease is called yellow patch because the leaves sometimes are etiolated and turn yellow. They appear in round-shaped patches of 8 to 20 inches (200 to 500 mm) in diameter. The color of the patches tends to become brown, and thus it also is called winter patch and winter brown patch.

Damage caused by yellow patch usually is not severe because the virulence of the pathogen is weak. But the loss of turf quality due to the browning cannot be overlooked. Young turfgrasses of 1 to 2 years after seeding tend to have severe damage with large, irregularly-shaped patches. Yellow patch also occurs on winter overseeded turfs of ryegrass, but the symptoms usually are not severe in these cases.

Environmental Effects. Yellow patch typically occurs in early to midwinter, with turf recovery occurring the next spring. The optimum temperature range for yellow patch disease is 50 to 59°F (10 to 15°C).

Causal Pathogen. Binucleate *Rhizoctonia* AG-D(I).
  teleomorph *Ceratobasidium cereale*.
  (syn. *Rhizoctonia cerealis*)

This pathogen attacks the shoots and sometimes the roots of grasses. The optimum temperature range for pathogenicity to bentgrass is between 41 and 68°F (5 and 20°C). The fungus loses pathogenicity at temperatures above 77°F (25°C). The pathogen survives saprophytically by bulbils, monilioid cells, and/or thick-walled mycelium in plant debris during periods unfavorable for growth. Local spread is by plant-to-plant contact. Dissemination is by mechanical means, such as turf cultivation and vertical cutting.

Host Cool-Season Turfgrasses:

    Major - annual bluegrasses (*Poa annua*).
              - bentgrasses (*Agrostis* species).
    Minor - Kentucky bluegrass (*Poa pratensis*).
              - ryegrasses (*Lolium* species).

Occurrence Documented: Europe, Japan, and North America.

Cultural Controls:

1. Apply certain plant growth regulator-containing fertilizers in early winter.

2. Maintain a sufficient, but not excessive, nitrogen (N) nutritional level.

3. Remove any excessive thatch when it forms, as by vertical cutting.

4. Provide sufficient watering during the winter to maintain a moist root zone.

Chemical Control. The application of a fungicide, such as tolclofos-methyl or flutolanil, in very late fall, just before yellow patch disease appearance, is suggested. Because of slow growth of the turfgrass during the winter, the application of fungicides after disease appearance occurs may leave patches that do not recover. In these cases, an application of certain plant growth regulators, such as cytokinin and gibberellin, stimulates plant growth, and may enhance turf recovery in the patches in about one week, if temperatures are not too low. Preventive application of a fungicide during the winter is not suggested for this disease.

Note: This pathogen also causes Rhizoctonia spring dead spot on C_4, warm-season turfgrasses, which is addressed in Chapter 7A.

Photo 17B-2. A ring-shaped, brown patch symptom of the yellow patch disease. The fringe of the patch turns brown, but the inside of the patch has recovered *(creeping bentgrass putting green; late winter).*

Photo 17B-1. A patch symptom of yellow patch disease that is brown in color *(creeping bentgrass putting green; late winter).*

Photo 17B-3. A light, yellow-brown patch symptom of yellow patch disease *(creeping bentgrass putting green; late winter).*

Photo 17B-4. A smoky-ringed, light-brown patch symptom of yellow patch disease *(creeping bentgrass putting green; late winter).*

Photo 17B-5 A smoky-ringed, yellow patch symptom of yellow patch disease *(perennial ryegrass tee; midwinter).*

Photo 17B-6. Irregular-shaped, extensive patches of yellow patch disease on young turfgrass. Seeding was made in late summer, with the patches occurring in early winter of the next year *(creeping bentgrass putting green; very early spring).*

Photo 17B-7. Yellow patch symptoms of yellow patch disease that occurred extensively on a winter overseeded turf. The zoysiagrass turf was winter overseeded with perennial ryegrass in September, with the patches appearing in mid-January of the next year *(tee; midwinter).*

CHAPTER 17C
Pseudo-Rhizoctonia Brown Patch

Disease Characteristics. This new disease is found on creeping bentgrass greens. Patches resembling Rhizoctonia brown patch that occur in late spring or in late fall may be this disease. Symptoms of this disease that appear in the midsummer cannot be distinguished from those of Rhizoctonia brown patch. Patches caused by pseudo-Rhizoctonia brown patch usually are not severe and turfgrasses in the patches do not become completely blighted.

The patches appear in a round shape of 8 to 20 inches (200 to 500 mm) in diameter. Irregular-shaped patches and a smoky ring also are observed. The color of the patches is light-brown to brown.

Environmental Effects. Rhizoctonia brown patch usually occurs from early to late summer, while pseudo-Rhizoctonia brown patch occurs over a longer period, from late spring to late fall. Factors affecting the occurrence and development of this disease are not yet clear.

Causal Pathogen. *Rhizoctonia circinata* var. *circinata*. teleomorph *Waitea circinata* var. *circinata*.

Determinations based on DNA analysis indicate that the pathogen is neither *Rhizoctonia oryzae* nor *Rhizoctonia zeae*, but is identical to *Rhizoctonia circinata* var. *circinata*, which had been proposed as the causal pathogen of Rhizoctonia disease on barley seedlings by Leiner and Carling in 1994. It had not been reported as a pathogen of creeping bentgrasses.

This pathogen attacks the shoots and sometimes the roots of grasses. It grows at temperatures between 59 and 95°F (15 and 35°C), with the optimum temperature range being 82 to 86°F (28 to 30°C). Strong pathogenicity on bentgrasses is observed at temperatures between 77 to 86°F (25 to 30°C), with the minimum temperature required for pathogenicity in the range of 50 to 59°F (10 to 15°C). The pathogen is considered to survive saprophytically by bulbils, monilioid cells, and/or thick-walled mycelium in thatch during periods unfavorable for growth. Local spread is by plant-to-plant contact. Dissemination is by mechanical means, such as turf cultivation and vertical cutting.

Host Cool-Season Turfgrasses:

Major - bentgrasses (*Agrostis* species).

Minor - (none known).

Occurrence Documented: Japan.

Cultural Controls:

1. Remove any excess thatch when it occurs, as by vertical cutting.
2. Avoid excessive watering.
3. Avoid unnecessarily close mowing, if possible.
4. Apply judicious nitrogen (N) fertilization.
5. Practice turf cultivation as needed, as by coring.

Chemical Control. Another important point that distinguishes this causal pathogen from the pathogen of Rhizoctonia brown patch is that the effective fungicides in inhibiting the mycelial growth of these two pathogens are distinctly different. Benomyl and pencycuron are effective on the causal pathogen of Rhizoctonia brown patch, but are not effective on the causal pathogen of pseudo-Rhizoctonia brown patch. Other fungicides, such as flutolanil, mepronil or polyoxin, are effective on both pathogens.

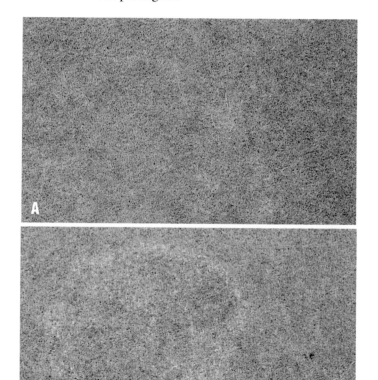

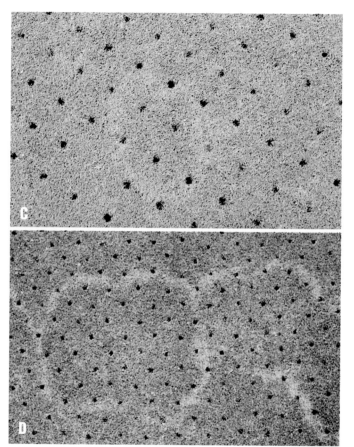

Photo 17C-1. Symptoms of pseudo-Rhizoctonia brown patch. Four types of symptoms are shown. Damage on turfgrasses is relatively light compared to those for Rhizoctonia brown patch *(creeping bentgrass putting green; late spring to midsummer)*.

A. faint appearance in irregular patches.

B. faint appearance of a smoky-ringed patch.

C. browning of the patches.

D. smoky-ringed patches with a clear, brown zone.

CHAPTER 18
Pythium Diseases

INTRODUCTION

In many parts of the world most of the diseases caused by *Pythium* species tend to be called Pythium blight, including Pythium red blight. But herein are discussed four specific Pythium diseases of C_3, cool-season turfgrasses as officially named and recognized in Japan. Typical symptoms of Pythium diseases vary among the various species. Pythium blight (I) which causes irregularly-shaped patches, primarily on seedling turfs, is discussed in Chapter 18B, while Pythium blight (II) disease which causes round-shaped patches is discussed in Chapter 18C.

The Pythium diseases are feared because of the rapidity with which severe damage can occur, such as in less than one day. While all turfgrasses can be attacked by *Pythium* species, the C_3, perennial, cool-season turfgrasses are the most susceptible. Pythium blight is commonly thought to be a disease of humid, hot weather. However, the environmental-seasonal occurrence can vary greatly among the various Pythium diseases.

The causal *Pythium* pathogen is transmitted rapidly by moving water via such structures as mycelium, oospores, and sporangia. The fungus also can spread from leaf-to-leaf by the rapid growth of cottony aerial mycelium, especially on closely-mowed turfgrasses.

Note. The Pythium diseases of C_4, warm-season turfgrasses are discussed in Chapters 8, 8A, 8B, and 8C. Also, Pythium snow blight of C_3, cool-season turfgrasses is discussed in Chapter 23C under the snow mold disease group.

Table 18-1. A Summary of the Pythium diseases, Causal Pathogens, and Host Turfgrasses.

Common name	Pythium causal pathogen(s)	Major host turfgrasses	Chapter
Pythium blight (I)*	*P. aristosporum*, *P. graminicola*, *P. ultimum*, & *P. vanterpoolii*	bentgrasses ryegrasses	18B
Pythium blight (II)*	*P. graminicola*	bentgrasses ryegrasses	18C
Pythium red blight*	*P. aphanidermatum*	bentgrasses ryegrasses	18A
Pythium yellow spot*†	*P. torulosum*	bentgrasses	18D
Pythium snow blight	*P. iwayamani* & *P. paddicum*	annual bluegrasses bentgrasses	23C
Irregular Pythium patch*	*P. graminicola* & *P. vanterpoolii*	manila zoysiagrass	8B
Pythium spring dead spot*††	*P. graminicola* & *P. vanterpoolii*	manila zoysiagrass	8A
Zoysia Pythium blight*	*P. periplocum*	manila zoysiagrass	8C

* Japanese common name.

† tentative name, as it is not yet approved by the Japanese Society of Plant Pathology. (?)

†† Occurs by double seasonal infection with *Microdochium nivale* or *Fusarium acuminatum* in the fall.

CHAPTER 18A
Pythium Red Blight

Disease Characteristics. Pythium red blight is feared as a warm-weather, patch disease capable of destroying a bentgrass green within one night in midsummer. The disease initially appears as a leaf blight consisting of small, red-brown patches of 0.8 to 1.2 inches (20 to 30 mm) in diameter, and develops rapidly to more than 8 inches (200 mm) in a few days. The disease is thought to develop rapidly, but in fact, many small patches coalesce with each other to quickly form large, irregularly-shaped patches within several days.

The symptom of red-browning is similar to the color tone caused by a partial scald, but Pythium red blight is clearly distinguished by a gray-purple ring at the perimeter of the patch. Further, turfgrasses in the center of the patches caused by Pythium red blight recover in a relatively short time, which results in a smoky ring symptom.

Because of the fast progress of this disease, diagnosis at the initial stage of disease development is the key to control. Pythium red blight can be diagnosed by careful examination of small patches of even 1 inch (25 mm) in diameter. Typical diagnostic symptoms during the initial stage of this disease are:

- leaves turn gray-purple.

- the surfaces of leaves are covered with a white, cob-webby mycelium.

- no dew-exudate appears on the leaves in the morning.

Environmental Effects. Pythium red blight occurs to a greater extent on putting greens characterized by a high humidity, poor soil drainage, and/or impaired air movement. Since the disease usually starts to develop after an extended rain during continuous night temperatures in the range of 73 to 77°F (23-25°C), special attention is necessary, especially after a prolonged rain, a thunderstorm, or a typhoon in early to midsummer. Because both high humidities and warm temperatures are required for disease appearance, the disease may not be seen if one of these conditions is absent.

Causal Pathogen. *Pythium aphanidermatum.*
   (syn. *Pythium butleri*)

This pathogen is able to attack all parts of the grass plant, but is primarily a foliar blighting disease. The optimum pathogen growth temperature range is from 86 to 95°F (30-35°C), while the fungus is pathogenic between 77 and 86°F (25-30°C).

Overwintering oospores in plants infected the previous season serve as the source of primary inoculum, with the fungus spreading during hot, wet conditions favorable for disease development. The disease spreads as a result of zoospores of the pathogen being washed over the turfgrasses, especially on putting greens, and also when mycelium formed on the surface of leaves is transmitted by mechanical means, such as mowers.

Host Cool-Season Turfgrasses: The fungus is pathogenic to a number of species of cool-season turfgrasses, but not to zoysiagrasses and bermudagrasses.

Major - bentgrasses (*Agrostis* species).
        - ryegrasses (*Lolium* species).

Minor - fescues (*Festuca* species).
        - bluegrasses (*Poa* species).

Occurrence Documented: Europe, Japan, and North America.

Cultural Controls:

1. Increase air flow over the turf canopy. In some cases, even the use of mechanical fans is effective.

2. Prevent water accumulation on the surfaces of turfgrasses.

3. Improve soil water drainage, as by coring.

4. Maintain the soil pH in the acid range. Also, the disease is increased by a calcium (Ca) deficiency.

5. Use a properly balanced (N-P-K-Fe) fertilization program.

6. Avoid dissemination of the pathogen from infected turf to uninfected turf on equipment. Diseased putting greens should be mowed last. Thoroughly clean all equipment after each usage.

Chemical Control. Preventive applications of fungicides several times at the beginning of the hot season have been practiced because of the fast development of Pythium red blight. However, preventive application without any observation of disease appearance should be minimized. Pythium red blight may not be seen if the conditions, especially a low humidity or a night temperature below 77°F (25°C), are not favorable for disease appearance. Upon detection of the initial stage of disease development, it is possible to control this disease completely by an immediate curative application of fungicide.

Fungicide applications at the initial stage of disease development cause the patches to disappear about 2 to 3 days following treatment. Even in severely infected areas, the turf usually recovers after 10 days. Multiple applications of a single group of fungicides, such as metalaxyl, should be avoided to reduce the risk of fungicide-resistant biotypes occurring. Alternating the use of fungicides with different modes of action, or the use of synergistic combinations, selected from fosetyl-Al, metalaxyl, and propamocarb, is very important.

Photo 18A-1. Severe patches of Pythium red blight have spread over the entire green within about 10 days *(creeping bentgrass putting green; midsummer)*.

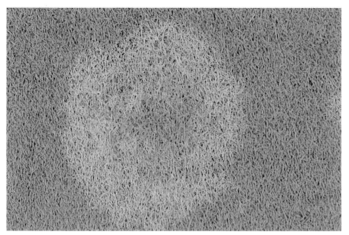

Photo 18A-2. A typical single patch of Pythium red blight, showing characteristics of a gray-purple ring at the fringe of the patch, and recovering grasses in the middle of the patch *(creeping bentgrass putting green; midsummer).*

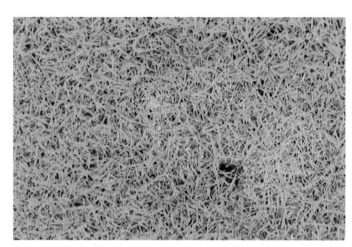

Photo 18A-3. A small, irregular patch of Pythium red blight *(creeping bentgrass putting green; midsummer).*

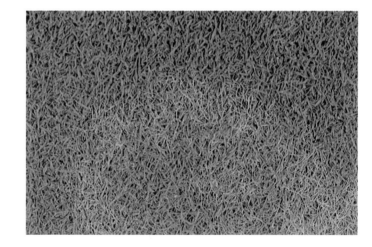

Photo 18A-4. An irregular-shaped patch of Pythium red blight. Most grass in the middle of the patch has recovered, with disease symptoms remaining at the fringe of the patch *(creeping bentgrass putting green; midsummer).*

Photo 18A-5. The coalescing of small patches of Pythium red blight. Multiple coalescing of patches have formed irregular shapes *(creeping bentgrass putting green; midsummer)*.

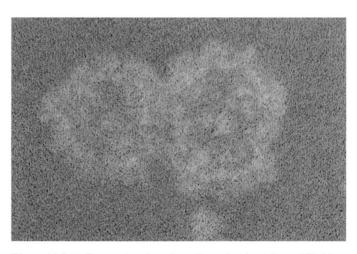

Photo 18A-6. The coalescing of medium-sized patches of Pythium red blight *(creeping bentgrass putting green; midsummer)*.

Photo 18A-7. Natural turf recovery in patches of Pythium red blight. Recovery of turfgrass starts from the center of the patches *(creeping bentgrass putting green; late summer)*.

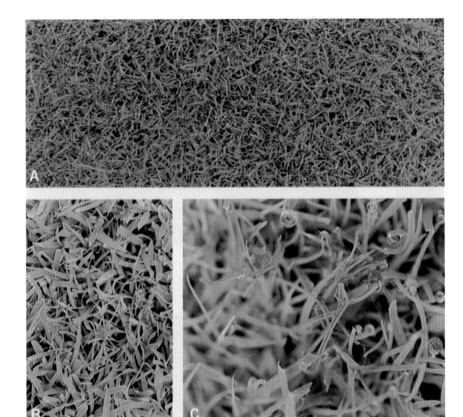

Photo 18A-8. A small patch of Pythium red blight at the initial stage of disease development:

  A: with detection at this stage of disease development, complete cure is possible within a few days.

  B: close-up of infected grass possessing gray-purple leaves.

  C: close-up of the patch with white, cobweb-like mycelium of the pathogen seen. Also, careful observation reveals no morning dew-exudate on the infected leaves (left) *(creeping bentgrass putting green; late summer).*

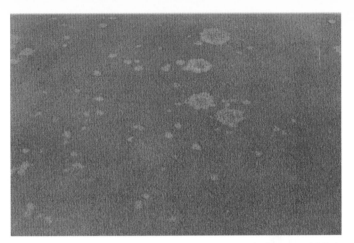

Photo 18A-9. A cluster of small patches of Pythium red blight surrounding larger patches. These small patches are the result of secondary infection *(creeping bentgrass putting green; midsummer).*

Photo 18A-10. A straight alignment of patches of Pythium red blight. The pathogen was disseminated by a mower, with the disease subsequently occurring in a straight line *(creeping bentgrass putting green; late summer).*

  left: older patches (7 days after appearance).
  right: new patches (3 days after appearance).

Photo 18A-11. A fungicide test for the control of Pythium red blight in Japan:

- **A:** the disease started to appear on July 12 and had spread over the entire putting green of creeping bentgrass by July 20.

- **B:** hymexazol + metalaxyl liquid formulation (1,000 times dilution, 24.5 gal/1,000 ft^2 or 100 liters/100 m^2) was applied on July 20.

Photos were taken just before (A) and 14 days after the chemical application (B), respectively.

Photo 18A-12. Partial leaf blight caused by scald. Symptoms caused by scald resemble those of Pythium red blight, but a smoky-ring is not formed on patches caused by scald, regardless of its size *(creeping bentgrass putting green; late summer).*

Photo 18A-13. Patches caused by scald:

- **A:** color tone of the patches caused by scald is similar to those of Pythium red blight.

- **B:** both can be clearly distinguished, however, by a gray-purple ring at the fringe of the patch, which occurs only on patches caused by Pythium red blight *(creeping bentgrass putting green; late summer).*

CHAPTER 18B
Pythium Blight (I)

Disease Characteristics. The typical symptoms of Pythium blight (I) are irregularly-shaped patches of light-brown to brown color that occur from early spring to late fall. The patch size initially is 1 inch (25 mm) in diameter and may coalesce to form irregular-shaped patches of more than 20 sq ft (2 m²). Patches sometimes can spread over an entire putting green.

Young plants of turfgrass within one year after seeding are more susceptible to Pythium blight (I), and the rate of disease spread can be severe. Seeding in mid- to late summer and in late fall should be done with caution because severe disease damage may occur to the grass seedlings in very early fall and in midwinter, respectively.

Turfs more than three years of age rarely have Pythium blight (I). It usually does not occur, except in areas having inappropriate cultural practices in terms of topdressing, fertilizer applications, or excessively close mowing.

Environmental Effects. In warm to hot seasons, conditions favorable for the occurrence of Pythium blight (I) include impaired air movement, a humid atmosphere, poor soil drainage, an alkaline soil pH, and improper cultural practices. In cool and cold seasons, the occurrence of the disease is correlated mainly with improper cultural practices.

Causal Pathogens:

- *Pythium vanterpoolii.*
- *Pythium graminicola.*
- *Pythium ultimum.*
- *Pythium aristosporum.*

The first two fungi also are the causal pathogens of Pythium spring dead spot and irregular Pythium patch on manila zoysiagrass turfs. In the USA and Europe, *Pythium ultimum* is considered an important causal pathogen of turfgrasses. In Japan, however, it is very rare to find this latter pathogen.

These pathogens are able to attack all parts of the grass plant, including distinctive crown and root rot phases. The pathogenicity of *Pythium vanterpoolii* occurs at temperatures between 41 and 68°F (5 and 20°C), and is most pathogenic to bentgrasses on putting greens between 50 and 59°F (10 and 15°C).

On the other hand, *Pythium graminicola* has pathogenicity at temperatures between 50 and 95°F (10 and 35°C), and is highly pathogenic over a wide range from 59 to 86°F (15 to 30°C). Because of these differences in optimum temperatures for pathogenicity of these two pathogens, both can infect during the cool season, but only *Pythium graminicola* also is active during the hot season.

The pathogenicity of *Pythium aristosporum* occurs at temperatures between 50 and 95°F (10 and 35°C). Severe damage by this pathogen has been observed in very early fall on perennial ryegrass seedlings.

The pathogens survive unfavorable conditions for growth as oospores in plant debris. Local spread is by plant-to-plant contact. Dissemination is by mechanical means, such as mowing, turf cultivation, and vertical cutting.

Host Cool-Season Turfgrasses:

    Major - bentgrasses (*Agrostis* species).
               - ryegrasses (*Lolium* species).

    Minor - annual bluegrasses (*Poa annua*).

Occurrence Documented: Europe, Japan, and/or United States; depending on the *Pythium* species.

Cultural Controls:

1. Young turfgrass seedlings tend to be more susceptible to Pythium blight (I) in both cold and hot seasons. Thus, it is preferable to avoid seeding in early to mid-summer and in late fall.

2. Improve the soil water drainage, as by coring. Rapid surface drainage also must be assured via proper contours.

3. Following proper cultural practices, such as topdressing, fertilization, and mowing, is essential.

4. Apply a balanced (N-P-K-Fe) fertilizer, based on an annual chemical soil test.

5. The use of calcareous sands should be avoided when topdressing and in constructing root zones.

Chemical Control. Special caution must be paid to turfgrasses in the first and second years after seeding. Appropriate application of fungicides, such as hymexazol + metalaxyl, fosetyl-Al + chloroneb, or propamocarb, at the initial stage of disease development is important during this period. First remove the dead grasses, and then apply the fungicide over a wide area around the infected patches. Reseeding is suggested after these treatments.

    Pythium blight (I) usually does not occur during the summer season on mature turfs of more than three years old, while it occurs during the winter season even on mature turfs. Try to establish the proper cultural practices on the mature turf to minimize the appearance of this disease and to reduce the need for fungicides.

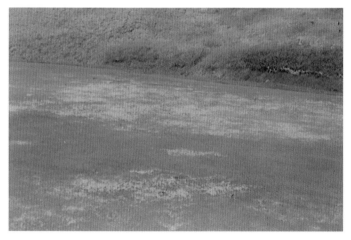

Photo 18B-1. Severe patches of Pythium blight (I) spread over the entire green of a young, one- to two-year old turf *(creeping bentgrass putting green; midsummer).*

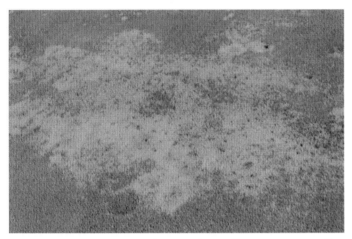

Photo 18B-2. Patches of Pythium blight (I) on young seedling turf. The irregularly-shaped patches consist of colorless, dead leaves *(creeping bentgrass putting green; midspring).*

Photo 18B-3. A patch of Pythium blight (I) on a mature turf several years after seeding. A local, irregularly-shaped patch occurs, and the soil is partially exposed. Improper cultural practices lead to the appearance of this disease on mature turfs *(creeping bentgrass green; early fall).*

Photo 18B-4. Patches of Pythium blight (I) *Pythium vanterpoolii,* occur on a creeping bentgrass turf during the winter season:

A: mature turf *(midwinter).*

B: young turf seeded in late fall of previous year *(midwinter).*

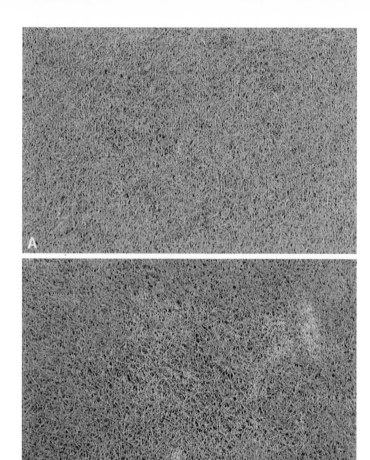

Photo 18B-5. Patches of Pythium blight (I), *Pythium aristosporum* on a perennial ryegrass tee. The causal pathogen was spread widely due to intense rain after seeding during the hot season:

A: irregular-shaped, large patches appear in those places where there had been problems with drainage.

B: after the turf died, a growth of algae is observed on the surface of the exposed soil. A whitish mycelial mass (arrow) also is observed *(tee; early fall).*

Photo 18B-6. An initial patch symptom of Pythium blight (I), *Pythium graminicola,* on a perennial ryegrass turf. The patches developed on a young turf seeded in late summer of the previous year:

A: smoky-ringed patch.

B: irregular-shaped patch.

In both cases, the color tones of the patches are relatively dark-brown *(tee; midsummer).*

Photo 18B-7. An initial patch of Pythium blight (I) *Pythium graminicola,* on a creeping bentgrass turf. Patches on a mature turf of several years after seeding sometimes exhibit a smoky-ring of light- brown *(putting green; late summer).*

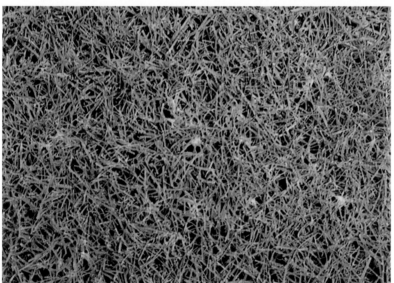

Photo 18B-8. Whitish mycelium of the Pythium blight (I) pathogen, *Pythium graminicola,* distributed extensively on the turf. The hyphae were spread by a greens mower from the infected turf. Under high atmospheric humidity conditions, growth of the whitish mycelium is formed rapidly *(perennial ryegrass tee; midsummer).*

CHAPTER 18C
Pythium Blight (II)

Disease Characteristics. Symptoms develop very rapidly, with many circular patches of 8 to 20 inches (200 to 500 mm) in diameter usually formed within a few days after an intense rain and resultant flooding. In some cases, the individual patches coalesce to form irregularly-shaped patches throughout the water-saturated areas on a green.

The patches of Pythium blight (II) are light-green during the initial stage, and later show symptoms similar to Rhizoctonia brown patch. Patches of Pythium blight (II), however, have a well-defined, dark-brown ring of 1 inch (25 mm) wide at the fringe of the patch, and the leaves and roots of turf in the patch die within several days. Further, a large number of oospores may be observed on the infected plant residues. These characteristics can be used to distinguish this disease from Rhizoctonia brown patch. After the turfgrasses have blighted, the patch often turns very dark-brown due to a secondary growth of algae.

Environmental Effects. Pythium blight (II) typically occurs on flooded turf areas in midsummer after 1 or 2 days of intense rain, plus daytime temperatures above 95°F (35°C). Severe development of Pythium blight (II) may occur in temperate climatic regions.

Turf damage caused by Pythium blight (II) is greater and the disease spreads faster than Pythium red blight under the specific conditions that are favorable to this pathogen, especially surface flooding. The disease also spreads to other areas by transport of the pathogen with infected grass clippings.

Causal Pathogen. *Pythium graminicola*.

The causal pathogen is a different strain from the *Pythium graminicola* that is described in the section on Pythium blight (I). The differences between these two strains have been confirmed by zymogram analyses with four enzymes. Also, there are differences in the optimum temperature for pathogenicity of the two. *Pythium graminicola* described in the section on Pythium blight (I) has a wide optimum temperature range for pathogenicity of from 59 to 86°F (15-30°C), while *Pythium graminicola* isolated from Pythium blight (II) is most pathogenic at 95°F (35°C) and becomes weak at 77°F (25°C).

This pathogen is able to attack all parts of the grass plant, but is primarily a foliar blighting disease. An assessment of the disease characteristics suggests this pathogen may be generally saprophytic, and the infection ability increases under conditions of both high humidity and high temperature. On the other hand, the resistance mechanisms of turfgrasses may be weakened under these conditions, and these factors may induce more disease occurrences. The population of the pathogen increases after establishment of the disease, and this becomes a primary inoculum for further disease development. Considerable zoospore formation is observed at 95°F (35°C), and dissemination is by these zoospores which actively move in water droplets, as by splashing. Also, dissemination may occur via infected plants and soil by mechanical means, such as mowing, turf cultivation, and vertical cutting.

Host Cool-Season Turfgrasses:

Major - bentgrasses (*Agrostis* species).

Minor - (none known).

Occurrence Documented: Japan.

Cultural Controls:

1. Improve the root zone drainage to minimize water accumulation on a putting green after an intense rain.

2. Remove any surface water that remains on a putting green turf immediately after a rain.

3. Increase air flow over the turf canopy. In some cases, even the use of mechanical fans is effective.

4. Maintain the soil pH in the acid range. Also, the disease is increased by a calcium (Ca) deficiency.

5. Use a properly balanced (N-P-K-Fe) fertilization program.

6. Avoid dissemination of the pathogen from infected turf to uninfected turf on equipment. Diseased putting greens should be mowed last. Thoroughly clean all equipment after each usage.

Chemical Control. Symptom development is extremely rapid after the initial appearance of patches. Intense symptom scouting is necessary in areas that tend to flood, especially after a thunderstorm or typhoon. A single application of fungicides, such as hymexazol + metalaxyl or fosetyl-Al + chloroneb, may be enough to control the disease, if the fungicide is applied at the initial stage of disease development. The turf should recover within several days if the treatment has been completed within 2 to 3 days after the first appearance of disease symptoms. Failure of treatments made at the initial stage may lead to disease development in the roots and lateral stems of infected turfgrasses. Reestablishment of the turf may be necessary in such situations.

Photo 18C-1. Severe patch symptoms of Pythium blight (II). The patches in the front possessing a dark-brown color are 4- to 5-days old. The patches behind these are just 2- to 3-days old, and have a light-brown color (*creeping bentgrass putting green; midsummer*).

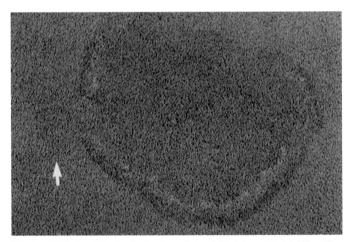

Photo 18C-2. Patches of Pythium blight (II) of various sizes. Very small patches and irregularly-shaped large patches (arrows) are observed on the putting green *(creeping bentgrass putting green; midsummer)*.

Photo 18C-3. Cloud-shaped patches of Pythium blight (II) appeared over a wide area. The causal pathogen had spread over the entire flooded area within a few days after a typhoon *(creeping bentgrass putting green; midsummer)*.

Photo 18C-4. A typical single patch of Pythium blight (II). The wide, dark-brown ring at the fringe is typical. The colored ring caused by *Rhizoctonia solani* is not as well defined and wide. The dark-brown ring can be seen even in the small patch (arrow) *(creeping bentgrass putting green; midsummer)*.

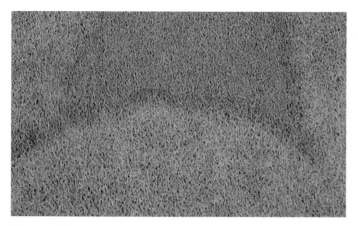

Photo 18C-5. A dark-brown ring at the fringe of a patch of Pythium blight (II). Well defined, dark-brown rings are observed on patches developed from three different directions *(creeping bentgrass putting green; late summer).*

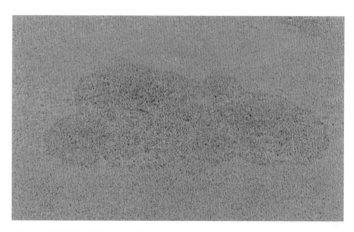

Photo 18C-6. The initial stage of a large-size patch of Pythium blight (II). Color tone of the patch is light because development is in the initial stage, but a darker ring at the fringe had already appeared *(creeping bentgrass putting green; midsummer).*

Photo 18C-7. The sporadic appearance of patches of Pythium blight (II). The causal pathogen in patches that occurred in flooded areas were disseminated by a greensmower to turf areas having no flooding *(creeping bentgrass putting green; late summer).*

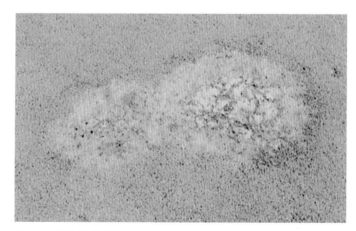

Photo 18C-8. Pythium blight (II) in the late stage of disease development. Grasses in the patch are dead, and algae have developed. Cracks in the soil are observed. A smoky ring is not formed *(creeping bentgrass putting green; late summer).*

Photo 18C-9. The rapid development of a patch of Pythium blight (II) on a creeping bentgrass putting green in Japan:

A: the initial symptom appeared on September 21, immediately after a typhoon passed on September 19.

B: the causal pathogen spreads within a few days, and extensive patches appeared on September 25 *(creeping bentgrass putting green).*

Photo 18C-10. A fungicide test for control of Pythium blight (II) on creeping bentgrass of the same golf course as Photo 18C-9:

A: patches appeared on August 15, two days after an intense rain. The same day a hymexazol + metalaxyl liquid formulation (1,000 times dilution) was sprayed a single time at 24.5 gal/1,000 ft^2 (100 liters/100 m^2).

B: complete cure of the disease was observed on August 29 *(creeping bentgrass putting green).*

CHAPTER 18D

Pythium Yellow Spot

Disease Characteristics. Pythium yellow spot occurs on creeping bentgrass putting greens. The patches usually are circular in shape, with a diameter of 2 to 4 inches (50 to 100 mm). The typical symptoms are yellowing of the leaves, and poor growth of the leaves and roots. Occasionally, browning of the patches also is observed. More than a thousand patches may be observed on a severely infected green, which reduces the surface uniformity. Even in such a case, turf recovery usually can be expected in late fall.

Disease symptoms of Pythium yellow spot resemble yellow tuft (Chapter 33) or yellow dwarf (Chapter 39). However, these latter two diseases can be easily distinguished because yellow tuft seldom appears during the midsummer, and yellow dwarf does not form oospores in the infected tissues.

The oospores of the causal fungus of Pythium yellow spot are one-half to one-third smaller than those of the causal pathogen of yellow tuft. The differences in the size of oospores can be useful in distinguishing these two diseases.

Environmental Effects. The Pythium yellow spot patches develop quickly in number under continuous, high temperatures above 95°F (35°C), usually in midsummer through early fall. As temperatures decrease below 77°F (25°C), the patches disappear.

Causal Pathogen. *Pythium torulosum.*

This pathogen is able to attack all parts of the grass plant. The fungus is known to have been isolated from the infected tissues and rhizosphere of Pythium diseases, but it usually has been considered nonpathogenic to turfgrasses. The results of inoculation tests indicate that the fungus is pathogenic at 86 to 95°F (30 to 35°C), while the pathogen loses pathogenicity at temperatures below 77°F (25°C). Survival under unfavorable conditions is by oospores in plant debris. Local spread is by plant-to-plant contact. Dissemination is via zoospores by mechanical means, such as turf cultivation and vertical cutting.

Host Cool-Season Turfgrasses:

Major - bentgrasses (*Agrostis* species).

Minor - (none known).

Occurrence Documented: Japan.

Cultural Controls:

1. Apply the minimum nitrogen (N) fertilization level needed during continuous high-temperature periods in the summer.

2. Apply a light rate of quick-acting nitrogen fertilizer to a green when the initial symptoms of this disease appear.

Chemical Control. When symptoms appear, application of a fungicide that is effective on *Pythium* species, such as metalaxyl or fosetyl-Al, should be sufficient to control Pythium yellow patch. Turfgrasses with a nitrogen (N) deficiency tend to have severe damage, and the application of a fungicide may not be enough under these conditions. A light application of a nitrogen (N) fertilizer, plus a fungicide, are effective in this case.

Photo 18D-1. Patches of Pythium yellow spot on a creeping bentgrass green:

    A: severe, yellow patches. Fewer patches appear outside the green at a higher mowing height.

    B: brown patches. Sometimes the yellow patches turn to a brown color.

Photo 18D-2. Dwarfing and yellowing are observed on the turfgrass infected with *Pythium torulosum* (left). The healthy grass is shown as the control (right).

CHAPTER 19
Fusarium Blight Diseases

Disease Characteristics. There are a number of *Fusarium* species that cause turf diseases in the forms of leaf spots, foliar blights, and root-crown rots. In Japan there are four species that can be classified into the two groups: one occurs in the midwinter to early spring and the other occurs in very early spring to early summer.

Winter Fusarium Blight. *Fusarium acuminatum* usually causes Fusarium blight disease in midwinter. It starts to occur in early to late winter, and continues to cause severe damage to turfgrasses until the spring.

The initial stage of disease development caused by *Fusarium acuminatum* is similar to the disease caused by *Microdochium nivale*, except the color of patches is a lighter tone after they develop to a larger size. In high precipitation areas, white or light-pink mycelial masses grow on the patch surface under high atmospheric humidity conditions. In this case, the mycelium can be transmitted by a mower, resulting in a straight alignment of patches.

The pathogen *Fusarium acuminatum* also occurs in a complex with *Microdochium nivale* or Microdochium patch to cause a winter blight disease.

Young seedling turfgrasses within one year of seeding tend to be severely injured by this disease. Turfgrasses die in the patches which usually become bare in this case. Replant-ing of the turf in the bare sites is necessary. The appearance of new patches may continue until early spring.

Spring Fusarium Blights. *Fusarium avenaceum, Fusarium oxysporum,* and *Fusarium tricinctum* cause Fusarium blight diseases on turfs in early to midspring.

Patches caused by these pathogens are not as severe as for the Fusarium blight disease occurring in the winter. Patches appear in circular shapes with a diameter of less than 20 inches (<500 mm), similar to yellow patch disease. The patches may form irregular-shaped areas by coalescing with each other.

The color of these patches gradually turns brown. Some of the grass leaves and roots die, resulting in a reduction in turfgrass shoot density. But the patches do not become bare like the winter Fusarium blight disease, and thus the turf will recover in late spring.

Environmental Effects. Poor drainage favors the develop-ment of Fusarium blights, along with high atmospheric and canopy humidities.

Causal Pathogens:

Winter Fusarium Blight:

- *Fusarium acuminatum.*
  teleomorph *Gibberella acuminata.*
  (syn. *Fusarium roseum*)

Spring Fusarium Blights:

- *Fusarium avenaceum.*
  teleomorph *Gibberella avenacea.*
- *Fusarium oxysporum.*
- *Fusarium tricinctum.*

These soil-borne pathogens are able to attack all parts of the grass plant. In general, *Fusarium* species grow at temperatures from 50 to 95°F (10 to 35°C), but in some cases, the pathogenicity of *Fusarium* species is expressed at relatively low temperatures. The pathogen causing disease in midwinter, *Fusarium acuminatum*, is most pathogenic at temperatures in the range of 48 to 59°F (8-15°C).

Pathogenicity of the pathogens causing the Fusarium diseases in the spring, *Fusarium avenaceum, Fusarium oxysporum,* and *Fusarium tricinctum*, is highest at temperatures in the range of 59 to 68°F (15 to 20°C). In all these cases, the optimal temperatures for pathogenicity are coincident with the temperatures favoring disease appearance.

Fusarium species usually are saprophytic in thatch and form chlamydospores to survive under environmental conditions unfavorable for growth. Local spread is by plant-to-plant contact. Dissemination is via mycelium in infected tissues or in thatch debris by mechanical means, such as turf cultivation and vertical cutting. Also, they are seed-borne.

Host Cool-Season Turfgrasses:

Major   - bentgrasses (*Agrostis* species).

Minor   - annual bluegrasses (*Poa annua*).
        - Kentucky bluegrass (*Poa pratensis*).
        - fescues (*Festuca* species).
        - ryegrasses (*Lolium* species).

Occurrence Documented: Japan and the United States.

Cultural Controls:

1. Remove any excessive thatch when it forms, as by vertical cutting.
2. Apply a well-balanced fertilization program based on an annual chemical soil test. The disease occurs much more severely on turfs with an excess or deficient nitrogen (N) nutritional level.
3. Avoid excessive humidity by enhancing air movement over the turf canopy.
4. Raise the mowing height, if possible.
5. Remove the leaf clippings.
6. Correct a developing soil compaction problem, as by coring.
7. Irrigate as needed to prevent plant water stress, especially on greens.

Chemical Control. A fungicide effective against *Fusarium* species, such as benomyl or thiophanate-methyl, should be sprayed on the small patches at the initial stage of disease development. The application of a fungicide after turfgrasses in the patches start to die has no effect on the control of Fusarium blight diseases.

Note: Fusarium blight of C_4, warm-season turfgrasses is discussed in Chapter 9. Also, it should be noted that in the United States there are summer Fusarium blights that are of concern on turfgrass areas. They tend to be especially active at high daytime air temperatures of 80 to 95°F (27-35°C) and with severe soil moisture deficits. These Fusarium blights include:

- *Fusarium culmorum.*
  (syn. *Fusarium roseum*)
- *Fusarium poae.*

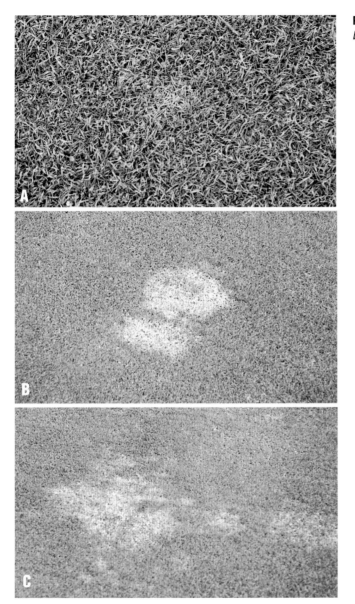

Photo 19-1. Patches caused by *Fusarium acuminatum (creeping bentgrass green)*

    A: small patches at an initial stage of the disease *(midwinter)*.

    B: large, circular patches. Turfgrasses in the patches die, and the color of patches turns white *(late winter)*.

    C: irregular-shaped patches and small patches *(winter)*.

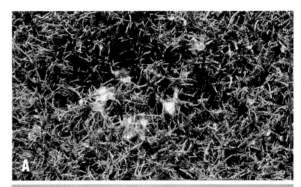

Photo 19-2. Patches caused by *Fusarium acuminatum*:

    A: white to light-pink mycelial mats are formed on the surface of a patch on a turf which had been covered with a thin cheesecloth *(creeping bentgrass nursery; early spring)*.

    B: straight alignment of patches occurred due to dissemination of mycelium of the pathogen by a mower *(creeping bentgrass nursery; early spring)*.

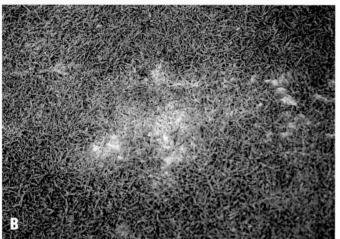

Photo 19-4. A fungicide test for the control of Fusarium blight caused by *Fusarium acuminatum* in Japan. Back side of an experimental plot (a) was sprayed once with benomyl wettable powder (750 times dilution, 50 gal/1,000 ft^2 or 100 liters/100 m^2) in early winter, when the patches began to appear. The patches in the treated plots were controlled almost completely, while the disease was very severe in the nontreated front plot. (b) The other plots had incomplete control from the use of other ineffective fungicides *(creeping bentgrass nursery)*.

Photo was taken in midspring of the year after the fungicide application.

Photo 19-3. Patches caused by *Fusarium tricinctum (creeping bentgrass green; midspring)*:

A: circular patches, similar to yellow patch disease.

B: irregular-shaped patches.

CHAPTER 20
Take-All Patch

Disease Characteristics. Take-all patch first appears as depressed, small, circular shapes of 2 to 3 inches (50-75 mm) in diameter, then may enlarge up to 24 inches (600 mm). The color tone of the initial patches is relatively light-green, and is uniform inside the patch edges. The roots are brown and necrotic. Shoot density of turfgrasses in the patches is reduced substantially, with the leaves turning yellow, then bronze, at the tip and progressing downward. Turfgrasses in the patches die within a few days under warm, drying weather conditions. Watering does not aid recovery of necrotic turfgrasses under these conditions. Subsequently, grass may recover in the center of the patch creating a ring symptom. Full, dense turf recovery is very slow. Take-all patch usually appears 2 to 4 years after planting, and after 5 to 7 years it declines as a biologically active soil forms. This is attributed to the emergence of antagonist soil microorganisms.

Black or dark-brown ectotrophic mycelium are formed on the lower leaf sheaths of grasses. The observation of these mycelium under a low-power magnifying glass (10x) is useful in diagnosis of take-all patch.

Environmental Effects. Take-all patch disease occurrence is severe in the range of 59 to 76°F (15 to 24°C). It usually occurs under cool, moist conditions in midspring to early summer on bentgrass greens and may disappear during midsummer, and again appears in the fall. Severe symptoms are frequently observed on newly-constructed greens with a high sand content and/or a pH above 6.5. A deficiency in phosphorus (P) and/or potassium (K) nutrition also may increase the severity of take-all patch.

Causal Pathogen. *Gaeumannomyces graminis.* var. *avenae.* Formerly named *Ophiobolus graminis.* var. *avenae.*

This fungus is classified, depending on the pathogenicity, into three varieties: *graminis, avenae,* and *tritici.* The causal pathogen of zoysia decline (Chapter 10) and of bermudagrass decline (Chapter 11) is var. *graminis,* while on cool-season turfgrasses it is the var. *avenae* in the United States. The variety of Japanese isolates still remains to be determined.

This soil-borne pathogen attacks the roots and crowns of grasses. The optimal temperature for pathogen growth is 70°F (21°C). The pathogen survives periods unfavorable for growth as dormant mycelium on the grass tissue and in plant debris as saprophytic mycelial strands. Local spread of mycelium may occur by plant-to-plant contact. Dissemination is by mechanical means, such as turf cultivation, vertical cutting, and sod transplanting. Also, it may be seed-borne.

Host Cool-Season Turfgrasses:

    Major   - bentgrasses (*Agrostis* species).

                - perennial ryegrass (*Lolium perenne*).

    Minor   - bluegrasses (*Poa* species).

                - fine-leaf fescues (*Festuca* species).

Occurrence Documented: Australia, Europe, Japan, and North America.

Cultural Controls:

1. Adjust the pH of the rhizosphere to between 5.5 and 6.0.

2. Provide adequate phosphorus (P) and potassium (K) levels by the appropriate fertilization, based on an annual chemical soil test.

3. Improve the root zone drainage, as by coring.

4. Irrigate immediately when leaf water stress appears on the diseased turfgrasses, as earlier loss of the roots accelerates the severity of patch symptom development via shoot desiccation.

5. Use a take-all patch tolerant turfgrass species, if possible.

Chemical Control. A single application of propiconazole or fenarimol in the spring is effective in controlling take-all patch.

Photo 20-1. Typical symptoms of patches of take-all patch (creeping bentgrass green).

A: typical patches *(early summer)*.

B, C: light symptoms during the initial appearance of the patches *(early fall)*.

D: smoky-ringed patches *(early fall)*.

Photo 20-2. Severe patches of take-all patch. Turfgrasses in the patch die within a few days under strong sunshine and heat following a prolonged rain. Turf recovery of the patches can not be expected in this case.

Photo 20-3. Extensive take-all patch occurrence on a creeping bentgrass putting green. *(Courtesy of Dr. Henry T. Wilkinson.)*

Photo 20-4. Take-all patch symptoms on a creeping bentgrass putting green when under heat stress. *(Courtesy of Dr. Henry T. Wilkinson.)*

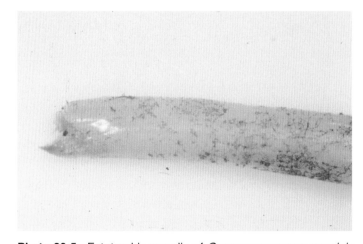

Photo 20-5. Ectotrophic mycelia of *Gaeumannomyces graminis* on the leaf sheath surface of creeping bentgrass.

CHAPTER 21
Summer Patch

Disease Characteristics. The initial symptoms of summer patch are small, circular patches of wilted to thinned turfs of 1 to 3 inches (25 to 75 mm) in diameter, that progress to yellow to gray-green, irregular-shaped patches ranging in size from 0.5 to 1.0 foot (150 to 300 mm), with some up to 3 feet (0.9 m) in diameter. Dark-brown roots may be evident from 4 to 6 weeks before the appearance of aboveground shoot symptoms. Severely infected plants turn gray-green and then straw-colored, starting at the leaf tip and progressing downward. Also, the roots and lateral stems turn black, necrotic, and brittle. The patches may coalesce into larger, irregular-shaped areas. Summer patch also may occur in ring and crescent-shaped patterns which appear in the second year as the original diseased patch reinitiates activity at the perimeter of the patch, with the inner portion being a green turf of recovered or invading grasses.

Environmental Effects. Symptoms of summer patch typically first appear in late spring to early summer during rainy, hot conditions at temperatures of 82 to 95°F (28 to 35°C). The patches may continue to enlarge during the summer and fall. The severity of patch development is greater in compacted, poorly drained soils and under close mowing.

Causal Pathogen. *Magnaporthe poae.*
Formerly named *Phialophora graminicola.*

This soil-borne pathogen attacks the roots of grasses. The optimum temperature for growth of *Magnaporthe poae* is 82 to 86°F (28 to 30°C). The pathogen is active at temperatures of less than 80°F (26°C). Dark-brown to dark-gray ectotrophic runner hyphae are found on the infected roots, crowns, and rhizomes. The pathogen may overwinter via mycelium in infected tissues and plant debris, such as thatch and mat. It is spread by plant-to-plant contact via roots and rhizomes. Dissemination of mycelium also may occur by mechanical means, such as coring, vertical cutting, and transplanted sod.

Host Cool-Season Turfgrasses:

Major - annual bluegrasses (*Poa annua*).
           - Kentucky bluegrass (*Poa pratensis*).
           - fine-leaf fescues (*Festuca* species).

Minor - creeping bentgrass (*Agrostis stolonifera* var. *stolonifera*).
           - perennial ryegrass (*Lolium perenne*).

Occurrence Documented: United States.

Cultural Controls:

1. Use a summer patch resistant turfgrass species and cultivar, especially for Kentucky bluegrass.

2. Avoid close mowing heights, if possible.

3. Maintain adequate nutrient levels, especially nitrogen (N), which sustains a moderate shoot growth rate.

4. Irrigate as needed to prevent an internal plant water stress. This may involve syringing daily at midday due to an inadequate root system in the patches, especially on greens.

5. Remove any excess thatch when it forms, as by vertical cutting.

6. Correct developing soil compaction, as by coring.

Chemical Controls. The demethylation inhibitor (DMI) fungicides, such as cyproconazole, propiconazole, or triadimefon, give good preventive control of summer patch. To maximize effectiveness the fungicide must be applied before symptom development in late spring-early summer. Some curative control is provided by the benzimidazole fungicides, such as benomyl or thiophanate-methyl, applied in multiple applications at 2- to 3-week intervals. Most of these fungicides must be drenched into the moistened root zone.

Photo 21-1. First-year patches of summer patch disease in a Kentucky bluegrass turf. *(Courtesy of Dr. Peter H. Dernoeden.)*

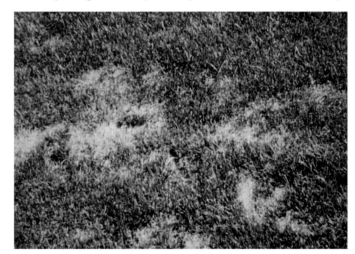

Photo 21-2. Second-year ring and crescent-shaped symptoms of summer patch disease in a Kentucky bluegrass turf. *(Courtesy of Dr. Peter H. Dernoeden.)*

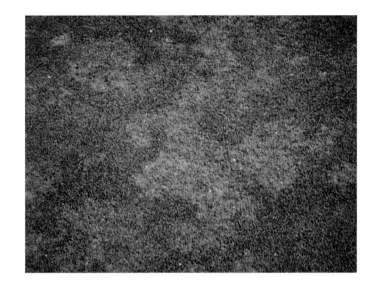

Photo 21-3. First-year patches of summer patch disease in annual bluegrass on a putting green. *(Courtesy of Dr. Peter H. Dernoeden.)*

Photo 21-4. Second-year rings and crescent-shaped symptoms of summer patch disease in annual bluegrass on a putting green. *(Courtesy of Dr. Peter H. Dernoeden.)*

CHAPTER 22
Necrotic Ring Spot

Disease Characteristics. Initial symptoms of necrotic ring spot are a yellow to light-green, small, circular spots of 2 to 4 inches (50 to 100 mm) in diameter. The leaves turn reddish-brown to bronze and then a light-straw color. The spots enlarge to between 0.5 and 1.0 foot (150 to 300 mm), and occasionally to more than 3 feet (0.9 m). Grass at the perimeter of the patch may be a dark reddish-brown color. Roots and rhizomes of infected plants turn black and die. The turfgrasses within the patch eventually die and the patch becomes sunken. Sometimes grass plants in the center recover to form an outer ring-like symptom. Individual patches may coalesce to form larger, irregular-shaped blighted areas.

Environmental Effects. This disease usually develops during cool, wet weather of the spring and fall. Necrotic ring spot symptoms may appear throughout the growing season, with turfgrass death in the patches being accelerated by hot, dry conditions that maximize water stress of the root-damaged turfgrasses. The patches may reappear each season in the same locations. Necrotic ring spot is most severe on 2- to 4-year-old turfs, and may subside in older turfs.

Causal Pathogen. *Leptosphaeria korrae.*
    Formerly named *Ophiobolus herpotrichus.*

This soil-borne pathogen attacks primarily the roots and crowns of grasses. The causal fungus grows in wet, cool weather by brown, septate, runner hyphae that grow along the surface of infected roots, crowns, and lateral stems. *Leptosphaeria korrae* has an optimum growth temperature range of 68 to 82°F (20 to 28°C), with growth cessation occurring above 86°F (30°C) and below 50°F (10°C). Both dark-brown, flattened sclerotia and black, flask-shaped pseudothecia may eventually develop on infected plants. Survival under conditions unfavorable for growth is by ascospores and mycelium in plant debris, such as thatch and mat. Dissemination is via infected plant debris and soil by mechanical means, such as mowing, turf cultivation, and vertical cutting.

Host Cool-Season Turfgrasses:

    Major - Kentucky bluegrass (*Poa pratensis*).
                - annual bluegrasses (*Poa annua*).
                - rough bluegrass (*Poa trivialis*).
    Minor - fescues (*Festuca* species).

Occurrence Documented: Northern North America.

Cultural Controls:

1. Use a necrotic ring spot resistant turfgrass species or cultivars, especially for Kentucky bluegrass.

2. Fertilize to ensure adequate nutritional levels at all times, especially nitrogen (N) applied in the form of a slow-release carrier.

3. Irrigate as needed to prevent an internal plant water stress. This may be daily at mid-day due to an inadequate root system in the patches.

4. Correct developing soil compaction, as by coring.

Chemical Controls. High rates of the benzimidazole group of fungicides, such as benomyl or thiophanate-methyl, have been used with varying success in controlling necrotic ring spot. They must be applied by drenching into the moistened root zone. Other fungicides that may provide more reliable control are cyproconazole, fenarimol, or propiconazole. Applications are best made in early to midspring.

Note: This pathogen also is one of the species that causes *Leptospaeria* spring dead spot on warm-season turfgrasses, which is discussed in Chapter 12.

Photo 22-1. Patches of necrotic ring spot on a Kentucky bluegrass turf. *(Courtesy of Dr. Joseph M. Vargas, Jr.)*

Photo 22-2 First year patches of necrotic ring spot on an annual bluegrass green. *(Courtesy of Dr. Henry T. Wilkinson.)*

Photo 22-3. Close-up of a second-year patch of necrotic ring spot on Kentucky bluegrass with turf recovering in the center. *(Courtesy of Dr. Joseph M. Vargas, Jr.)*

CHAPTER 23
Snow Mold Diseases

INTRODUCTION

Snow mold is the general term for overwintering diseases and their causal pathogens. Symptoms of each individual disease within the snow mold group are different. Occurrences for most of these diseases are typically limited to regions that receive snow, with regional distributions depending on the characteristics of each disease. In general, favorable conditions for these diseases can be found in regions having snow cover for more than 40 days annually. One exception to the snow association is Microdochium patch.

The optimum temperatures for occurrence of each snow mold disease closely match the temperatures in the regions where each disease commonly occurs. These pathogens inhabit particular sites in the turf with their own type of survival structures, and the same type of disease usually occurs at the same sites every year. A key aid in the diagnosis of these snow molds is by the characteristics of the sclerotia and hyphae of the causal fungus.

The determination of the particular pathogen of snow mold that commonly occurs on the turf area and selection of the pathogen-specific fungicide effective against the pathogen are important. The disease may not spread over the entire turf area, and applications of nonselective fungicides to the entire area without a diagnosis of the type of pathogen is useless. Application of a specific fungicide effective against the pathogen that commonly occurs on that area is the best strategy to control the disease.

The addition of an adhesive agent tends to increase the stability of the fungicide effects. Use of a fungicide or fungicides specific to the particular pathogen or pathogens increases the efficiency of the chemicals. Application of a granular formulation also is effective.

Table 23-1. A Summary of Snow Mold Diseases, Causal Pathogens, and Host Turfgrasses

Common name	Causal pathogen(s)	Major host turfgrasses	Chapter
Microdochium patch (pink snow mold)	*Microdochium nivale*	annual bluegrasses bentgrasses	23A
Pythium snow blight	*Pythium iwayamai* & *Pythium paddicum*	annual bluegrasses bentgrasses	23C
Snow scald	*Myriosclerotinia borealis*	bentgrasses fine-leaf fescues ryegrasses	23D
Typhula blights (gray snow molds)	*Typhula incarnata* & *Typhula ishikariensis*	annual bluegrasses ryegrasses bentgrasses	23B
Coprinus snow mold	*Coprinus psychromorbidus*	annual bluegrasses bentgrasses fine-leaf fescues	——

Note: In some locations more than one type of snow mold disease may occur, such as Microdochium patch and Typhula blights. In this situation it is preferable to select a persistent, systemic fungicide that is effective on both diseases.

CHAPTER 23A
Microdochium Patch
(Pink Snow Mold)

Disease Characteristics. The symptoms of Microdochium patch occur in two forms, depending on whether there is an associated snow cover or not.

On snow-free turfs, Microdochium patch appears as circular, water-soaked patches of 1 to 2 inches (25 – 50 mm) in diameter. They typically enlarge up to 12 inches (300 mm), with a yellow to orange-brown color which then turns tan. During wet conditions, a pink to white ring of mycelium may be seen around the edge of the patch. The patches may coalesce to form larger, irregular-shaped areas.

Patches formed in association with a snow melt will initially tend to be white in color, 3 to 12 inches (75 – 300 mm) in diameter, and may be covered with a sparse, white mycelium that tends to form a mat with the grass leaves. The color of the patches will turn pink, especially at the margins, due to a color change in the mycelium when exposed to sunlight, thus the name pink snow mold. The patches may coalesce to form larger, irregular-shaped areas.

Environmental Effects. Microdochium patch is favored by high atmospheric humidities and air temperatures in the 32 to 45°F (0-7°C) range. Also, it occurs at air temperatures up to 65°F (18°C) under persistent wet drizzle or foggy conditions.

The occurrence of Microdochium patch is not limited to a snow cover association even though it also is called pink snow mold. It may occur during wet, cool to cold conditions of the fall or spring, and during the winter in regions with mild weather and minimal snowfall or even in the summer in colder regions. Microdochium patch occurs more on soils with good drainage when compared to Typhula blight. It also is enhanced on turfs that have a thick thatch, a high nitrogen nutritional level, and/or a soil pH above 6.5.

Causal Pathogen. *Microdochium nivale*.

teleomorph *Monographella nivalis*.

Formerly named *Fusarium nivale*.

This pathogen, an ascomycetes, attacks the shoots of grasses. The mycelium is cobwebby, and salmon to rose colored. The optimum pathogenicity temperature range for the pathogen is 32 – 44°F (0-6°C). The key survival structures under unfavorable conditions for growth are conidia and dormant mycelium in infected live plants and dead plant debris. Dissemination is by conidia, especially via water splash dispersal among the leaves, and as mycelium in leaves or soil by mechanical means, such as mowing, turf cultivations, and vertical cutting. Also, *Microdochium nivale* is seed-borne.

Host Cool-Season Turfgrasses:

Major   - annual bluegrasses (*Poa annua*).
          - bentgrasses (*Agrostis* species).

Minor   - fescues (*Festuca* species).
          - Kentucky bluegrass (*Poa pratensis*).
          - rough bluegrass (*Poa trivialis*).
          - ryegrasses (*Lolium* species).

Occurrence Documented: Northern Europe, Japan, North America, and southern Australia and New Zealand.

Cultural Controls:

1. Use a Microdochium patch resistant turfgrass species and cultivars, especially for Kentucky bluegrass.

2. Avoid nitrogen (N) fertilizations that stimulate lush shoot growth, especially in the fall.

3. Provide surface drainage for rapid removal of excess water.

4. Maintain a soil reaction in the acidic range of less than 6.5 pH.

5. Enhance air circulation over the turf canopy.

6. Remove any excess thatch when it occurs, as by vertical cutting.

Chemical Control. Fungicides for the control of Microdochium patch include systemics such as benomyl, cyproconazole, fenarimol, iprodione, mancozeb, propiconazole, thiophanate-methyl, triadimefon, or vinclozolin. Applications should be made during rainy, cold periods typical of the fall, with multiple treatments possibly needed. Also, they may be needed during midwinter thaws as well as in early spring.

Photo 23A-1. Microdochium patch. Each single patch has a round shape, but occurrence of many patches results in their coalescing to form larger, irregularly-shaped patches *(annual bluegrass fairway; early spring)*.

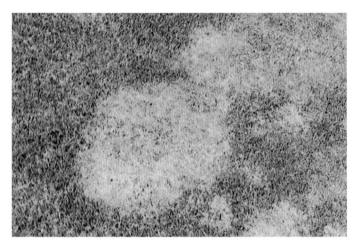

Photo 23A-2. A typical patch caused by Microdochium patch. Note the pinkish pattern along the edges of the patches *(annual bluegrass fairway; early spring)*.

Photo 23A-3. Rot symptoms of a turf infected by Microdochium patch. The pink color is more distinct under humid atmospheric conditions. *(Courtesy of Dr. Hironori Koga.)*

Photo 23A-4. Two types of patches caused by *Typhula ishikariensis* and *Microdochium nivale* appear as a mixed symptom. Snow molds usually do not occur on all areas of a golf course. Examination of all types of pathogens in the diseased area and treatment with a specific fungicide effective against the pathogen are very important in controlling these diseases *(annual bluegrass fairway; early spring)*.

CHAPTER 23B
Typhula Blights
(Gray Snow Mold)

Disease Characteristics. The initial symptoms of Typhula blight usually appear as snow thaw on the turf surface is occurring. Circular, light yellow to grayish-brown patches ranging from 2 – 30 inches (50 – 750 mm) in diameter appear, with most from 6 – 12 inches (150 – 300 mm). A grayish-white mycelium may be seen growing over or at the perimeter of the patch, especially during humid, wet periods. During drying the leaves become matted together, turn silvery-white, and become encrusted. The patches may coalesce to form larger, irregular-shaped areas. Depending on the conditions affecting the severity of the *Typhula* pathogen infection, only the leaves may be killed or both the leaves and meristematic node areas may be killed. Only the former situation allows shoot recovery.

Sclerotia of 1 to 5 mm in diameter form on the infected leaves. Mature sclerotia are useful in distinguishing the causal agent of the apparent disease, since *Typhula incarnata* forms orange-brown to pink sclerotia, and *Typhula ishikariensis* forms dark-brown to black sclerotia. Furthermore, the former pathogen forms pink fruiting bodies or sporocarps, while the latter pathogen forms grayish-white to light-brown ones in the fall.

Environmental Effects. Typhula blight occurs most commonly in high snowfall areas, although it is known to occur in wet, cold weather with little snow cover at temperatures of 36 to 40°F (2-5°C). The most severe attacks are associated with a deep snow on unfrozen turf-soil. *T. ishikariensis* occurs more in regions with a longer cover of snow and also causes more turf damage, when compared to *T. incarnata*. The disease severity increases with the duration of snow cover. It is more damaging on turfs maintained at a high nitrogen level and/or with an excessive thatch. The disease tends to reoccur on the same sites.

Causal Pathogens.
- *Typhula incarnata.*
- *Typhula ishikariensis.*

These pathogens attack the shoots of grasses. The *Typhula* species are basidiomycetes which have clamp connections on the mycelium. The optimum temperature range for mycelial growth is 48 – 59°F (9 – 15°C), but it also can grow at low temperatures of 34 – 36°F (1 – 2°C). The survival structure under unfavorable conditions for growth is via sclerotia on and in infected plant tissues. Dissemination is primarily by basidiospores that are dispersed via wind and rain.

Host Cool-Season Turfgrasses:

Major - annual bluegrasses (*Poa annua*).
- bentgrasses (*Agrostis* species).
- ryegrasses (*Lolium* species).

Minor - fescues (*Festuca* species).
- Kentucky bluegrass (*Poa pratensis*).

Occurrence Documented: Northern portions of Asia, Europe, Northern Japan, and North America.

Cultural Controls:

1. Use a Typhula blight resistant turfgrass species and cultivar, especially for bentgrass.

2. Avoid fall nitrogen (N) fertilizations that stimulate lush shoot growth.

3. Control thatch accumulation when it occurs, as by vertical cutting.

4. Provide rapid surface and subsurface root zone drainage.

5. Place snow fence to reduce snow accumulations on key turf areas.

6. Remove snow drifts in early spring on key turf areas.

Chemical Controls. Iprodione or tolclofos-methyl controls both species of *Typhula*, while chloroneb, cyproconazole, fenarimol, flutolanil, PCNB, propiconazole, or triadimefon effectively control mainly *Typhula incarnata*. Apply a preventive fungicide before the first permanent snowfall.

Photo 23B-1. Patches of Typhula blight caused by *Typhula ishikariensis*. Each single patch has a round shape. But occurrence of many patches results in coalescing to form irregularly-shaped patches *(creeping bentgrass nursery; early spring).*

Photo 23B-2. Typhula blight caused by *Typhula ishikariensis*:

  A: initial symptom (Type I).

  B: advanced symptom (Type II).

(annual bluegrass fairway; early spring)

Photo 23B-3. The sclerotia of *Typhula ishikariensis*. The black granules observed on the blighted leaves are the sclerotia of *Typhula ishikariensis*. *(Courtesy of Dr. Takao Araki.)*

Photo 23B-4. The whitish fruiting bodies of *Typhula ishikariensis* that are formed in late fall. They usually are not observed on creeping bentgrass *(perennial ryegrass turf)*. *(Courtesy of Dr. Naoyuki Matsumoto.)*

Photo 23B-5. Typhula blight caused by *Typhula incarnata*. Large, irregularly-shaped patches occurred on a timothy turf. *(Courtesy of Dr. Takao Araki.)*

Photo 23B-6. The brown granules observed on the blighted leaves are the sclerotia of *Typhula incarnata*. *(Courtesy of Dr. Hironori Koga.)*

Photo 23B-7 The pinkish fruiting bodies of *Typhula incarnata* formed in late fall. They usually are not observed on creeping bentgrass *(perennial ryegrass turf)*. *(Courtesy of Dr. Naoyuki Matsumoto.)*

CHAPTER 23C
Pythium Snow Blight

Disease Characteristics. Initially small, round, tan to orange spots may appear. Necrosis starts at the leaf tips. Pythium snow blight then forms irregularly-shaped, light- to dark-brown patches ranging up to 6 inches (15 mm) in diameter. They may coalesce to form irregularly-shaped, large blighted turf areas of 2 to 6 feet (0.6 to 1.8 m) in diameter that appear after the snow thaws. Rotting of the grass shoots can be observed, involving a brown to tan color, with the rotted tissues filled with oospores.

Environmental Effects. Pythium snow blight occurs more commonly under highly humid areas with prolonged, deep snow on unfrozen soil, and is more extensive on water-saturated sites with poor soil drainage. It also is favored by high soil fertility levels.

Causal Pathogens:

- *Pythium iwayamai.*
- *Pythium paddicum.*

These pathogens, both being oomycetes, attack primarily the shoots and crowns of grasses. Their optimum temperature range is 30 to 32°F (-1 to 0°C). The survival structure under unfavorable conditions is via oospores in dead plant debris. Dissemination is by water movement and by mechanical means, such as turf cultivation and vertical cutting.

Host Cool-Season Turfgrasses:

Major - annual bluegrasses (*Poa annua*).
            - bentgrasses (*Agrostis* species).
Minor - fine-leaf fescues (*Festuca* species).

Occurrence Documented: Both northern Japan and North America.

Cultural Controls:

1. Provide adequate surface and subsurface root zone drainage.

2. Maintain a moderate to low soil fertility level when entering the period associated with the first permanent snowfall.

Chemical Control. Apply fungicides that are effective on oomycetes before the first permanent snowfall. Metalaxyl is most effective.

Photo 23C-1. Pythium snow blight causes a rotting of the infected tissues, and the tissues turn brown. *(Courtesy of Dr. Hironori Koga.)*

CHAPTER 23D
Snow Scald

Disease Characteristics. Snow scald causes irregularly-shaped patches ranging up to 6 inches (150 mm) in diameter that appear after snow melting. The individual patches may coalesce to form very large, irregularly-shaped areas.

Initially, the lesions on the leaves appear water-soaked and are covered with sparse, gray mycelium and tan sclerotia. The leaves then die and turn white. The crowns may become rotted under severe infections.

The fungus sporadically forms small, black sclerotia with a flat shape in the spring after the snow thaws and brown fruiting bodies in late fall. The sclerotia turn from cream to dull- black in color at maturity. They are found on the surface of leaves and within the leaf sheaths.

Environmental Effects. Snow scald is most severe on turfs under prolonged, deep snow on a frozen soil. Water-saturated soils reduce snow scald development.

Causal Pathogen. *Myriosclerotinia borealis.*

(syn. *Sclerotinia borealis*)

This is a weak pathogen, an ascomycetes, that attacks the shoots of grasses. The mycelium is gray in color. The sclerotia range in shape from round to oval to flake-like, with a 0.5 to 0.7 mm length. Ascospores are produced and dispersed in the fall. The optimum growth temperature for *Myriosclerotinia borealis* is 32°F (0°C). The survival structure under unfavorable conditions for growth is via sclerotia in plant debris. Local spread of mycelium is by plant-to-plant contact under a snow cover. Dissemination is by wind-borne ascospores and mechanical means, such as turf cultivation and vertical cutting.

Host Cool-Season Turfgrasses:

    Major - bentgrasses (*Agrostis* species).
                    - fine-leaf fescues (*Festuca* species).
                    - ryegrasses (*Lolium* species).
    Minor - most other cool-season turfgrasses.

Occurrence Documented: Northern areas of Europe, Japan, and North America.

Cultural Controls:

1. Select a more snow scald tolerant turfgrass species, such as Kentucky bluegrass.

2. Ensure a nitrogen (N) nutritional level that sustains moderate shoot growth in the fall and early spring, but avoid excessive nitrogen fertilization.

3. Use snow fence to prevent deep snow drifts on important turf areas, if possible.

4. Remove excessively deep snow accumulations from important turf areas, if possible.

5. Enhance snow thawing in late winter-early spring.

Chemical Control. Make two preventive fungicide applications, such as with benomyl, thiophanate-methyl or tolclofos-methyl, before the first permanent snowfall.

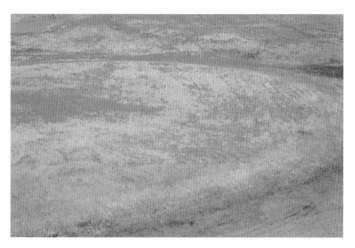

Photo 23D-1. Severe appearance of snow scald which has damaged the entire putting green. Most of the grass was dead. *(Courtesy of Dr. Takao Araki.)*

Photo 23D-2. The sclerotia of *Myriosclerotinia borealis*. Relatively large- sized, black granules are observed. *(Courtesy of Dr. Akitoshi Tajimi.)*

Photo 23D-3. The fruiting bodies of *Myriosclerotinia borealis* formed in late fall *(perennial ryegrass turf). (Courtesy of Dr. Naoyuki Matsumoto.)*

CHAPTER 24
Red Thread

Disease Characteristics. Initial symptoms of red thread appear as water-soaked lesions on the leaves. The lesions enlarge across the leaf which causes blighting to a tan to light-straw color. The resultant round patches in the turf are 1 to 2 inches (25 – 50 mm) in diameter. The patches may enlarge and coalesce to form irregular shapes up to 18 inches (450 mm) in diameter.

Red thread can be easily identified by the observation of pink to yellow to red, branched, stranded sclerotia extending up to 10 mm above the leaf tips and by pink to red, cottony flocks of mycelium up to 10 mm in diameter on the leaf blades, especially under humid conditions.

Turf damage by red thread may be limited, because the infection usually is on the leaf and stem parts, but it does not infect the roots. Turf recovery can be expected from species with a creeping growth habit.

Environmental Effects. Red thread usually occurs from midspring to early summer and in early fall on slow-growing turf, especially under humid conditions. It can be severe on bluegrasses during the summer in humid, cool climatic regions and on ryegrasses and fescues during the winter in mild-marine climates. A water-saturated atmosphere associated with prolonged, light rains and ground fog, plus 65 to 75°F (18-24°C) temperatures, favor red thread development. Slow shoot growth, as caused by a nitrogen deficiency and/or water stress, also favors red thread.

Causal Pathogen. *Laetisaria fuciformis.* Formerly named *Corticium fuciforme.*

This disease had been misidentified as pink patch caused by *Limonomyces roseipellis.* But these are completely different diseases.

This pathogen attacks the leaves of grasses. The mycelium do not have clamp connections. *Laetisaria fuciformis* grows at temperatures between 32 and 86°F (0 – 30°C), with the optimum growth being between 68 and 77°F (20 – 25°C). The survival structure during unfavorable periods for growth is via resting sclerotia on infected shoots and via mycelium in plant debris, such as thatch and mat. Dissemination is by wind-borne arthroconidia and by mycelium that are spread by water splash, wind, and mechanical means, such as via mowing, turf cultivation, and vertical cutting.

Host Cool-Season Turfgrasses:

Major - fine-leaf fescues (*Festuca* species).
- ryegrasses (*Lolium* species).

Minor - bentgrasses (*Agrostis* species).
- bluegrasses (*Poa* species).

Occurrence Documented: Australia, Europe, Japan, New Zealand, and North America.

Cultural Controls:

1. Use a seed blend of red thread resistant turfgrass cultivars, especially for the fine-leaf fescues and perennial ryegrass.

2. Increase the nitrogen (N) nutritional level judiciously, to sustain a moderate shoot growth rate.

3. Maintain adequate phosphorus (P) and potassium (K) levels, based on an annual chemical soil test.

4. Practice clipping removal during major infections.

5. Raise the mowing height, if possible.

Chemical Control. Cyproconazole, fenarimol, flutolanil, iprodione, propiconazole, triadimefon, or vinclozolin is effective in controlling red thread. A spot spray of the fungicide onto the patch at the initial stage of disease development should be sufficient for minor infections.

Photo 24-1. The sporadic occurrence of patches of red thread *(fairway of cool-season turfgrasses; midspring)*.

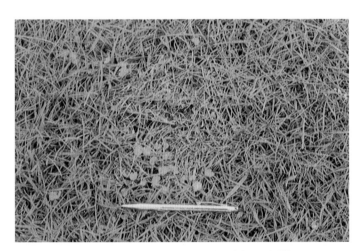

Photo 24-2. An initial patch symptom of red thread. The symptom is only a leaf blight *(fairway of cool-season turfgrasses; late spring)*.

Photo 24-3. A small patch symptom caused by red thread on a red fescue turf.

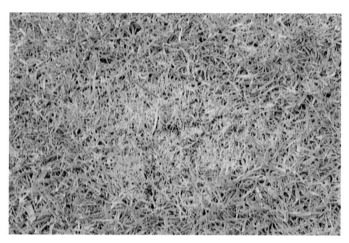

Photo 24-4. An advanced patch symptom of red thread with dead leaves and stems, and the soil partially exposed *(perennial ryegrass fairway; midspring).*

Photo 24-5. The red mycelial strings (arrow) and whitish mycelial mass (in center) are characteristics of the red thread causal pathogen *(perennial ryegrass; midspring).*

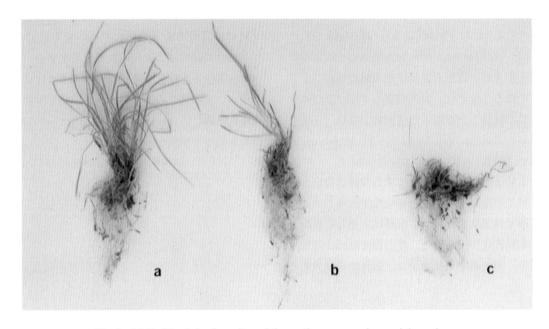

Photo 24-6. The infection sites of the pathogen causing red thread are the leaves and stems, while the roots are not infected by this pathogen:

a: healthy grass, **b:** early disease symptoms, **c:** severely diseased grass *(creeping bentgrass; artificially inoculated).*

CHAPTER 25
Pink Patch

Disease Characteristics. Pink patch occurs in light-green to reddish-brown, slightly thinned turf patches with a circular shape and a diameter of 8 to 24 inches (200 – 600 mm). The patches spread slowly. The color of patches may turn brown due to blighting of the grass shoots. Yellowing sometimes occurs, along with a smoky-ring shape. A gelatinous, pink to reddish film of hyphae forms on the leaves under high atmospheric humidity conditions after a prolonged rain. The leaves die from the tip downward. The disease is slow developing and rarely causes severe turf thinning. Pink patch was once considered to be red thread, but they are different diseases. Mycelium growth on the leaves, as observed with red thread, is not formed on pink patch.

Environmental Effects. Pink patch typically is severe in mid- to late spring and midfall, and is especially active in cooler climates. It is most severe on slow-growing plants, and especially under low nitrogen levels and infrequently mowed turfs.

Causal Pathogen. *Limonomyces roseipellis.* Formerly named both *Corticium fuciforme* and *Athelia fuciformis.*

This pathogen attacks the shoots of grasses. The formation of clamp connections at most septa aids in the identification of this fungus, as red thread does not have clamp connec-

tions. Optimum growth of *Limonomyces roseipellis* is at 77°F (25°C), while the pathogenicity to turfgrasses is high in the temperature range between 60 and 68°F (16 – 20°C), especially with extended periods of leaf wetness. Young leaves are less prone to infection than old leaves. The pathogen survives conditions unfavorable for growth saprophytically in plant residues, such as thatch, and starts to infect the turfgrass when the temperature rises into the favorable range. Dissemination is mainly via infected plant debris. It also is seed-borne.

Host Cool-Season Turfgrasses:

    Major - bentgrasses (*Agrostis* species).
                - fescues (*Festuca* species).
                - ryegrasses (*Lolium* species)
    Minor - bluegrasses (*Poa* species).

Occurrence Documented: Europe, Japan, and North America.

Cultural Controls:

1. Provide an adequate nitrogen (N) nutritional level that sustains a moderate shoot growth rate.

2. Remove any excess thatch when it occurs, as by vertical cutting.

3. Maintain proper soil water drainage, as by coring.

4. Prevent a deficiency of phosphorus (P) via fertilization as needed, based on a chemical soil test.

Chemical Control. Pink patch can be controlled by an application of tolclofos-methyl or propiconazole during the initial symptom development stage. A preventive application of iprodione, fenarimol, or triadimefon also is effective. Note that benomyl is effective in controlling red thread, but is ineffective on pink patch.

Photo 25-2. Close-up of pink patch. The turfgrass leaves are blighted, but the leaf blades still remain intact *(perennial ryegrass tee; midspring)*.

Photo 25-1. A severe pink patch occurrence involving a mixture of brown and yellow patches *(perennial ryegrass tee; midspring)*.

Photo 25-3. Gelatinous massing of hyphae on pink patch affected turf areas *(perennial ryegrass tee; midspring)*.

CHAPTER 26
Dollar Spot

Disease Characteristics. The origin of this disease name is based on the size of its patch which is similar to a U.S. silver dollar coin. On closely mowed turfs the symptoms are small, circular, sunken patches that seldom are larger than 2 inches (50 mm). The spots initially are brown and then turn a bleached-straw color. Once the dollar spots occur extensively, the patches coalesce with each other to form irregular shapes. However, this symptom will not develop to a large size like other diseases, with the size of a coalesced patch usually being only up to 6 inches (150 mm). When morning dew is present, a white cobweb-like growth of mycelium may be seen.

Lesions may be seen on infected leaves, especially on higher mowed turfs. They initially appear as small, yellow-green chlorotic spots, that turn a tan to bleached-straw color. Typically the lesions have a reddish-brown border and will enlarge across the full width of the leaf blade. Multiple lesions may occur which can cause blighting of the entire leaf.

Environmental Effects. Warm, humid days and cool nights that enhance dew formation, plus a humid turf canopy, will favor dollar spot occurrence. Dollar spot usually appears sporadically in midspring, with severe development observed from late spring to early summer. Its incidence typically declines during midsummer, but increases again in late summer and continues until mid- to late fall. The reduction of dollar spot during midsummer results from hot temperatures, but symptoms may still develop in cooler, shaded areas even during this period. A nitrogen deficiency and/or water stress increases dollar spot occurrence.

Causal Pathogen. Not clarified, thus will continue to use the name *Sclerotinia homoeocarpa*.

The European race has been known to form sclerotia, while the American race does not form this structure. The pathogen in Japan seems to be the American race, as the fungus has not been found to overwinter as sclerotia.

This pathogen attacks the leaves of grasses. It can grow between 50 and 95°F (10 – 35°C), with the optimum temperature for growth in a wide range of 68 to 86°F (20 – 30°C). Pathogenicity of the fungus occurs at temperatures as low as 50°F (10°C), but the fungus is most severe between 59 and 77°F (15 – 25°C). The pathogen survives unfavorable conditions for growth via mycelium on plant debris and as sclerotia. Dissemination is primarily as infected plant debris by mechanical means, such as mowing, turf cultivation, and vertical cutting. The patches sometimes appear in a straight line, which indicates this pattern has resulted from movement of the pathogen via a mower.

Host Cool-Season Turfgrasses: This pathogen has a wide host range.

Major - bentgrasses (*Agrostis* species).
              - fine-leaf fescues (*Festuca* species).

Minor - bluegrasses (*Poa* species).
              - tall fescue (*Festuca arundinacea*).

Occurrence Documented: Australia, Central America, Europe, Japan, New Zealand, and North America.

Cultural Controls:

1. Use a dollar spot resistant turfgrass cultivar, especially for bentgrass.

2. Ensure a sufficient nitrogen (N) nutritional level to sustain a moderate shoot growth rate, especially in the spring and early summer.

3. Remove dew and exudate from the leaves in early morning, especially on closely mowed turfs.

4. Avoid plant water stress by timely irrigation, scheduled as infrequently as possible.

5. Time irrigations to minimize the duration of leaf wetness.

6. Raise the height of cut, if possible.

7. Provide good air movement across the turf canopy.

Chemical Control. This is the most common disease requiring control on golf courses throughout much of the world. Dollar spot can be controlled by many contact, nonsystemic and systemic fungicides, such as benomyl, fenarimol, iprodione, procymidone, propiconazole, thiophanate-methyl, triadimefon, or vinclozolin. However, tolerant *Sclerotinia homoeocarpa* biotypes have developed to the benzimidazole and dicarboximide fungicide groups, such as benomyl, iprodione, fenarimol, propiconazole, thiophanate-methyl and triadimefon. The development of tolerant biotypes may be minimized by practicing a fungicide program that alternates among fungicides with different modes of action and that involves using fungicide combinations which are synergistic.

Spot application of a fungicide onto the diseased areas may be enough to control dollar spot during certain times of the year in some locations. When a sign of severe disease occurrence is observed in the rainy season, an application of fungicide to the entire area is necessary. Furthermore, treatment to the entire turf area during very late summer may be needed under normal weather conditions. Afterwards, spot treatments on the infected areas may be sufficient. In those years or locations with rainy summers, application to the entire turf area is necessary in midsummer.

Note: Dollar spot of C_4, warm-season turfgrasses is discussed in Chapter 14.

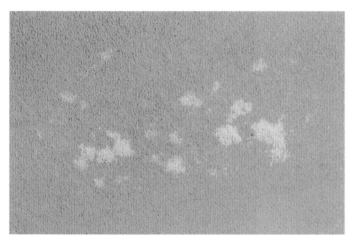

Photo 26-1. Typical patches of dollar spot appeared sporadically. The typical size of a patch is about the size of a U.S. silver dollar coin *(creeping bentgrass putting green; late spring).*

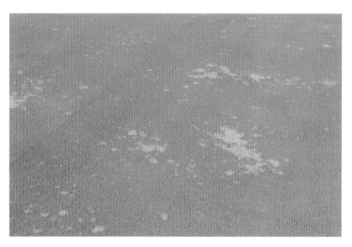

Photo 26-2. Severe patches of dollar spot. The patches may coalesce to form a large, irregular patch *(creeping bentgrass putting green; very early summer).*

Photo 26-3. Patches of dollar spot occurred on the edge of a putting green. The patches sometimes appear not only on the closely mowed green, but also on the higher-cut turf *(creeping bentgrass putting green; early summer).*

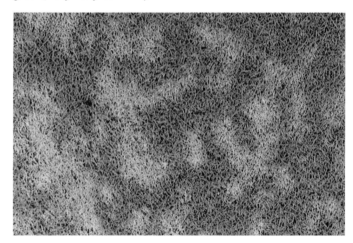

Photo 26-4. Patches of dollar spot in midsummer. The causal pathogen continues to spread even in midsummer on an area with more shade. Coalesced patches may form striped shapes *(creeping bentgrass putting green; midsummer).*

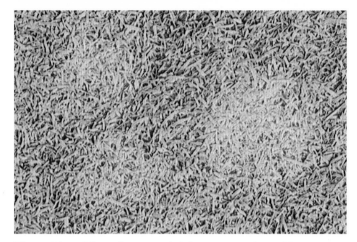

Photo 26-5. The color tone of dollar spot patches. The patches are buff colored equally at both the fringe and the inside of the patch *(creeping bentgrass putting green; very early summer).*

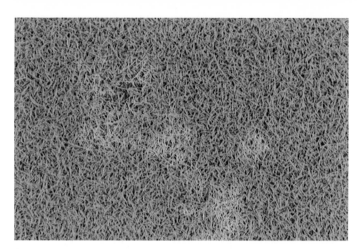

Photo 26-6. A patch of dollar spot at the initial stage. This patch looks similar to the symptom of leaf spot, but it is easy to distinguish by a simple humid identification method *(creeping bentgrass putting green; late spring).*

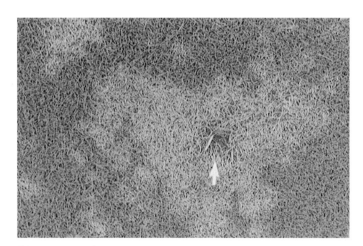

Photo 26-7. Several patches of dollar spot are coalesced into each other. The arrow indicates severe damage to the crowns. The dollar spot patch never forms a smoke-ring *(creeping bentgrass putting green; early summer).*

Photo 26-8. Trace of a patch of dollar spot that occurred in the fall. Note the disappearance of the grass and exposure of the bare soil *(creeping bentgrass putting green; late fall).*

Photo 26-9. Aligned patches of dollar spot that were produced by the pathogens being disseminated via a greens mower *(creeping bentgrass putting green; midsummer)*.

Photo 26-10. Severe damage caused by an iprodione-resistant strain of dollar spot *(creeping bentgrass putting green; late summer)*.

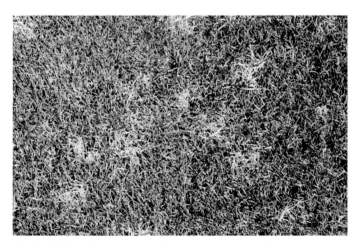

Photo 26-11. Patches of dollar spot on a perennial ryegrass tee *(late summer)*.

Photo 26-12. Patches of dollar spot on a tall fescue turf *(late summer)*.

Photo 26-13. A fungicide test (I) for the control of dollar spot in Japan:

  a: untreated control.

  b: iprodione wettable powder (1,000 times dilution, 24.5 gal/1,000 ft^2 or 100 liters/100 m^2) applied twice.

Photo was taken two weeks after the second application (late spring).

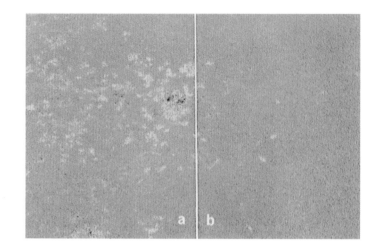

Photo 26-14. Fungicide test (II) in Japan for the control of dollar spot on a turf composed of an iprodione-resistant strain:

  a: thiophanate-methyl wettable powder (1,000 times dilution, 24.5 gal/1,000 ft^2 or 100 liters/100 m^2) applied once.

  b: untreated control.

Photo was taken two weeks after the application (late spring).

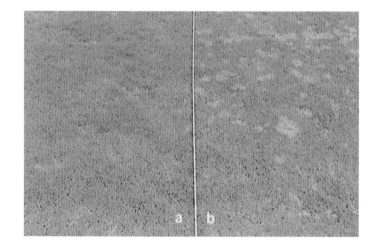

CHAPTER 27
Anthracnose

Disease Characteristics. The fungus forms dark, elongated setae from acervuli on the infected tissue surface. The observation of setae using a low-power magnifying glass (10x) is useful for rapid diagnosis of anthracnose. The symptoms of anthracnose disease can vary depending on the environmental and cultural conditions.

Basal Rot. Under wet, cool conditions anthracnose symptoms appear as a basal rot with a dark-brown discoloration on the lower portions of leaf sheaths. Water-soaked stem lesions may appear and then turn yellow to brown. Then the crown turns black and the shoot can be easily detached. Annual bluegrass is especially susceptible, with irregular patches up to 6 inches (15 mm) in diameter. Rooting is poor within the patch.

Foliage Blight. Under wet, warm conditions the initial anthracnose symptoms are elongated, reddish-brown lesions, which may enlarge, coalesce, and cover the entire leaf. The leaf turns yellow to light-tan to brown and dies. Older leaves are especially prone to attack. The disease progresses to irregular-shaped patches in the turf of 2 inches to 6 feet (25 mm to 2 meters) in width. The patch color turns from reddish-brown to yellow to tan to brown.

HAS Syndrome. A disease complex of *Colletotrichum graminicola* and *Bipolaris sorokiniana* has been described on senescing leaves of annual bluegrass at high night temperatures, above 80°F (27°C).

Environmental Effects. Anthracnose usually occurs in the spring to early summer and also during the fall. The disease severity is most pronounced between 59 and 77°F (15 – 25°C). Infection occurs primarily when the plant is stressed. Severe anthracnose often occurs on bentgrass greens with poor soil drainage and under high atmospheric humidities after an intense or prolonged rain. A deficiency of phosphorus (P) and/or potassium (K) also favors the occurrence of anthracnose.

Causal Pathogen. *Colletotrichum graminicola* teleomorph *Glomerella graminicola.*

This pathogen attacks the shoots and roots of grasses. Optimum mycelium growth of this pathogen is at 77°F (25°C). Conidia formed on the surface of leaves are spread via raindrops. Their infection site depends on the season. Older leaves tend to be infected in the warmer season, while the stem base is the site during cool seasons. Survival of *Colletotrichum graminicola* during conditions unfavorable for growth is as a saprophyte on plant debris or as mycelium in live plant tissue. Dissemination is by rain splash, wind and mechanical means, such as turf cultivation and vertical cutting.

Host Cool-Season Turfgrasses: Anthracnose has a wide host range among the grasses, but there may be some host specificity among the fungi, including both species and cultivars of turfgrasses.

Major   - annual bluegrasses (*Poa annua*).
             - fescues (*Festuca* species).

Minor   - bentgrasses (*Agrostis* species).
             - perennial ryegrass (*Lolium perenne*).

Occurrence Documented: Europe, Japan, and North America.

Cultural Controls:

1. Provide a nitrogen (N) nutritional level that sustains a moderate shoot growth rate.

2. Remove any excessive thatch when it occurs, as by vertical cutting.

3. Irrigate in early morning to minimize the length of time free water remains on the surface of turfgrass shoots.

4. Maintain a properly balanced fertilization program, with phosphorus (P) and potassium (K) applied based on an annual chemical soil test.

5. Replace the annual bluegrass with a less susceptible turfgrass species/cultivar.

6. Correct soil compaction via turf cultivation, as by coring.

Chemical Control. Fungicides, such as fenarimol, propiconazole, tolclofos-methyl, or triadimefon, are effective in anthracnose control.

Photo 27-1. The acervuli of *Colletotrichum graminicola* with hair-like setae (a) can be observed with a low-power magnifying glass (10x) as black spots on the surface of leaves infected by anthracnose, and (b) magnified setae as observed with a high-power microscope (400x). This former observation is useful for a rapid diagnosis.

Photo 27-2. Mature acervuli with setae occurring in rows in the interveinal areas of the leaf blade of annual bluegrass. *(Courtesy of Dr. Joseph M. Vargas, Jr.)*

Photo 27-3. Types of patches caused by anthracnose:

    A: cluster of typical patches *(creeping bentgrass green; late spring).*

    B: smoky-ring shape of patch *(creeping bentgrass green edge; late spring).*

    C: advanced, larger, irregular-shaped patches *(creeping bentgrass green; late spring).*

    D: post-disease damaged annual bluegrass fairway *(courtesy of Dr. Joseph M. Vargas, Jr.).*

CHAPTER 28

Drechslera/Bipolaris Diseases:

Brown Blight, Leaf Spot, Melting-Out, & Net Blotch

INTRODUCTION

Diseases of turfgrasses caused by the *Drechslera* and *Bipolaris* genera were known by the group name of Helminthosporium diseases. They cause leaf, crown, lateral stem, and root rots.

The *Drechslera* species attack mainly Pooid, C_3, cool-season turfgrasses, with one exception which is zonate leaf spot of the Chloridoid bermudagrasses. These fungi have mycelium, conidia, and conidiophores that range from clear to yellowish to brown in color, depending on the species. The mycelium can grow both inside live plant tissues and along the leaf surface. It also can grow saprophytically on dead plant tissues.

The *Bipolaris* genus of turfgrass diseases also was included within the group of Helminthosporium diseases. The genus is specific in attacking C_4, warm-season turfgrasses such as the Chloridoid and Panicoid, with one exception. It is *Bipolaris sorokiniana* which is a nonspecific pathogen on most species of turfgrasses.

Note: Bipolaris leaf blotch of C_4, warm-season turfgrasses is discussed in Chapter 16.

Table 29-1. A Summary of the Drechslera/Bipolaris Diseases, Causal Pathogen, and Host Turfgrasses

Common name	Causal pathogen	Host turfgrasses	Chapter
Brown blight	*Drechslera siccans* (syn. *Helminthosporium siccans*)	perennial ryegrass annual ryegrass tall fescue	28A
Bipolaris Leaf spot	*Bipolaris sorokiniana* (syn. *H. sativum*)	annual bluegrasses bentgrasses fine-leaf fescues Kentucky bluegrass perennial ryegrass tall fescue	28B
Melting-out	*Drechslera poae* (syn. *H. vagans*)	Kentucky bluegrass	28C
Net blotch	*Drechslera dictyoides* (syn. *H. dictyoides*)	fine-leaf fescues tall fescue perennial ryegrass Kentucky bluegrass	28D
Bipolaris leaf blotch	*Bipolaris cynodontis* (syn. *H. cynodontis*)	bermudagrasses	16
Red leaf spot	*Drechslera erythrospila* (syn. *H. erythrospilum*)	bentgrasses	———
Zonate leaf spot	*Drechslera gigantea* (syn. *H. giganteum*)	bermudagrasses	———

CHAPTER 28A
Brown Blight

Disease Characteristics. The initial symptoms are small, brown, multiple spots on the leaf blades of grass. Dark-brown, elongated streaks also may appear on the blades. The lesion center may turn light-brown to white as the lesion enlarges. The entire leaf blade may become necrotic if the infection is severe. This is followed by crown and root rots, resulting in thinning of the turf.

Environmental Effects. Brown blight leaf lesions occur mainly during moist, cool periods of the spring and fall. Free water on the leaf surface is required for spores to form germ tubes and invade the leaves of grasses. The crown and root rots appear primarily during the summer.

Causal Pathogen. *Drechslera siccans*.
teleomorph *Pyrenophora lolii* Dovaston.
(syn. *Helminthosporium siccans*)

This pathogen attacks the shoots, crowns, and roots. *Drechslera siccans* is characterized by light-yellow to golden-brown conidia and chestnut-brown conidiophores. It survives unfavorable periods for growth as dormant mycelium in the infected tissues of live plants and saprophytically in dead tissue, such as the thatch and mat. Dissemination is by infected leaf clippings and by spores via wind, water splash, machines, and animals.

Host Cool-Season Turfgrasses:

Major   - perennial ryegrass (*Lolium perenne*).

Minor   - annual ryegrass (*Lolium multiflorum*).
    - tall fescue (*Festuca arundinacea*).

Occurrence Documented: Australia, Europe, New Zealand, and North America.

Cultural Controls.

1. Use a seed blend of brown blight resistant turfgrass cultivars, especially for perennial ryegrass.

2. Maintain adequate nitrogen (N) nutritional levels to sustain moderate shoot growth, especially in the spring and fall.

3. Schedule irrigations so free water remains on the leaves as short a time as possible.

4. Raise the height of cut, if possible.

5. Remove any excess thatch as it occurs, as by vertical cutting.

Chemical Control. Iprodione, mancozeb, and vinclozolin may be effective in the control of brown blight. Avoid continuous, excessive applications of certain fungicides in the demethylation inhibitor (DMI) and benzimidazole groups.

CHAPTER 28B
Bipolaris Leaf Spot

Disease Characteristics. The initial symptoms of Bipolaris leaf spot are multiple, small, purple to dark-brown spots on the leaf blades. The lesions expand to 3 to 6 mm, with the centers turning a light-tan color and they may coalesce. The entire blade may develop a purplish, water-stressed appearance, and turn straw-colored. Severe infections can extend to the crowns, lateral stems, and roots that become rotted; resulting in thinning of the turf in irregular-shaped, brownish patches in a relatively short time of 4 to 5 days.

On bentgrasses, a smoky-blue appearance develops in 12 to 40 inch (300-1,000 mm) diameter, irregular patches; followed by yellowing and then death of plants in matted areas. The leaf lesions consist of yellow flecks that progress to oval spots and then to water-soaked blotches.

Environmental Effects. Bipolaris leaf spot usually occurs during the rainy, humid, warm- to hot- weather of summer. The leaf spot phase appears at temperatures of 70°F (21°C), while advanced leaf blight begins to occur at 86°F (30°C). Extensive turf thinning occurs at 95°F (35°C) and above. The saprophytic growth of the fungus and spore production is enhanced by cycles of wetting and drying of the plant debris. Plant water stress and/or a high nitrogen level increase the severity of Bipolaris leaf spot.

Causal Pathogen. *Bipolaris sorokiniana.* teleomorph *Cochliobolus sativus.* (syn. *Helminthosporium sativum.*)

This pathogen attacks the leaves, crowns, lateral stems, and roots of grasses. *Bipolaris sorokiniana* is characterized by dark-brown mycelium, olive-brown conidia, and brown conidiophores. Survival during unfavorable periods for growth is by dormant mycelium in infected plant tissues and saprophytically in dead plant debris, such as thatch and mat. Dissemination is primarily by spores produced on infected leaf clippings via wind, water, machines, and animals. It also is seed-borne.

Host Cool-Season Turfgrasses:

Major - Kentucky bluegrass (*Poa pratensis*).
- bentgrasses (*Agrostis* species).
- fine-leaf fescues (*Festuca* species).

Minor - annual bluegrasses (*Poa annua*).
- ryegrasses (*Lolium* species).
- tall fescue (*Festuca arundinacea*).

Occurrence Documented: Northern Europe, and Northern North America.

Cultural Controls:

1. Use a seed blend of Bipolaris leaf spot resistant turfgrass cultivars, especially for Kentucky bluegrass.

2. Maintain adequate nitrogen (N) nutritional levels to sustain moderate shoot growth during the summer.

3. Ensure high soil phosphorus (P) and potassium (K) levels based on chemical soil tests.

4. Raise the height of cut to 2 inches (50 mm) or higher, if possible.

5. Remove the leaf clippings.

6. Remove any excess thatch when it occurs, as by vertical cutting.

7. Irrigate as needed to avoid drought stress.

Chemical Control. Both contact and penetrant fungicides are available to control the Bipolaris leaf spot disease. The contact fungicides include iprodione, mancozeb, or vinclozolin; while the localized penetrant fungicides include propiconazole. Apply when night air temperatures do not fall below 70°F (21°C) and the relative humidity is above 85%. Multiple applications in both the spring and fall may be required.

Note: This pathogen also occurs on seedling grasses, with severe damage likely.

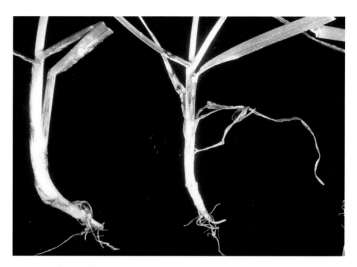

Photo 28B-2. Shoots of Kentucky bluegrass infected with Bipolaris leaf spot. *(Courtesy of Dr. Phillip F. Colbaugh.)*

Photo. 28B-1. Various phases of turf loss on a creeping bentgrass green caused by Bipolaris leaf spot. *(Courtesy of Dr. Malcolm C. Shurtleff.)*

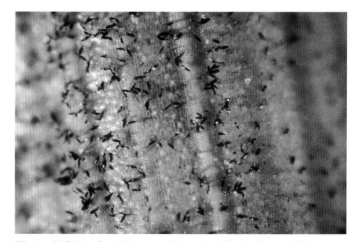

Photo 28B-3. Conidial sporulation by *Bipolaris sorokiniana* on leaf clippings of Kentucky bluegrass. *(Courtesy of Dr. Phillip F. Colbaugh.)*

CHAPTER 28C
Melting-Out

Disease Characteristics. The initial symptoms of melting-out are small, water-soaked spots that turn purple/brown/black in appearance on the leaf blades, and then the leaf sheaths. The lesions enlarge in an elongated shape of 6 to 9 mm with a necrotic brown to tan center, and may have a yellowish border. An extensive infection of the leaf sheaths results in girdling and abscission of the leaves. This event is the origin of the expression "melting-out." Severe infections spread to produce rotting of the crowns, rhizomes, and roots. The turf appearance becomes yellowish to reddish-brown, and is seriously thinned.

Environmental Effects. Optimum leaf lesion development occurs at air temperatures of 65 to 75°F (18-24°C), high atmospheric humidities, and cloudy, low sunlight conditions. The melting-out lesion stage typically develops during rainy, wet, cool conditions in the spring and fall, with the crown and root rot stages and resultant turf thinning occurring during the warm weather of late spring-early summer. Infected plants are more prone to wilting, even in moist soils.

Causal Pathogen. *Drechslera poae*.
   (syn. *Helminthosporium vagans*)

   This pathogen attacks the shoots, crowns, rhizomes, and roots of grasses. *Drechslera poae* is characterized by hyaline to buff-colored mycelium, olive-brown to dark-brown conidia, and light yellow-brown conidiophores. Survival is by conidia and dormant mycelia in infected live plant tissue and saprophytically in dead tissue, such as thatch and mat. Leaf clippings are a major source of conidia for infection, which is most severe when the leaf surface is wet. Mowing is a primary means of conidia dislodging and dispersal. Dissemination is by infected leaf clippings, especially from mowing, and by spores via wind, water splash, animals and machines. It also is seed-borne.

Host Cool-Season Turfgrasses:

   Major - Kentucky bluegrass (*Poa pratensis*).

   Minor - other bluegrasses (other *Poa* species).
          - ryegrasses (*Lolium* species).

Occurrence Documented: Europe, and Northern North America.

Cultural Controls:

1. Use a seed blend of melting-out resistant turfgrass cultivars, especially for Kentucky bluegrass.

2. Raise the cutting height to at least 2 inches (50 mm), if possible.

3. Maintain an adequate nitrogen (N) nutritional level needed to sustain moderate shoot growth.

4. Irrigate as needed to avoid plant water stress.

5. Remove any excess thatch when it occurs, as by vertical cutting.

6. Remove leaf clippings.

Chemical Control. The preferred approach is to use a seed blend of two to four of the many melting-out resistant Kentucky bluegrass cultivars. The fungicides effective in controlling Bipolaris leaf spot, iprodione, mancozeb, propiconazole and vinclozolin, also are effective in the management of melting-out disease, with multiple applications in the spring and fall usually involved.

Photo 28C-1. Typical thinning symptoms of melting-out in a Kentucky bluegrass turf. *(Courtesy of Dr. Malcolm C. Shurtleff.)*

Photo 28C-2. Irregular-shaped damage to a Kentucky bluegrass turf caused by melting-out. *(Courtesy of Dr. Joseph M. Vargas, Jr.)*

Photo 28D-1. Close view of net blotch lesions on the leaves of tall fescue. *(Courtesy of Dr. Phillip F. Colbaugh.)*

Photo 28D-2. View of net blotch lesions on the leaves of tall fescue. *(Courtesy of Dr. Nichole R. O'Neill.)*

CHAPTER 28D
Net Blotch

Disease Characteristics. The initial symptom of net blotch is small, reddish-brown to black, irregular-shaped spots on the leaf blade. They expand across the width of the blade of fine-leaf fescues causing death of the upper leaf. Small, irregular-shaped, 2 to 4 inch (50 — 100 mm) patches of tan-colored, dead shoots occur in the turf.

On tall fescue the lesions appear as dark-purple to brown-black, irregular, transverse strands or streaks, resembling a net which may extend across the leaf. The shoots turn yellow, then brown, and die back from the tips. Turf thinning and irregular-shaped patches of dead shoots can occur.

Environmental Effects. Net blotch leaf lesions and both crown and root rots occur primarily during moist, cool weather in the spring and fall, and also in the summer in cool temperate climates.

Causal Pathogen. *Drechslera dictyoides*.
        teleomorph *Pyrenophora dictyoides*.
        (syn. *Helminthosporium dictyoides*.)

This pathogen attacks the shoots, crowns, rhizomes, and roots of grasses. *Drechslera dictyoides* is characterized by light to buff-colored mycelium, nearly colorless to yellowish-brown conidia, and dark-brown to olive-brown conidiophores.

The survival mechanism during conditions unfavorable for growth is by dormant mycelium in live plant tissue and saprophytically in dead tissues, such as thatch and mat. Dissemination is by spores via wind, water, machines, and animals.

Occurrence Documented: Australia, Europe, New Zealand, and North America.

Host Cool-Season Turfgrasses:

Major - fine-leaf fescues (*Festuca* species).
      - tall fescue (*Festuca arundinacea*).
      - perennial ryegrass (*Lolium perenne*).
Minor - Kentucky bluegrass (*Poa pratensis*).

Cultural Controls:

1. Use a seed blend of net blotch resistant turfgrass cultivars, especially for red fescue.

2. Use minimal amounts of nitrogen (N) fertilizer, especially in the spring.

3. Maintain adequate levels of phosphorus (P) and potassium (K) based on an annual chemical soil test.

4. Irrigate infrequently and modestly to sustain minimal needed soil moisture levels.

5. Raise the height of cut, if possible.

6. Remove any excess thatch as it occurs, as by vertical cutting.

Chemical Control. Fungicides usually are not used on these low-maintenance fescue turfs. Certain fungicides can provide control of net blotch lesions, such as iprodione, mancozeb, or vinclozolin.

CHAPTER 29
Powdery Mildew

Disease Characteristics. The initial sign of powdery mildew appears as individual colonies or tufts of fine, white mycelium on the leaves. The colonies then enlarge and coalesce to eventually cover most of the leaf. The result is a grayish-white, dusty or powdery appearance on the leaves. Symptoms may occur as severe infections which cause the leaves to turn yellow to tan to brown. These severely infected plants are weakened, and may die if exposed to additional stresses. Older leaves are more severely damaged than younger leaves. Severe infections may cause a general thinning of the turf, especially in shaded sites.

Environmental Effects. Powdery mildew typically occurs in the spring and fall seasons. It is favored by humid, cloudy weather. The optimum temperature range is 60 to 72°F (15 — 22°C). The disease attacks with the most severity those grasses that are under environmental stress, especially shade environments with a low light intensity, high humidity, and poor air movement.

Causal Pathogen. *Erysiphe graminis.*

This fungus is an obligate parasite that attacks the leaves and shoots of grasses. The fungus penetrates the epidermal cell walls, and then feeds by a special structure, the hausto-rium, that extends into the lamea of the epidermal cells. *Erysiphe graminis* survives unfavorable growth conditions for growth primarily via mycelium on living plant tissue. In very cold climates it overwinters as ascospores in brown to black cleistothecia on infected plants. Dissemination is relatively rapid, primarily by conidia via wind.

Host Cool-Season Turfgrasses: Highly specialized races of this pathogen can develop, with each race being specific to a single grass cultivar.

Major - Kentucky bluegrass (*Poa pratensis*).
- fine-leaf fescues (*Festuca* species).

Minor - bentgrasses (*Agrostis* species).
- ryegrasses (*Lolium* species).

Occurrence Documented: Europe, North America, and Northern Japan.

Cultural Controls:

1. Avoid nitrogen (N) and irrigation levels that produce succulent, lush leaf growth.

2. Mow the turfgrass at a high height, if possible.

3. Selectively prune tree limbs to enhance sunlight levels and air movement under the tree canopy.

4. Use a polystand of shade-adapted turfgrass species and cultivars.

Chemical Control: Powdery mildew can be controlled with the demethylation inhibitor (DMI) fungicides, such as cyproconazole, fenarimol, propiconazole, or triadimefon. Unfortunately, *Erysiphe graminis* strains will eventually develop resistance to benzimidazole fungicides.

Photo 29-1. Powdery mildew on a Kentucky bluegrass turf. *(Courtesy of The Scotts Company.)*

Photo 29-2. A Kentucky bluegrass turf thinned by powdery mildew. *(Courtesy of Dr. Lee L. Burpee.)*

Photo 29-3. Close view of powdery mildew on leaf blades of Kentucky bluegrass. *(Courtesy of Dr. Lee L. Burpee.)*

Photo 29-4. Two leaves of Kentucky bluegrass severely infected with the white powdery appearance of powdery mildew. *(Courtesy of Dr. Ralph S. Byther.)*

CHAPTER 30
Rust Diseases:
Crown, Leaf, Stem, and Stripe

Disease Characteristics. Typical symptoms of the rust diseases include initial light-yellow flecks on the leaf blades and sheaths, which enlarge, elongate, and turn yellow. These infection areas become raised above the epidermis and eventually rupture as yellow to orange to reddish-brown spores protrude. The spores release when contacted. The leaf blade turns yellow starting at the tip and progressing to the base. Under a severe rust infection the shoot growth is slowed, a yellowish to red-brown appearance develops, and the turf is thinned as individual plants die.

Environmental Effects. The occurrence of rust disease may start in early spring or some time through midsummer, depending on the north-south site location. Infection is favored by moist, low-sunlight conditions. The optimal temperature range for rust is between 65 and 86°F (18 and 30°C), depending on the rust species. Spore release typically is very active during early to late spring and late summer to midfall. The rust infection is most severe on slow-growing grasses, and especially under low nitrogen (N) nutritional levels and/or plant water stress.

Causal Pathogens: There are many *Puccinia* species that cause rust diseases on turfgrasses, with four being major pathogens of turfgrasses (Table 30-1).

Uromyces dactylidis causes problems by forming large amounts of yellow-brown urediniospores, while *Puccinia striiformis* is characterized by uredinia formation on leaves without abundant production of spores.

Rust disease injury on bentgrass leaves caused by *Puccinia coronata* var. *coronata* generally occurs on unmowed areas, and rarely on the edges of mowed turf areas where it causes minimal thinning of the turf. Also, abundant urediniospores of *Puccinia coronata* var. *coronata* are produced on tall fescue leaves in tall-growing areas.

These pathogens attack the leaves and shoots of grasses. Rust fungi have narrow host ranges, and are pathogenic to specific cultivars of turfgrasses. These pathogens are obligate parasites, and cannot saprophytically overwinter in dead plant residues. Thus, survival during unfavorable conditions for growth is via mycelium in diseased grass plants and as teliospores. The sporulation of urediniospores is active between 50 and 77°F (10 and 25°C), and the spores spread the disease by becoming airborne. A high atmospheric humidity is required to germinate the spores and also for infection through the stomata in leaf blades.

Occurrence Documented: Africa, Asia, Australia, Europe, Japan, New Zealand, North America, and South America.

Cultural Controls:

1. Select a seed blend of turfgrass cultivars that are resistant to the rusts found in that location, especially for Kentucky bluegrass and perennial ryegrass.

   The interactions between specific resistant genes of each cultivar of a grass and the specific genes of fungi determine the disease occurrence for a given cultivar. There is no cultivar of turfgrass immune to all races of rust fungi. Since many turfgrass cultivars possess different resistant genes, seeding a blend of cultivars possessing a specific resistant gene to the pathogen of a specific region is possible. Determination of an avirulence gene of each race of fungus distributed in each region can lead to identification of a resistant cultivar that is suitable to the region.

2. Maintain an adequate nitrogen (N) level that sustains a moderate shoot growth rate, but avoid excessively high application rates.

3. Avoid excessively close mowing heights, if possible.

4. Remove clippings.

5. Reduce any excessive thatch depth as it occurs, as by vertical cutting.

6. Minimize the time moisture remains on the leaf surface, by proper scheduling of irrigation.

Chemical Control. Certain fungicides can be used to manage rust diseases, such as fenarimol, mancozeb, myclobutanil, propiconazole, or triadimefon.

Note: Zoysia rust of zoysiagrasses is discussed in Chapter 15.

Table 30-1. A Summary of the Four Major Rust Diseases, Causal Pathogens, and Host Turfgrasses

Common name	Scientific name	Major host	Minor host	Uredenia color/pattern
Crown rust	*Puccinia coronata*	perennial ryegrass (*Lolium perenne*) tall fescue (*Festuca arundinacea*)	bentgrass (*Agrostis* spp.) Kentucky bluegrass (*Poa pratensis*)	orange/scattered
Leaf rust	*Uromyces dactylidis*	bluegrass (*Poa* spp.)	bentgrass (*Agrostis* spp.) fescues (*Festuca* spp.)	yellow-brown/stripes
Stem or black rust	*Puccinia grammis*	ryegrass (*Lolium* spp.) bluegrass (*Poa* spp.)	bentgrass (*Agrostis* spp.) fescues (*Festuca* spp.)	brown/long stripes
Stripe or yellow rust	*Puccinia striiformis*	Kentucky bluegrass (*Poa pratensis*)	bentgrass (*Agrostis* spp.) perennial ryegrass (*L. perenne*)	yellow/stripes

Photo 30-1. Severe rust disease symptoms on perennial ryegrass that had been winter overseeded onto a manila zoysiagrass turf *(very early spring)*.

Photo 30-2. Urediniosori of rust on leaves of Kentucky bluegrass. *(Courtesy of The Scotts Company.)*

Photo 30-3. The symptoms of rust on bentgrass:

A: orange-colored areas appear on an unmowed, tall-growing rough *(creeping bentgrass, midfall)*.

B: thinning at the edge of a creeping bentgrass green caused by rust disease *(midfall)*.

Photo 30-4. Fungicide test for the control of rust in Japan:

A: the central block possessing green grass was treated with myclobutanil emulsifiable concentrate (3,000 times dilution, 7.37 gal/1,000 ft² or 30 liters/100 m²) applied twice.

B: close-up of (left) treated; (right) untreated control *(annual bluegrass putting green; midspring)*.

CHAPTER 31
Stripe Smut

Disease Characteristics. The first symptom of stripe smut is yellow-green, narrow, elongated streaks on stiff, erect leaf blades and sheaths. As the disease progresses the leaf blade curls, with parallel, gray to black stripes extending the length of the leaf. Black, soot-like puffs of spores are released from sori in the silver-gray stripes, especially when touched. Older, infected leaves become split, twisted, and shredded from the tips downward. The infection may occur in individual plants scattered throughout the turf or may be concentrated in large patches. Turfgrass root growth and tillering are reduced. Infected turfs gradually decline in density over a period of 4 to 5 years.

The identification of stripe smut on closely mowed bentgrasses is more difficult due to the lack of large, distinct sori pattern development.

Environmental Effects. Symptoms of stripe smut typically appear in the cool weather of the spring and fall at temperatures in the 50 to 60°F (10 — 16°C) range. Turfgrass loss is accelerated in older turfs by hot, dry weather, especially when improperly fertilized. An excessive thatch accumulation increases the severity of stripe smut attacks.

Causal Pathogen: *Ustilago striiformis.*

This pathogen attacks the meristematic buds on the crowns, stolons, and rhizomes of grasses. The fungus behaves as a systemic, perennial pathogen within infected plants. Sori-containing spores form below the leaf epidermis and eventually rupture the epidermis. The teliospores of *Ustilago striiformis* occur singly. Survival under conditions unfavorable for growth is via spores in infected tissues, thatch, mat and soil; and by mycelium in vegetative plant parts. Dissemination is by seed, wind, water, soil, machine, animals, and infected live plants.

Host Cool-Season Turfgrasses: Numerous subspecies of *Ustilago striiformis* occur with each having a high host specificity.

Major - Kentucky bluegrasses (*Poa pratensis*), certain cultivars.
- bentgrasses (*Agrostis* species), certain cultivars.

Minor - annual bluegrasses (*Poa annua*).

Occurrence Documented: Europe and North America.

Cultural Controls:

1. Use a seed blend of stripe smut resistant turfgrass cultivars, especially for Kentucky bluegrass.

2. Avoid high nitrogen (N) fertility levels, especially in the summer. Apply only enough nitrogen to sustain moderate leaf growth.

3. Maintain a balanced (N-P-K-Fe) fertility level, based on an annual chemical soil test.

4. Irrigate as needed to prevent drought stress.

Chemical Control. A systemic demethylation inhibitor (DMI) fungicide, such as cyproconazole, fenarimol, propiconazole or triadimefon, is effective in managing stripe smut.

Note: Flag smut caused by *Urocystis agropyri* is a related disease with symptoms similar to those of stripe smut.

Photo 31-1. Stripe smut disease symptoms on a turf of Kentucky bluegrass. *(Courtesy of The Scotts Company.)*

Photo 31-2. Lateral view of a Kentucky bluegrass turf severely damaged by stripe smut. *(Courtesy of Dr. Ralph S. Byther.)*

Photo 31-3. Elongated streaks of stripe smut on severely infected leaf blades of Kentucky bluegrass. *(Courtesy of The Scotts Company.)*

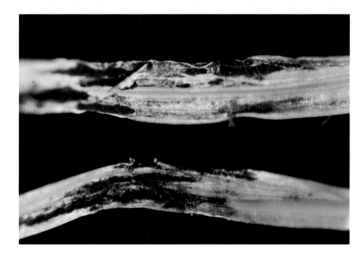

Photo 31-4. Close-up of two Kentucky bluegrass leaves that are severely infected with stripe smut. *(Courtesy of Dr. Ralph S. Byther.)*

CHAPTER 32
Leptosphaerulina Leaf Blight

Disease Characteristics. Discolored, irregular-shaped areas in the turf without a well-defined border between the healthy and diseased areas, or small patches with a brown color and a diameter of 2 to 4 inches (50 — 100 mm) are the typical symptoms of Leptosphaerulina leaf blight. Leaf symptoms involve a yellowing of the tips which turn water-soaked, then brown, and can extend down the leaf sheath. Turf recovery of the patches usually occurs in the warmer season.

Environmental Effects. Leptosphaerulina leaf blight is favored by extended periods of hot, wet weather. This disease occurs at high atmospheric humidities, and especially on soils with poor drainage. It can be severe on grasses that have been weakened by unfavorable environmental conditions or by herbicides that are only partially selective. The appearance of this disease often is increased on turfgrasses that have been weakened by nutrient deficiencies.

Causal Pathogens: *Leptosphaerulina australis.*
    Leptosphaerulina trifolii.
    (syn. *Pleospora gaumannii* and *Pseudoplea gaumannii*)

This pathogen attacks the leaves of grasses. Infection occurs primarily on senescing leaves. Abundant ascospores are formed on the infected leaves. Leptosphaerulina leaf spot is easily diagnosed by the microscopic observation of these ascospores. Tiny, brown perithecia form in the dead lesions on grass leaves. *Leptosphaerulina* mainly survive saprophytically during periods unfavorable for growth via perithecia or mycelium in plant debris. Dissemination is primarily by mowing activities.

Host Cool-Season Turfgrasses: Leptosphaerulina leaf blight has relatively weak pathogenicities to a wide range of plant hosts.

  Major - bentgrasses (*Agrostis* species).

  Minor - bluegrasses (*Poa* species).
      - fescues (*Festuca* species).
      - ryegrasses (*Lolium* species).

Occurrence Documented: Australia, Europe, Japan, and North America.

Cultural Controls:

1. Apply a balanced (N-P-K) fertilizer, with the phosphorus (P) and potassium (K) rates determined by an annual chemical soil test.

2. Remove any excess thatch when it occurs, as by vertical cutting.

3. Improve the soil drainage, as by coring.

Chemical Control. The application of fungicides is not needed for Leptosphaerulina leaf blight. Implementation of the proper cultural practices, especially nitrogen (N) and phosphorous (K) fertilizers, prevents severe appearance of this disease.

Photo 32-1. The appearance of a discolored turf caused by Leptosphaerulina leaf blight (*creeping bentgrass tee; midspring*).

Photo 32-2. Brown-colored patches of Leptosphaerulina leaf blight appeared together as discolored areas without defined borders (*Kentucky bluegrass fairway; late summer*).

Photo 32-3. The application of nitrogen (N) and phosphorous (P) fertilizers erases the discolored area caused by Leptosphaerulina leaf blight, and only patches remain (*Kentucky bluegrass fairway; very early fall*).

Photo 32-4. The turfgrass plants die in diseased patches of Leptosphaerulina leaf blight, and browning of the turf is observed (*Kentucky bluegrass fairway; very early fall*).

Part IV
DISEASES COMMON
TO BOTH
WARM- AND COOL-
SEASON
TURFGRASSES

CHAPTER 33
Downy Mildew
(Yellow Tuft)

Disease Characteristics. The patches of downy mildew on cool-season turfs occur in circular shapes with a diameter of 1 to 4 inches (25 – 100 mm). Dwarfing and yellowing are the typical symptoms of infected shoots.

On new seedling turfs, especially bentgrass greens, the initial symptoms appear as individual clusters or tufts of dense, yellow shoots originating from a single node or terminal stem apex. This type of symptom usually disappears within 2 to 3 years.

On St. Augustinegrass, the downy mildew symptoms are much different than on cool-season grasses. The initial symptoms are white streaks that form parallel to the leaf veins. The epidermis over the streaks is raised and a white, downy growth of sporangia appears during wet conditions. The general turf appearance is a whitish surface that appears stunted in growth, and the turf may become thinned.

Environmental Effects. Downy mildew typically occurs first in wet, poorly drained, depressional areas. It usually occurs on cool-season turfgrasses during early to late spring and mid- to late fall. The symptoms may disappear in early summer because the pathogen is inactivated by high temperatures. On St. Augustinegrass, the downy mildew occurs primarily in the summer during humid weather, and can be especially severe in shaded areas.

Causal Pathogen. *Sclerophthora macrospora*.
    (syn. *Sclerospora macrospora*)

This pathogen is an obligate parasite belonging to the oomycetes that attacks the shoots of grasses. *Sclerophthora macrospora* forms oospores in the infected tissues with a diameter of 50 to 75 μm, which is about 2 to 3 times larger than those of the *Pythium* species. The fungus also forms lemon-shaped sporangia that release zoospores under humid atmospheric and canopy conditions. It persists as systemic mycelium in infected shoots, crowns and stems, and as oospores. Local dissemination is by infection spores in free water.

Host Turfgrasses:

> Major - bentgrasses (*Agrostis* species).
> - bluegrasses (*Poa* species).
> - St. Augustinegrass (*Stenotaphrum secundatum*).
>
> Minor - fescues (*Festuca* species).
> - perennial ryegrass (*Lolium perenne*).
> - rough bluegrass (*Poa trivialis*).

Occurrence Documented: Australasia, Europe, Japan, and North America.

Cultural Controls:

1. Use a downy mildew resistant turfgrass cultivar, especially for bentgrass and St. Augustinegrass.

2. Improve soil water drainage, as by coring.

3. Avoid excessive atmospheric and canopy humidities by enhancing air circulation.

4. Minimize water accumulation and movement on the surface of turfgrasses after a rain, by proper surface contours.

5. Avoid high to excessive nitrogen (N) fertility levels.

Chemical Control. A fungicide, such as metalaxyl, should be sprayed as a soil drench to control downy mildew, and is most effective when applied as a preventive program.

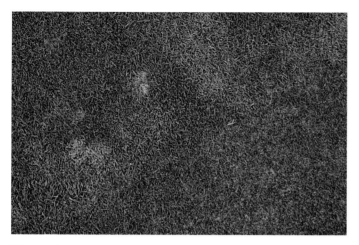

Photo 33-1. Yellow patches of yellow tuft on a putting green turf *(creeping bentgrass green; midspring).*

Photo 33-2. Dwarfing and yellowing of creeping bentgrass caused by yellow tuft (left), and a healthy turfgrass that is not infected (right).

Photo 33-3. Yellow patches of yellow tuft on a Kentucky bluegrass turf. *(Courtesy of Dr. Henry T. Wilkinson.)*

Photo 33-4. Close view of a yellow patch symptom of yellow tuft on a Kentucky bluegrass turf. *(Courtesy of Dr. Henry T. Wilkinson.)*

CHAPTER 34
Gray Leaf Spot

Disease Characteristics. The symptoms of gray leaf spot vary between the warm- and cool-season turfgrasses.

St. Augustinegrass. The initial symptoms of gray leaf spot are tiny, brown spots on the leaves and stems that enlarge rapidly, turn bluish-gray, and become oval or elongated in shape with a 6 to 8 mm length. Occasionally, a gray mold may be seen covering the lesions during very hot, humid conditions. The mature lesions have tan to gray, depressed centers with irregular, purple to brown margins. A yellow border may also be present. A severe infection results in leaves with a scorched or burned appearance, and the turf density becomes thinned.

Cool-Season Turfgrass Species. The symptoms take more the form of a melting-out. Perennial ryegrass seedlings, and sometimes mature plants, can be severely injured during late summer and fall. Gray lesions with a brown border form along the margins of infected leaves. The leaf blades often are twisted and die back from the tips. The turf may become thinned, especially under hot, humid conditions.

Environmental Effects. Gray leaf spot is most severe during prolonged rainy, humid, hot periods which typically occur in midsummer. The optimum temperature range is 80 to 90°F (26 – 32°C). Gray leaf spot is favored by high nitrogen nutritional levels and by any other factor that stresses the grass, such as an inappropriate herbicide application, drought, and/or soil compaction. Turfgrasses under infertile conditions with minimal growth exhibit little gray leaf spot.

Causal Pathogen. *Pyricularia grisea.*
    teleomorph *Magnaporthe grisea.*

This pathogen attacks the leaves and shoots of grasses. The pathogen forms gray conidiophores that appear as protuberances from infected tissues. *Pyricularia grisea* survives periods unfavorable to growth via dormant mycelium and conidia on infected leaves and on plant debris, such as thatch. Dissemination is by spores via wind, water, equipment, and animals.

Host Turfgrasses:

    Major - St. Augustinegrass (*Stenotaphrum secundatum*).
           - perennial ryegrass (*Lolium perenne*).

    Minor - bermudagrasses (*Cynodon* species).
           - centipedegrass (*Eremochloa ophiuroides*).
           - fescues (*Festuca* species).

Occurrence Documented: Africa, Asia, Australasia, Europe, North America, and South America.

Cultural Controls:

1. Use a gray leaf spot resistant turfgrass cultivar, especially for St. Augustinegrass and perennial ryegrass, if available.

2. Avoid medium to high nitrogen (N) levels during midsummer.

3. Irrigate as needed to minimize plant water stress, but allow free water to remain on the leaf surfaces as short a time as possible by proper timing of irrigation.

4. Minimize the presence of plant debris by vertical cutting to remove excess thatch accumulations.

Chemical Control. A fungicide, such as propiconazole, is used to manage gray leaf spot. Isoprothioran also may be effective in controlling this disease.

Photo 34-1. Extensive gray leaf spot damage to a St. Augustinegrass turf. *(Courtesy of Dr. Phillip F. Colbaugh.)*

Photo 34-2. Initial spot symptoms of gray leaf spot on a St. Augustinegrass turf. *(Courtesy of Dr. Peter H. Dernoeden.)*

Photo 34-3. Gray leaf spot lesions on the leaf blades of St. Augustinegrass. *(Courtesy of Dr. Monica L. Elliott.)*

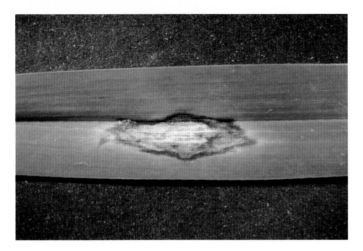

Photo 34-4. Close-up of a lesion of gray leaf spot on a St. Augustine grass leaf. *(Courtesy of Dr. Gordon E. Holcomb.)*

Photo 34-5. Initial symptoms of gray leaf spot on perennial ryegrass. *(Courtesy of Dr. Peter H. Dernoeden.)*

Photo 34-6. Symptoms of gray leaf spot on a perennial ryegrass fairway. *(Courtesy of Dr. Peter H. Dernoeden.)*

Photo 34-7. Advanced stage of gray leaf spot damage on a perennial ryegrass fairway. *(Courtesy of Dr. Peter H. Dernoeden.)*

CHAPTER 35
Fairy Rings

Disease Characteristics. The causal agents may or may not produce aboveground mushroom and puff ball basidiocarps. These fungi inhabit the root zone of turfgrasses forming hymenia in the soil. Rings or patches form along the developing hymenia of some fungal species. Typically there is a distinct outer ring of either dark-green turf or brown-dead turf, depending on the specific causal agent (Table 35-1). When individual rings come into contact with one another, their activities cease due to antagonistic effects. The patch shapes have different characteristics depending on the species. For example:

- *Lepista sordida* forms a circular patch of 17 to 66 feet (5 – 20 m) in diameter, and occasionally may have the shape of a fan of 66 to 170 feet (20 – 50 m) or more in length.
- *Marasmius oreades* develops round-shaped rings of 7 to 33 feet (2 – 10 m) in diameter.
- *Lycoperdon perlatum* develops wavy-shaped rings of 2 to 7 feet (0.5 – 2 m) in diameter, and also may develop wave-shaped belts with a length of 7 to 33 feet (2 – 10 m) or more.
- *Agaricus campestris* causes circular patches of 7 to 17 feet (2 – 5 m) in diameter, and sometimes wave-shaped belts with lengths of 7 to 33 feet (2 to 10 m) or more.

Some causal agents, such as *Chlorophyllum molybdites*, form fruiting bodies, but do not form patches except in very rare cases. Contrary to this, other causal pathogens form only ring-shaped patches, but not fruiting bodies. A mushroom growing in a turf does not necessarily indicate that a fairy ring is present.

Fairy rings tend to occur in the same locations every year, and spread gradually to outer areas from these sites. One exception is *Lycoperdon perlatum* which sometimes causes symptoms suddenly during the summer, and large areas of a green may be seriously damaged. Occurrence of the patches may become pronounced by frequent irrigation of water contaminated with algae from a storage reservoir. Continuous use of undecomposed organic materials in topdressing also may increase the occurrence of certain fairy rings.

Environmental Effects. During high humidity periods, turfgrasses within the ring turn darker green, and the growth of grasses may be stimulated. However, in rainless periods, the drying mycelium in the soil becomes hydrophobic, and drought stress of the turfgrasses occurs because of impaired water movement to the roots. Subsequent blight of grasses usually occurs in the summer, and it is not unusual to see these symptoms on cool-season turfgrasses even in the winter in mild climates.

Causal Agents. Basidiomycetes of more than 40 species are considered to be capable of causing fairy ring. Causal agents of fairy rings around the world include:

- *Agaricus* species - *A. campestris.*
- *Chlorophyllum molybdites.*
- *Collybia* species.
- *Hygrocybe* species.

- *Lepiota* species.
- *Lepista* species - *L. sordida*.
- *Lycoperdon* species - *L. perlatum*.
- *Marasmius* species - *M. oreades*.
- *Psalliota* species.
- *Scleroderma* species.
- *Tricholoma* species - *T. sordidum*.

These fungi survive saprophytically on plant debris. The fungal mycelium grow around the roots of turfgrasses, usually to a soil depth of 4 to 6 inches (100 – 150 mm) if plant residues are present. The formation of fruiting bodies, such as mushrooms and puff balls, tends to occur in midspring to late spring and in late summer to early fall. In contrast, *Lycoperdon perlatum* forms fruiting bodies more actively during midsummer. Dissemination of the fungus usually is as contaminated soil by mechanical means, such as sod, machines, and human activities.

Turfgrasses Affected:

All turfgrasses.

Occurrence Documented: Worldwide wherever turfgrasses are grown.

Cultural Controls:

1. Excessive plant residues, such as woody limbs and roots, should not be allowed to remain in the soil during construction of turf sites.
2. Avoid the use of root zone mixes containing large amounts of undecomposed organic materials.
3. Control any excessive thatch accumulation when it forms, as by vertical cutting.

4. Maintain appropriate watering to avoid a plant water deficit. A dark-green pattern will still remain, but timely watering can prevent the desiccation of turfgrasses in the ring.
5. An application of nitrogen (N) fertilizer can be used to mask the dark-green ring of some types of fairy rings, but can increase the incidence of certain fairy rings, such as *Tricholoma sordidum*.

Chemical Control. In the past, deep fumigation with methyl bromide onto the fairy ring affected areas has been the main control approach used. Now fungicides effective on basidiomycetes, such as bicoral, flutolanil or polyoxin, have been effective on a number of species that cause fairy rings. Because the fungi inhabit the soil to a depth of 4 inches (100 mm), a drench of the fungicide solution at a rate of 2.2 to 4.4 gal/sq yard (10 – 20 liters/m²) with a fungicide concentration of three times higher than the normal rate is required to effectively treat the infected turf area. Limited success can be achieved in controlling certain fairy ring species by treatment with a normal fungicide solution rate of 0.44 gal/sq yard (2.0 liters/m²), but repeated applications are required in this case.

Table 35-1. The Many Types of Fairy Ring Have Been Visually Characterized into Three Distinct Groups as Follows:

Type I.	Rings exhibit a zone of dead or severely injured grass, one or two zones of darker green, stimulated grass, and basidiocarps.
Type II.	Rings exhibit a single ring of darker green, stimulated grass and basidiocarps.
Type III.	Rings appear occasionally as a circular arrangement of basidiocarps, and have no visible effects on grass growth.

Mixtures with surfactants or wetting agents will overcome the hydrophobic nature of the mycelial mats and help to thoroughly distribute the fungicides. Since some fungicides are toxic to bentgrasses, repeated applications with lower concentrations are suggested for this turfgrass.

The fungicide should be applied during early spring to early summer and very late summer to midfall, as treatment during midsummer is less effective. The frequency of chemical treatments for the complete cure of fairy ring depends on the species of pathogen. *Lepista sordida* and *Lycoperdon perlatum* usually can be controlled by a few applications, but *Marasmius oreades* may need additional applications of 4 – 6 times.

Note: Fairy rings in Southern Alberta, Canada, have been measured with diameters of up to 2,600 feet (800 m) or about 0.5 mile. They were estimated to be over 1,000 years old.

Photo 35-1. Extensive rings of *Tricholoma sordidum* fairy ring on a Kentucky bluegrass turf. *(Courtesy of Dr. James B Beard.)*

Photo 35-2. The growth of grasses becomes active along the ring formed by an infection of *Lepista sordida*. The growth of grasses at the infected soil sites becomes even better than in other areas during high-humidity periods *(zoysiagrass fairway; midfall)*.

Photo 35-3. The fruiting bodies of *Lepista sordida* *(zoysiagrass fairway; late spring)*.

Photo 35-4. The shapes of rings caused by *Lepista sordida*:

A: large size of a folding fan shape *(zoysiagrass fairway; early fall).*

B: medium size of folding fan shape *(Japanese zoysiagrass primary rough; very late spring).*

C: nearly straight shape *(manila zoysiagrass putting green; early fall).*

D: straight shape *(manila zoysiagrass putting green; early fall).*

Photo 35-5. Anthocyanin in turfgrass leaves at the fringe of a ring caused by *Lepista sordida*. The anthocyanin is rarely observed in the fall when the leaves are growing actively *(manila zoysiagrass fairway; midfall)*.

Photo 35-6. Fruiting bodies of *Marasmius oreades* formed along the circular fairy ring *(manila zoysiagrass fairway; very late spring)*.

Photo 35-7. The fruiting bodies of *Marasmius oreades:*

A: immature *(Japanese zoysiagrass rough; late spring)*.

B: mature *(manila zoysiagrass fairway; late spring)*.

Photo 35-8. The shapes of rings caused by *Marasmius oreades*. Every fairy ring shown here is round shaped:

A: the zone of dead leaves forms the shape of a ring during the dry season *(manila zoysiagrass fairway; midsummer)*.

C: grasses become darker-green in parts of the rings due to frequent watering *(manila zoysiagrass green; very early fall)*.

B: grasses in the ring become necrotic because of little rainfall *(manila zoysiagrass fairway; midspring)*.

D: grasses in the ring maintain their green color on turf during partial winter dormancy *(hybrid bermudagrass fairway; midwinter in a subtropical area)*.

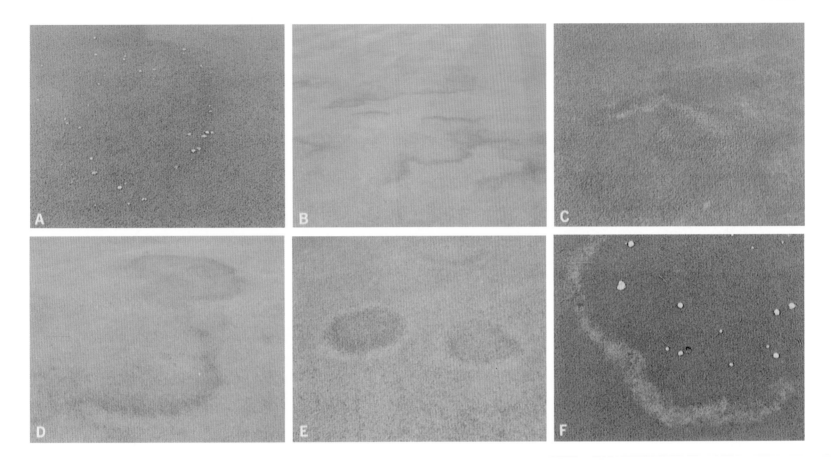

Photo 35-9. The shapes of rings caused by *Lycoperdon perlatum*:

(A, B, D) manila zoysiagrass putting green, **(C,E,F)** creeping bentgrass putting green. Various shapes can be observed:

A, B, D: patterns of darker green can be seen during the rainy season or in places given frequent watering.

C, E, F: zones of dead leaves form the shapes of rings during the dry season or in places given insufficient watering.

White fruiting bodies can be observed in the photos of A and F (early to midsummer).

Photo 35-10. Young mushroom fruiting bodies of *Lycoperdon perlatum*. Old fruiting bodies turn darker brown, and give rise to powdery spores from inside the bodies.

Photo 35-11. Extensive rings caused by *Lycoperdon perlatum* on a creeping bentgrass putting green. The symptoms occurred under dry conditions caused by a shortage of rain *(midsummer)*.

Photo 35-12. The fruiting bodies of *Agaricus campestris*. Note the relatively large size.

Photo 35-13. Cluster of fruiting bodies of *Agaricus compestris*. The formation of a ring is prevented by sufficient rain during the development period *(zoysiagrass fairway; early fall)*.

Photo 35-14. Large fan-shaped, green patches caused by *Chlorophyllum molybdites*. Development of circular patch symptoms is seldom observed *(zoysiagrass fairway; midfall)*.

Photo 35-15. The fruiting bodies of *Chlorophyllum molybdites*:

A: this pathogen usually does not form rings. But since the shape and size of the mushroom is similar to that of a golf ball, occurrences of these fruiting bodies cause problems when playing golf *(Japanese zoysiagrass; early summer)*.

B & C: close-ups of mushrooms.

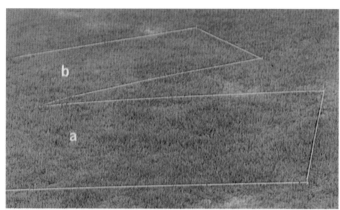

Photo 35-16. Fungicide tests for the control of fairy rings in Japan:

  A: ring caused by *Lepista sordida*:

    a: mepronil (250 times dilution, 245.5 gal/1,000 ft^2 or 1,000 liters/100 m^2) applied twice.

    b: mepronil (500 times dilution, 245.5 gal/1,000 ft^2 or 1,000 liters/100 m^2) applied twice.

    Between a and b is an untreated control.

    Osmac (a surfactant at 300 times dilution) was added to both solutions *(zoysiagrass fairway; very late spring)*.

    The fungicide was applied in midfall and the photos were taken in late spring of the next year.

  B: rings caused by *Lycoperdon perlatum*:

    a: untreated control.

    b: bitertanol (1,000 times dilution, 245.5 gal/1,000 ft^2 or 1,000 liters/100 m^2) applied twice *(creeping bentgrass putting green; midsummer)*.

The fungicide was applied during the initial stage of ring development. (Photos were taken 2 weeks after application.)

CHAPTER 36
Superficial Fairy Rings

Disease Characteristics. The numerous types of superficial fairy rings exhibit varying visual symptoms that have been characterized into three distinct groups (Table 36-1).

Superficial fairy ring may appear as patches with felted, white mycelium on the turfgrasses. The border between healthy and affected areas is well defined because of the very dense mycelial mats. A ring with a width of about 1.0 inch (20 – 30 mm) at the border area sometimes can be observed. The patches may appear sunken due to rapid decomposition of an accumulated thatch layer. A green, smoky ring may occur on turfs growing in high humidities. The lower turfgrass leaves in the patches die on some occasions, but the turfed patches are not blighted.

Environmental Effects. Superficial fairy ring patches generally appear in the summer season and disappear in the cooler seasons. However, the patch symptoms tend to remain even in the winter if the turf is not properly managed. An accumulation of thatch and/or a deficiency of nutrients may cause more severe symptoms.

Causal Agents. Superficial fairy rings are caused mostly by basidiomycetes with clamp connections on their hyphae. Included are:

- *Clavaria* species.
- *Clitocybe* species.
- *Coprinus* species - *C. kubickae.*
- *Hygrophorus* species.
- *Melanotus phillipsii* called white blight when on tall fescue.
- *Psilocybe* species.
- *Trechispora alnicola* called yellow ring.
- *Trechispora cohaerens.*
- *Trechispora farinacea.*

These superficial fairy rings appear to be saprophytic fungi without any particular host range. They are primarily inhabitants of the thatch and pseudothatch-turf canopy, which distinguishes them from the fairy ring causal agents. Dissemination is via fungus infected turfs and soil by mechanical means such as sod, machines, human activities, wind, and water.

Turfgrasses Affected:

All turfgrasses.

Occurrence Documented: Worldwide, especially in cool, moist climates where turfgrasses are grown.

Cultural Controls:

1. Remove any excess thatch when it occurs, as by vertical cutting.

2. Practice topdressing and turf cultivation, as appropriate for thatch/mat control.

3. Improve the drainage of the root zone, as by coring.

Chemical Control. Applications of a fungicide effective on the causal agent of certain superficial fairy rings, such as polyoxin or mepronil, may be effective in controlling certain species of superficial fairy ring. One application of this fungicide after symptom appearance may be sufficient to eliminate the rings on turfs.

Note: The use of benomyl is thought to control antagonistic fungi and other organisms which appear to result in increased superficial fairy ring symptoms.

Table 36-1. The Various Superficial Fairy Rings Have Been Visually Characterized into Three Groups

Type A.	Sparse to copious mycelia are produced, with or without fruiting bodies, on the shoot bases of turfgrasses and in the thatch. There is minimal visual effect on grass growth.
Type B.	Turfgrass growth is visually stimulated and/or shoot discoloration occurs, but the grass is not severely injured. Thatch decomposition is evident.
Type C.	Severe turfgrass injury is evident, and adjacent turfgrass growth may or may not be stimulated.

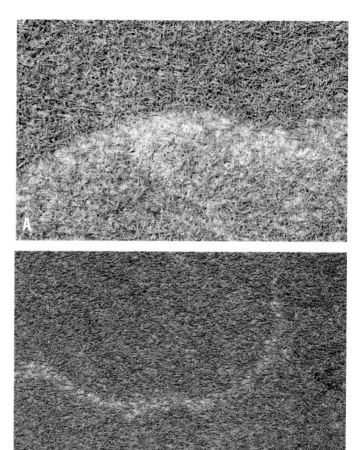

Photo 36-1. Severe patches of superficial fairy ring. The patches are very pronounced on the site because of improper turf cultural practices *(creeping bentgrass nursery; midsummer).*

Photo 36-2. White mycelium of superficial fairy ring on the surface of infected turf:

A: a mycelial mat covering the surface of patches. The mycelium density is higher at the edge of patches between healthy and diseased areas *(creeping bentgrass green; midsummer).*

B: a mycelial mat remaining as a fine-ring shape *(creeping bentgrass green; early summer).*

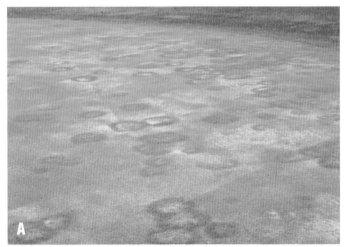

Photo 36-3. A green ring of superficial fairy ring:

A: a growth of turf stimulated at the site of infection, with enhanced greenness observed.

B: close-up of a smoky-ring patch *(creeping bentgrass green; midsummer).*

Photo 36-4. The presence of a superficial fairy ring causal agent in the rhizosphere of turfgrass to a soil depth of about 0.5 inch (12 mm) can be observed at 68°F (20°C) under a high atmospheric humidity. Fruiting bodies also may be observed in the turf.

CHAPTER 37
Slime Molds

Disease Characteristics. Slime molds appear as slimy masses of brightly colored spots ranging from 0.5 to 24 inches (10 – 600 mm) in diameter on the turf. Sometimes the slimy, spore cluster symptoms of white, gray, yellow, purple or brown on the leaves form a straight line. This is caused by the manner in which the slimy zoospores are formed on the surface of leaves. The turfgrass leaves may become chlorotic or yellow due to sunlight exclusion by the accumulated slimy plasmodia masses. The symptoms naturally disappear under continuous, sunny, dry weather conditions. The slime mold masses may reappear in the same locations.

Environmental Effects. Slime molds typically occur during the cool, rainy season under high atmospheric and canopy humidities and wet surface canopy conditions.

Causal Agents.

Many species including:

- *Mucilago crustacea.*
- *Mucilago spongiosa.*
- *Physarum* species - *P. cinereum.*

The occurrence of these fungi, the myxomycetes, are limited to the surface of turfgrass. The fungi do not infect the grass tissues. The plasmodia feed on living bacteria, fungi, and decaying organic matter. Large numbers of white/gray/purplish-brown, pin-sized, sporangia or fruiting bodies of the fungus can be formed suddenly on grass leaves. There is no parasitic activity, only sunlight exclusion to the green leaves by masses of slimy plasmodia. Survival during unfavorable weather conditions for growth is by spores. Dissemination is primarily by wind-borne spores.

Turfgrasses Affected:

All turfgrasses.

Occurrence Documented: All parts of the world characterized by wet conditions and mild temperatures.

Cultural Controls:

1. Washing larger, dense slimy masses off the leaves and shoots with a stream of water may prove beneficial in minimizing the chlorosis of grass leaves caused by sunlight exclusion, especially during drying conditions.

2. During prolonged, wet weather an alternate approach of reducing the slimy masses is by mechanical removal, such as raking or brushing.

3. Remove any excess thatch when it occurs, as by vertical cutting.

4. Ensure adequate surface and subsurface soil drainage.

Chemical Control. Control by a fungicide usually is not necessary.

Photo 37-1. An area affected by slime mold on a turf. *(Photo courtesy of The Scotts Company.)*

Photo 37-2. A large mass of slime mold in a Kentucky bluegrass turf. *(Photo courtesy of Dr. Ralph S. Byther.)*

Photo 37-3. Close view of slimy spore clusters of slime mold on leaf blades. *(Photo courtesy of Dr. Arthur H. Bruneau.)*

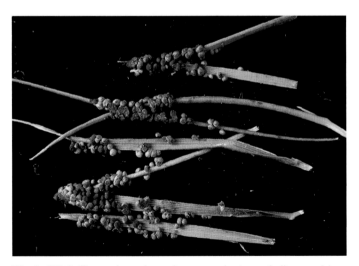

Photo 37-4. Close view of purple spore clusters of slime mold on leaf blades. *(Photo courtesy of Dr. Ralph S. Byther.)*

CHAPTER 38
Bacterial Wilt

Disease Characteristics. Bacterial wilt first appears as blue-green, wilted symptoms on the leaf blades. The leaves shrivel and turn a reddish-brown or purple color, followed by root dysfunction. Red to copper-colored spots form in the turf due to death of individual plants. The spots coalesce and enlarge, and may cause death of large, irregular-shaped areas quite rapidly under ideal conditions.

Environmental Effects. Bacterial wilt symptoms are most severe on closely mowed turfs, during wet, cool-to-warm periods, which typically occur in the spring and fall. It seldom causes turf loss on areas mowed at high cutting heights, when compared to greens.

Causal Pathogen. Pathovar of *Xanthomonas campestris*.

Grass injury is caused by clogging of the xylem vessels by the bacteria. *Xanthomonas campestris* is characterized as having a short, rod shape of about 0.5 x 1 to 2 µm. The bacteria move via water films on the leaf surface, and thus can be transferred by intense rainfall and streams of irrigation water.

Host Turfgrasses:

    Major - creeping bentgrass (*Agrostis stolonifera* var. *stolonifera*), certain cultivars- Toronto, Seaside, and Cohansey.
           - annual bluegrasses (*Poa annua*).

    Minor - bermudagrasses (*Cynodon* species) certain cultivars -Tifgreen.
           - fescue (*Festuca* species).
           - perennial ryegrass (*Lolium perenne*).

Occurrence Documented: North America.

Cultural Control:

Use bacterial wilt resistant cultivars, if available.

Chemical Control. The antibiotic, oxytetracycline applied at high rates, has provided alleviation of the bacterial disease problem. However, this usually is only a short-term solution that is high in cost and impractical.

Photo 38-1. A putting green of Toronto creeping bentgrass with injury by bacterial wilt in the foreground. *(Courtesy of Dr. David Roberts.)*

Photo 38-2. Close view of a putting green of Toronto creeping bentgrass seriously injured by bacterial wilt. *(Courtesy of Dr. David Roberts.)*

CHAPTER 39
Mycoplasma-Like Organisms (MLOs)

Disease Characteristics. Mycoplasma-like organisms (MLOs) are very tiny organisms that have the cytoplasm contained by a membrane, but no cell wall. They possess both RNA and DNA and are thought to reproduce by budding. MLOs usually are transmitted by insects, and then spread systemically through the plant. Other plants located around a turf facility, especially grasses, may serve as sources of inoculum. However, the alternate hosts and insect vectors are not known at this time.

The initial symptom associated with a mycoplasma-like organism (MLO) is a whitening of individual shoots, due to the loss of chlorophyll. This symptom is particularly common on bermudagrasses during the first 3 to 4 years following vegetative planting. A tuft composed of a dense proliferation of leaves from a single node may develop. Yellow-green, small spots of 2 to 4 inches (50 – 100 mm) in diameter may eventually appear on bentgrass turfs. There are no lesions evident on the shoots. The greenness of the grasses can be lost on a severely-infected putting green, the width of infected leaf blades tends to narrow, and extreme ranking or dense leaf proliferation from a single node of infected grass leads to poor uniformity of turfs on putting greens.

Environmental Effects. The MLO symptoms usually start to occur on creeping bentgrass putting greens in late spring. Severe symptoms are observed in midsummer to late summer, but disappear in midfall. The disease may reoccur again at the same sites the next year.

Causal Pathogen. A mycoplasma-like organism (MLO) or phytoplasma.

Mycoplasmas may be transmitted by insects. Rice, wheat, and vegetable farms located close to a golf course, and also grassy weeds on the turf facility, may be primary sources of inoculum. There is a possibility that the MLO may be transported through the infected seeds of turfgrasses.

Occurrence Documented: Japan and Southeast Asia.

Host Turfgrasses:

Major - bentgrasses (*Agrostis* species).
- bermudagrasses (*Cynodon* species).
Minor - manila zoysiagrass (*Zoysia matrella*).

Cultural Control. Not understood, but should involve sanitary practices.

Note: Recently it has been proposed that the name mycoplasma be changed to phytoplasma, because the MLO that is parasitic on plants does not grow on culture media like the mycoplasma isolated from animal tissues.

Chemical Control. There are no chemicals available to cure turfgrasses of MLO-related diseases. MLOs are sensitive only to antibiotics of the tetracycline group, as the MLO does not possess a cell wall. However, the preventive application of these antibiotics over the long term is excessively costly, impractical, and unsound.

The best way to control this disease may be the identification of the insect that transmits this disease and the control of the insect vector by certain insecticides. Unfortunately, such a control method is still lacking.

Yellow dwarf caused by an MLO is becoming a major problem on creeping bentgrass putting greens in Japan. The first occurrence of this disease was several years ago on creeping bentgrass. Since then, similar symptoms have been observed on other golf courses in several areas of Japan

White leaf is an MLO-like disease that occurs on vegetatively propagated bermudagrasses in southeast Asia. Individual plants lose chlorophyll and turn white, resulting in a random, white speckling of the turf, especially on closely mowed greens.

Photo 39-1. Patches of yellow dwarf disease occur sporadically:
  A: on a manila zoysiagrass putting green *(early fall)*.
  B: on a creeping bentgrass putting green *(early summer)*.

Photo 39-2. A typical single patch of yellow dwarf disease, where yellowing of leaves can be observed, but do not die *(creeping bentgrass putting green; midsummer).*

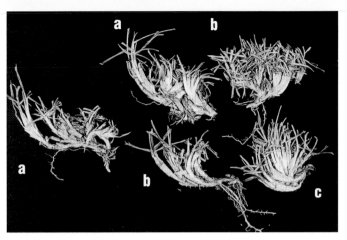

Photo 39-3. Typical symptoms of yellow dwarf are leaf yellowing, shoot dwarfing, and ranking or leaf proliferation from a node:

   TOP: creeping bentgrass:
      a: healthy.   **b:** diseased.
   BOTTOM: manila zoysiagrass:
      a: healthy.   **b:** partially affected.   **c:** diseased.

Photo 39-4. White leaf disease on a Tifdwarf hybrid bermudagrass green. *(Courtesy of Dr. James B Beard.)*

Photo 39-5. Close view of white leaf disease symptoms on individual plants on a Tifdwarf hybrid bermudagrass green. *(Courtesy of Dr. James B Beard.)*

CHAPTER 40
Virus Diseases

INTRODUCTION

Viruses are tiny, parasitic organisms that require live cells in which to multiply. They are composed of nucleic acids with a protein coat, and can only be seen through an electron microscope. They spread systemically throughout the plant. Most viruses are transmitted from plant-to-plant via the feeding activities of an insect or nematode vector. A primary approach to control of many viruses is by control of its vector.

ST. AUGUSTINEGRASS DECLINE (SAD)

Disease Characteristics. Initial symptoms are a yellow, mottled or mosaic pattern on the leaf blades. As the chlorosis becomes more severe the leaf growth is slowed. Eventually there may be a reduction in the shoot density, plus shortened stolons. Any significant loss of turf usually will not occur until after three years, and sometimes may not occur.

Environmental Effects. The occurrence of St. Augustinegrass decline typically is on lawns, primarily in the southwestern United States. Any environmental stress, such as water or shade stress, that weakens the host turfgrass, also will enhance the potential for additional injury by the virus disease.

Causal Pathogen. A strain of Panicum mosaic virus, group CMMV.

This is one of the few turfgrass diseases whose causal pathogen is documented as a virus. It is a spherical RNA virus. The virus requires a living host to multiply. Transmission of the virus is via mechanical means in plant sap, such as by mowers, turf cultivation, vertical cutting, and sod.

Host Warm-Season Turfgrasses:

Major - St. Augustinegrass (*Stenotaphrum secundatum*).
- centipedegrass (*Eremochloa ophiuroides*).

Minor - (none known).

Occurrence Documented: Southern North America.

Cultural Controls:

1. Use a SAD resistant turfgrass cultivar of St. Augustinegrass, such as Floratam, Floralawn, Raleigh, and Seville, if adapted to the region. All existing cultivars of centipedegrass are susceptible.

2. Follow sanitary practices that prevent introduction of the virus via infected plant parts on soil and machines.

3. Sustain a moderate leaf growth rate and the associated recuperative ability through adequate nitrogen (N) fertilization and irrigation.

4. Select other cultural practices that maintain healthy plants, which will delay the progress of the virus disease.

5. Do not mow grasses when the shoots are wet.

Chemical Control. None known.

Photo 40-1. A chlorotic, weedy turf of St. Augustinegrass that has been thinned by St. Augustinegrass decline. *(Courtesy of Dr. Gordon E. Holcomb.)*

Photo 40-2. Advanced St. Augustinegrass decline symptoms on a St. Augustinegrass turf. *(Courtesy of Dr. Gordon E. Holcomb.)*

Photo 40-3. Close-up of the mottled symptoms of St. Augustinegrass decline on the leaf blades of St. Augustinegrass. *(Courtesy of Dr. Gordon E. Holcomb.)*

VIRUS DISEASES OF ZOYSIAGRASS

Disease Characteristics. Zoysia dwarf virus, zoysia mosaic virus, and stripe leaf roll virus have been known as virus diseases of turfgrasses in Japan. These viruses occur on Japanese zoysiagrass, but severe turf damage caused by these diseases has not been reported.

Environmental Effects. They most commonly occur on slow-growing, high cut and unmowed turfs, such as golf course roughs, low-maintenance lawns, and roadsides.

Causal Pathogens:

- zoysia dwarf virus - wheat mottle dwarf virus (WMDV).
- zoysia mosaic virus - zoysia mosaic virus (ZMV).
- stripe leaf roll virus - specific causal pathogen not identified.

Host Warm-Season Turfgrasses:

Major - Japanese zoysiagrass (*Zoysia japonica*).

Minor - (none known).

Occurrence Documented: Japan

Cultural Controls:

1. Use of a resistant turfgrass cultivar is the preferred approach, if available.
2. Follow cultural practices that maintain the best possible plant health of the turfgrasses in order to impair and slow severe disease development.

Chemical Control. No chemical control is known.

Photo 40-4. Yellow spot lesion on Japanese zoysiagrass leaves caused by zoysia mosaic virus.

Photo 40-5. Leaf roll symptoms of the stripe leaf roll virus on Japanese zoysiagrass. (*Courtesy of Dr. Satoru Ohgi.*)

Part V
SIMPLE METHODS FOR DISEASE DIAGNOSIS

CHAPTER 41
Disease Diagnosis

The diagnosis of turfgrass disease sometimes requires considerable experience because the cultural and natural conditions often change the appearances of disease symptoms. Individuals with less experience may need the help of experts if the typical symptoms of disease do not appear. This section describes the conventional methods for disease diagnosis and provides information necessary to reduce the possibility of incorrect approaches to disease control.

Foliar Attacking Pathogens.   Most foliar attacking diseases exhibit visible symptoms on the leaves and/or shoots relatively early in the disease development process. The symptoms include:

1. *Local leaf/shoot lesions* - such as blight, blotch, fleck, leaf spot, mosaic, mottle, spot, stippling, streak, stripe, and zonate; with varying sizes and colors.

2. *Fungal structures visible* - such as basidiocarps (mushrooms and puff balls), flock, mold, pustule, sclerotia, and sori; with varying sizes and colors.

3. *Whole leaf/shoot symptoms* - such as bleached, chlorosis, desiccate, dieback, necrosis, rot, water-soaked, and yellows.

4. *Turf symptoms* - such as distinct patches, general turf thinning, seedling damping-off, and turf decline; with varying sizes and colors.

Descriptions for each of these symptom types are described in the Appendix Glossary.

Root Attacking Pathogens.   The diagnosis of root diseases is much more difficult than for the foliar attacking diseases. Also, less is understood about the root diseases. Root attacking diseases exhibit few distinguishing symptoms. The only foliar symptom is leaf death that occurs from the tip downward. By the time this aboveground symptom appears it is already too late. Regular examinations of the root profile may be practiced, but the root attacking diseases usually occur in random patches that are difficult to detect. Accordingly, significant turf injury may occur in the first year, with effective control measures initiated early in the second year.

Microscopic Diagnosis.   Since many golf courses provide a microscope for disease diagnosis, necessary information on the handling of the microscope and some characteristics of pathogens for simple identification also are described in this section. Microscopic observation of pathogens is one of the powerful methods for disease diagnosis. However, the identification of causal agents achieved with only microscopic examinations sometimes is risky. In cases of turfgrass diseases, many fungi including nonpathogens of the disease may be isolated from the infected parts of grasses. *Fusarium* or *Curvularia* can always be isolated, while *Rhizoctonia* and *Pythium* also cause secondary infection and often are isolated from the infected parts of grasses.

Further, the identification of a genus of fungus sometimes is not a sufficient diagnosis of the pathogen to select a control for the disease. For example, *Rhizoctonia* has different species, such as *Rhizoctonia solani*, *Rhizoctonia oryzae*, or *Rhizoctonia cerealis*, and a fungicide effective against the first one may have no effect on the second and third ones. In this case, the effective chemical control is dependent on the precise identification of the species of *Rhizoctonia*. Considering these facts, the following methods are simplified diagnostic approaches, but are not perfect identification methods to cover all the problem situations. It must be emphasized that accurate diagnosis is based on knowledge of the disease characteristics and environmental conditions favoring disease appearance. Confusing cases should be examined by an expert to avoid misjudgment in the disease diagnosis.

CHAPTER 41A
A Simple Inoculation Method

Similarities of symptoms across certain diseases lead to mistakes in diagnosis, and inappropriate fungicides often are used to control the apparent-disease. Differences between two similar-appearing diseases, such as (a) Pythium red blight and scald, (b) Rhizoctonia brown patch and severe Pythium blight (II), and (c) dollar spot and Curvularia leaf blight, seem to be especially difficult to distinguish. The following method describes a simple procedure to distinguish these diseases by using fungicides that are highly selective to each pathogen. Examples of selective diagnostic fungicides for individual pathogens are listed in Table 41A-1.

Materials:

Photo 41A-1. Plastic bags, turf sods (can be taken from the nursery), sprayers, petri dishes, water bottle, rubber bands, and distilled or deionized water (water should not contain any bleaching reagents).

Table 41A-1. Pathogen-Selective Fungicides That Can Be Used for Diagnosis

Disease (Pathogen)	Fungicide (Active Ingredient)	Concentration
Oomycetes:		
Pythium red blight (*Pythium aphanidermatum*)	metalaxyl liquid formulation	1,000 times dilution
Pythium blight (*P. graminicola & P. vanterpoolii*)	hymexazol liquid formulation	300 times dilution
	propamocarb-HCl liquid formulation	300 times dilution
Ascomycetes:		
Dollar spot pathogen	fenarimol wettable powder 48	1,000 times dilution
Basidiomycetes:		
Rhizoctonia brown patch (*Rhizoctonia solani*)*	pencycuron wettable powder	500 times dilution
	flutolanil wettable powder	500 times dilution
	mepronil wettable powder	500 times dilution

* Perfect stage expected.

Methods:

1. Spray the highly selective fungicide in a higher concentration (a few times higher than normal use) thoroughly on the surface of turfgrass seedlings in each pot (Photo 41A-2).

2. Inoculate the infected parts from the sample turf (Photo 41A-3) by transferring it to the center of the healthy sod with forceps (Photo 41A-4).

3. Place a pot of the inoculated sod onto the petri dish, and cover the whole unit in a plastic bag. Sufficient watering is necessary (Photo 41A-5).

4. Fill the plastic bag with air, and close (Photo 41A-6).

5. Incubate it under certain conditions. Outdoors may be acceptable if in a shaded area.

The fungicide that prevents the development of disease on the inoculated sod is effective in control of the pathogen, and this combination of fungicide and pathogen can be used for the diagnosis of the causal pathogen. For example, Pythium blight (II) shows symptoms similar to brown patch on turf, and the distinction of these two diseases sometimes is difficult. However, it can be easily examined by using this method.

Photo 41A1-7 illustrates the results of this method for the identification of Pythium blight (II) caused by *Pythium graminicola*. The pathogen of Pythium blight is sensitive to fungicides effective

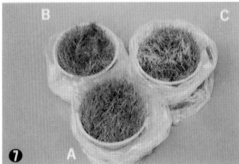

Photo 41A1–7

against oomycetes, such as metalaxyl, but not to fungicides effective against ascomycetes or basidiomycetes.

Photo 41A-7-(A) was treated with metalaxyl, while Photo -(B) and -(C) were treated with fenarimol which is effective against ascomycetes and with pencycuron which is effective against the Rhizoctonia brown patch pathogen *Rhizoctonia solani*. This pathogen developed symptoms on both (B) and (C) pots, but not on (A) pot, indicating that the tested sample was Pythium blight caused by *Pythium* species, but not Rhizoctonia brown patch caused by *Rhizoctonia* (basidiomycetes).

In the case of Rhizoctonia brown patch, symptom development will be prevented on sod treated with pencycuron which is effective against *Rhizoctonia solani*.

The same combinations of fungicides can be used to distinguish Pythium red blight and scald, as well as dollar spot and Drechslera/Bipolaris diseases. Symptom developments will be restricted only on sod treated with metalaxyl for Pythium red blight, and no symptom development will be observed on any sods damaged by scald. The causal pathogen of dollar spot will show the symptoms only on sod treated with fenarimol instead.

This simple method also can be used for the detection of a new fungicide-resistant strain. The appearances of fungicide-resistant strains of *Pythium* species and the dollar spot pathogen have been reported. A list of fungicides effective against these fungi is shown in Table 41A-2. To use this

Table 41A-2. Fungicides Can Be Used for the Detection of the Appearance of Fungicide-Resistant Strains

Diseases	Fungicide (Active Ingredient)
Pythium diseases (*Pythium* species)	metalaxyl liquid formulation
	hymexazol liquid formulation
	fosetyl-aluminum wettable powder
	propamocarb-HCl liquid formulation
Dollar spot pathogen	thiophanate-methyl wettable powder
	iprodione wettable powder
	triflumizole wettable powder
	iminoctadine triacetate liquid formulation

method for the detection of fungicide-resistant strains, the concentrations and application volumes of the two fungicide solutions must be adjusted to match those used in the field.

Unfortunately, this method is not applicable for the diagnosis of all pathogens, and considerable numbers of pathogens cannot be distinguished by this method. Most pathogens of zoysiagrasses tend to be difficult in terms of the induction of their symptoms by this inoculation method. The pathogens of certain diseases, such as take-all patch and necrotic ring spot on cool-season grasses, also are sometimes difficult to diagnosis by this method for the same reasons. Sophisticated techniques are required for successful inoculation of these pathogens.

CHAPTER 41B
A Simple Diagnostic Method

Materials:

Photo 41B-1. Plastic bags, plastic cups, petri dishes, water bottle, tissue paper (or cotton), rubber bands, and distilled water (water should not contain any bleaching reagents).

Procedures:

1. Remove a sod plug containing infected parts of turf by a hole cutter or a soil sampler, and place the sod in a plastic cup. The border of the infected part and healthy part must be in the center of the sod plug.

2. Sufficient watering is necessary (Photo 41B-2).

3. Place a pot of the inoculated sod onto the petri dish, and add some water in the petri dish (Photo 41B-3).

4. Cover the whole unit in a plastic bag (Photo 41B-4).

5. Soak a few sheets of tissue paper or cotton with water (Photo 41B-5).

6. Place the wet paper in the plastic bag (Photo 41B-6).

7. Fill the plastic bag with air (Photo 41B-7).

8. Close the bag tightly with a rubber band (Photo 41B-8).

9. Incubate it under certain conditions. An outdoor site may be acceptable if in a shaded area.

Photo 41B1–8.

Photo 41B-9. Pythium spring dead spot. Development of aerial mycelium of *Pythium graminicola*.

Photo 41B-10. Dollar spot (A, B). Development of aerial mycelium of the dollar spot pathogen.

Photo 41B-11. Development of aerial mycelium of *Fusarium* (A, B). Sometimes this can develop as a secondary infection, and not due to the primary causal agent.

Photo 41B-12. Development of aerial mycelium of *Marasmius oreades* around the roots (left) and *Pythium* on the surface of the soil (right). Note that the mycelium of the pathogens causing fairy ring are distributed over the depth of the roots, but *Pythium* mycelium survive only on the soil surface.

Note: These mycelium developments cannot be seen on the inoculations of *Rhizoctonia* species, *Curvularia* species, or *Drechslera/Bipolaris* species. But production and development of mycelium and/or spores become active by this method under highly humid conditions, making microscopic examinations easier.

Photo 41B-13. Fungicide tests on fairy ring - pathogen: *Marasmius oreades*:

> **Middle:** untreated control.
> **Left:** flutolanil + isoprothiolane wettable powder (600 times dilution, 20 liters/m^2), plus Osmac surfactant (300 times dilution) addition.
> **Right:** flutolanil + isoprothiolane (600 times dilution, 20 liters/m^2).
> **A:** April 29 *(just after the first application)*.
> **B:** May 14 *(15 days after the first treatment)*.
> **C:** July 14 *(21 days after the fourth treatment)*.

Application of fungicides effectively controls disease development (B), but treatment with the fungicides without the addition of a surfactant (Osmac) leads later to reappearance of the disease (C).

CHAPTER 42
Microscopic Examination of Pathogens

USE OF THE MICROSCOPE:

Materials:

Photo 42-1. Slide glass, cover glass, dropper bottle (water or staining solution), inoculation needle (can be prepared by fixing a needle to a stick), forceps, magnifying glass (5x to 20x), alcohol burner, petri dish (for water), cheesecloth, and filter paper.

Procedures:

1. Abundant spores or mycelia to be observed can be prepared by the methods described in Chapter 41B on "A simple diagnostic method."

2. Ignite the alcohol burner (Photo 42-2).

3. Clean a slide glass and a cover glass with cheesecloth (Photo 42-3).

4. Place a drop of water or staining solutions from the dropper bottle on the slide glass (Photo 42-4).

5. Sterilize the tip of a pair of forceps by heating with the burner (Photo 42-5).

6. Cool the tip by immersing in water (Photo 42-6).

7. Take the sample segments with the forceps while observing the procedure with a magnifying glass (Photo 42-7).

8. Place the sample onto the water drop on the slide glass (Photo 42-8).

9. Sterilize the inoculation needle by using the burner (Photo 42-9), and cool by immersing it in water.

10. Press the sample segments with the forceps, and break the segments by using the inoculation needle (Photo 42-10).

11. Place the cover glass onto the sample (Photo 42-11).

12. Absorb excess water or staining solutions using a filter paper (Photo 42-12).

13. Place the slide glass on the microscope stage (Photo 42-13).

14. Start the examination (Photo 42-14).

Examination Procedure with a Microscope:

1. Adjust the position of the mirror to direct sufficient light to the lens.

2. Adjust the condenser to have the right intensity of light.

3. Start with the low-power objective (10x) and ocular (10x).

4. Move the objective to a higher power, as appropriate.

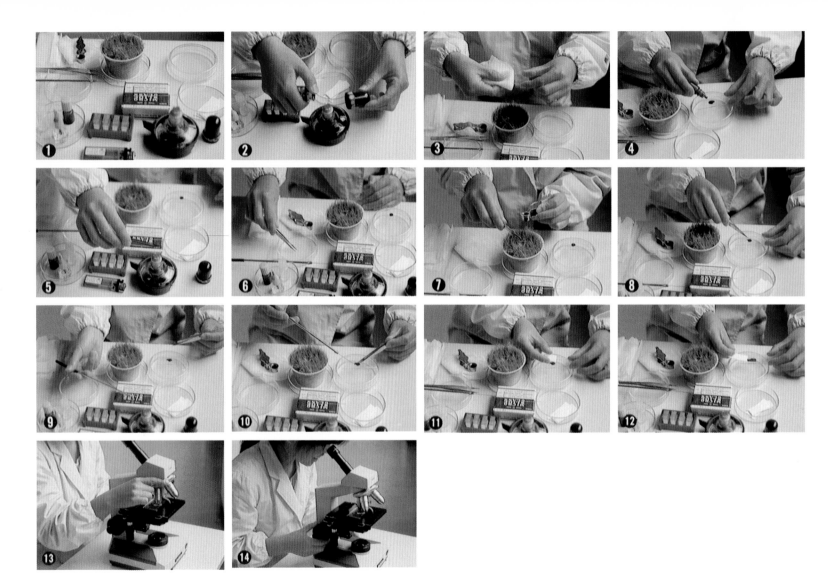

Photo 42-1 to 14.

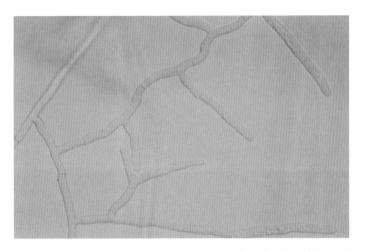

Photo 42-15. Mycelium of *Rhizoctonia* species. Typical T-formed cells. Relatively larger mycelium with a diameter of 4 to 7 µm.

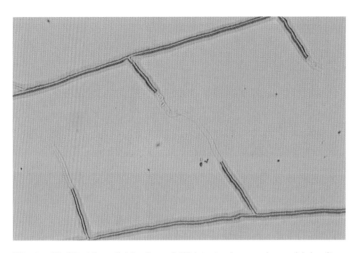

Photo 42-16. Mycelial fusion of *Rhizoctonia* species, which often occur between the same strains. This can be used as one of the characteristics to identify *Rhizoctonia* species.

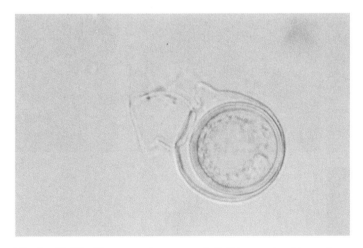

Photo 42-17. The sexual organs of *Pythium aphanidermatum*. Fertilization of oogonium (right) by the antheridium (left). *(Courtesy of Dr. Takiro Ichitani.)*

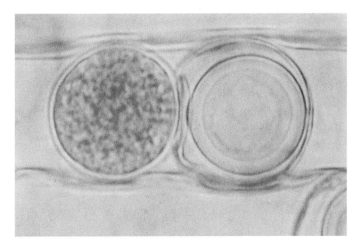

Photo 42-18. Oogonium (left) and oospores (right) of *Pythium aphanidermatum. (Courtesy of Dr. Takiro Ichitani.)*

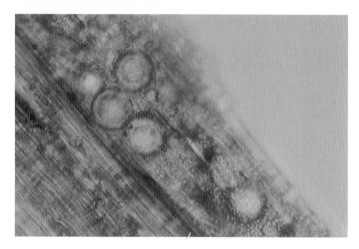

Photo 42-19. Oospore formation of *Pythium aphanidermatum* in the leaf tissue of creeping bentgrass. The observation of oospores is helpful in the diagnosis of Pythium red blight.

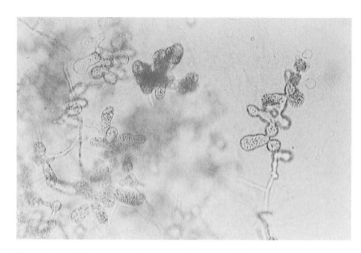

Photo 42-20. Inflated sporangium of *Pythium graminicola*. *(Courtesy of Dr. Takirou Ichitani.)*

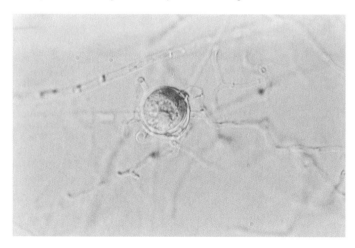

Photo 42-21. Monoclinous (arrow) antheridium of *Pythium graminicola*. *(Courtesy of Dr. Takirou Ichitani.)*

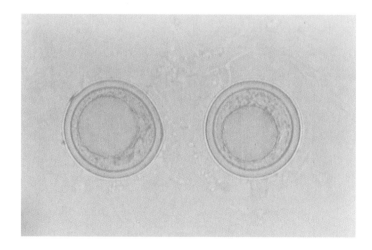

Photo 42-22. Mature oospores of *Pythium graminicola*. *(Courtesy of Dr. Takirou Ichitani.)*

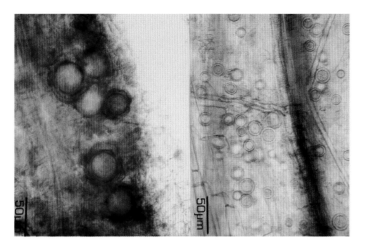

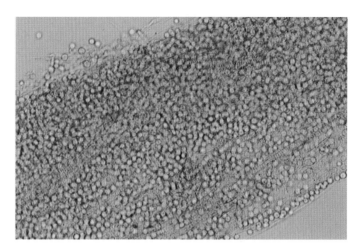

Photo 42-23. Oospores of *Pythium torulosum* (right) and *Sclerophthora macrospora* (left).

Photo 42-24. Abundant oospore formation of *Pythium graminicola* in the leaf tissue of creeping bentgrass. Pythium blight (II) can be easily distinguished from Rhizoctonia brown patch by this observation.

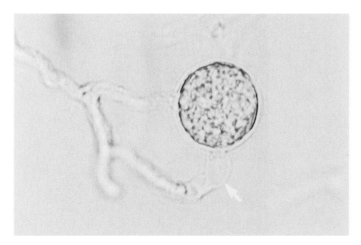

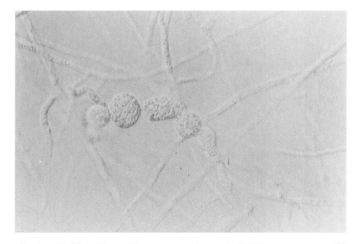

Photo 42-25. Oogonium with spherical-shape and antheridium (arrow) of *Pythium vanterpoolii. (Courtesy of Dr. Takirou Ichitani.)*

Photo 42-26. Chain-like sporangium of *Pythium vanterpoolii. (Courtesy of Dr. Takirou Ichitani.)*

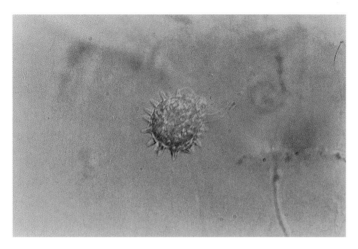

Photo 42-27. Echinulated or spiny oogonium of *Pythium periplocum. (Courtesy of Dr. Takirou Ichitani.)*

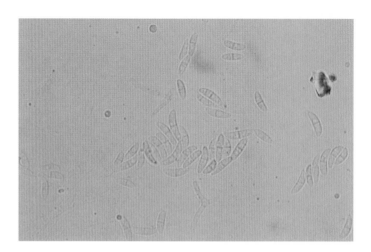

Photo 42-28. Conidia of *Microdochium nivale.*

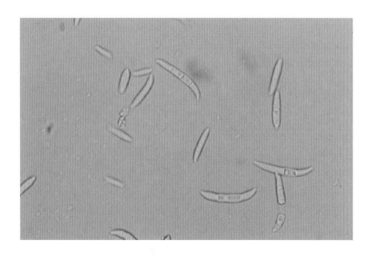

Photo 42-29. Conidia of *Fusarium acuminatum.*

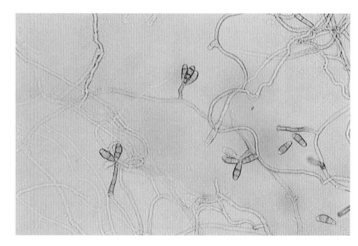

Photo 42-30. Conidia of *Curvularia* species on conidiophores.

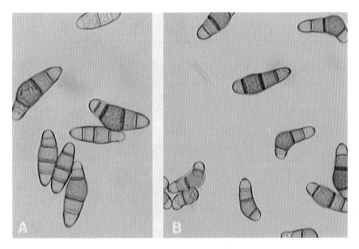

Photo 42-31. Conidia of *Curvularia* species:
A: geniculata type (mostly 5-septate cells).
B: lunata type (mostly 4-septate cells).

Photo 42-32. Surface electron microscopic views of the conidia of *Curvularia lunata* showing rough surface (right) and *C. lunata* var. *aeria* showing smooth surface (left), respectively.

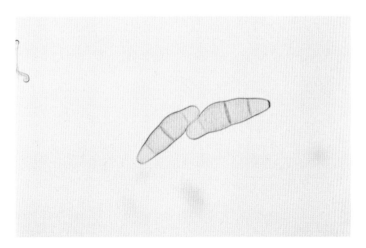

Photo 42-33. Conidiophores of *Curvularia verructilosa*.

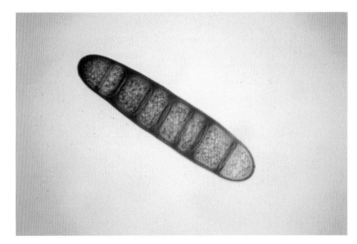

Photo 42-34. Conidium of *Drechslera poae*. *(Courtesy of Dr. Joseph M. Vargas, Jr.)*

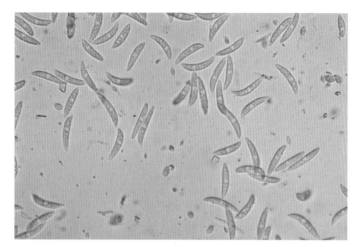

Photo 42-35. Conidiospores of *Colletotrichum graminicola*.

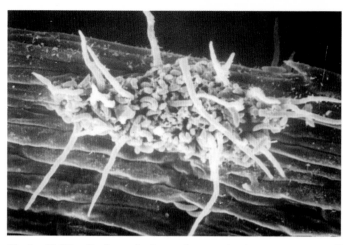

Photo 42-36. Surface electron micrograph of a mature acervuli of *Colletrotrichum graminicola* with setae and spores present. *(Courtesy of Dr. Joseph M. Vargas, Jr.)*

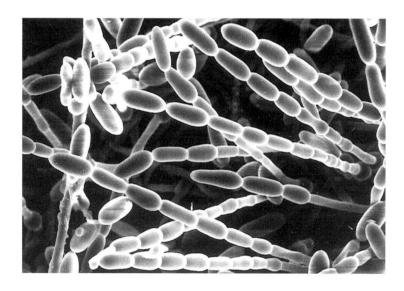

Photo 42-37. Surface electron micrograph of conidiospores of *Erysiphe graminis. (Courtesy of Hitishi Kunoh.)*

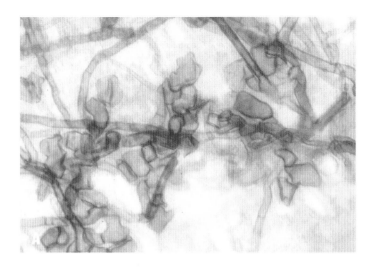

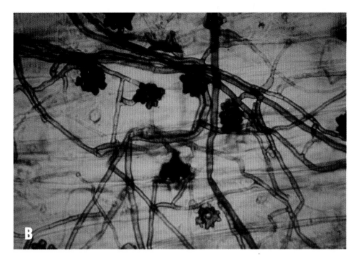

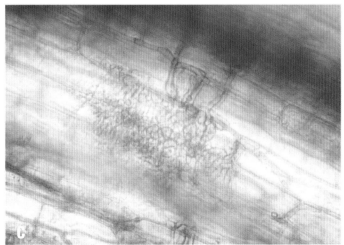

Photo 42-38. Hyphopodia and ectotrophic mycelium of *Gaeumannomyces graminis* on a leaf sheath surface:

A: *Gaeumannomyces graminis* var. *graminis* on manila zoysiagrass.

B: *Gaeumannomyces graminis* var. *graminis* on bermudagrass. *(Courtesy of Dr. Peter J. Landshoot.)*

C: *Gaeumannomyces graminis* var. *avenae* on creeping bentgrass. Lobed and unlobed hyphopodia are characteristic signs of var. *graminis* and var. *avenae*, respectively.

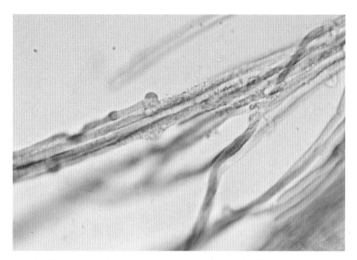

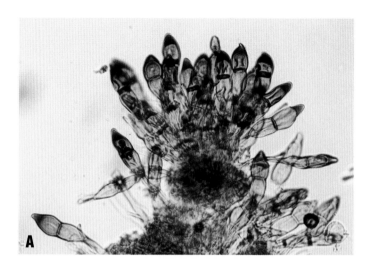

Photo 42-39. Hyphae of *Limonomyces roseipellis* bearing clamp connections.

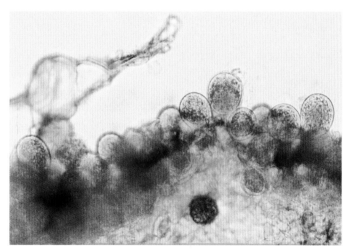

Photo 42-40. Uredinia of a rust fungus on urediniosori.

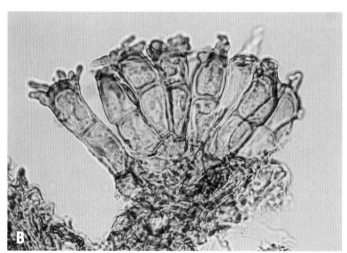

Photo 42-41. Teleutospores of rust fungi:
A: *Puccinia graminis* type.
B: *Puccinia coronata* type.

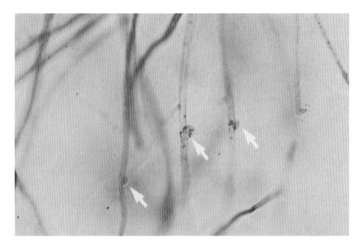

Photo 42-42. Mycelium of *Lepista sordida*. The clamp connections (arrows) are clearly observed in the mycelium of this fungus.

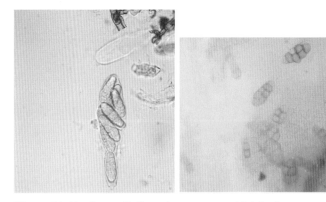

Photo 42-43. Ascus (left) and ascospores (right) of *Leptosphaerulina trifolii*.

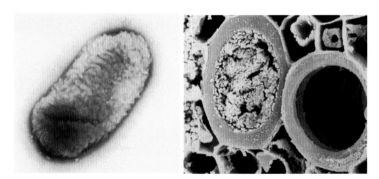

Photo 42-44. Scanning electron micrographs of the bacterium *Xanthomonas campestris* which causes bacterial wilt disease (left) and the nonfunctional xylem of a Toronto creeping bentgrass plant that is clogged with the bacteria (right). *(Courtesy of Dr. David Roberts.)*

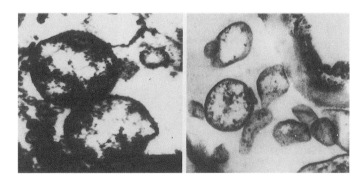

Photo 42-45. Mycoplasma-like organism (MLO) that causes yellow dwarf as viewed via an electron microscopic: left x 57,000 and right x 30,000.

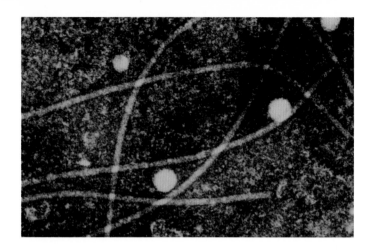

Photo 42-46. Thirty nanometer, spherical particals of Panicum mosaic virus. *(Courtesy of Dr. Gordon E. Holcomb.)*

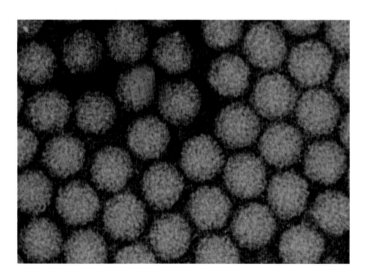

Photo 42-47. Wheat mottle dwarf virus (WMDV), the cause of zoysia dwarf virus, viewed via an electron microscope with a magnification of 5×10^5. *(Courtesy of Dr. Shuichi Yamashsita.)*

CHAPTER 43

Diagnostic Color Plates of Pathogen Mycelial Mats

The following photos illustrate the mycelial growths of 22 pathogenic fungi. The fungi were grown on PDA plates that were placed in the dark at their optimal growth temperature. Each photo was taken of two plates that represent the views of mycelial mats from the top surface (left) and the bottom side (right), respectively. It should be noted that the typical growth patterns are not always the same between different strains of the same fungus.

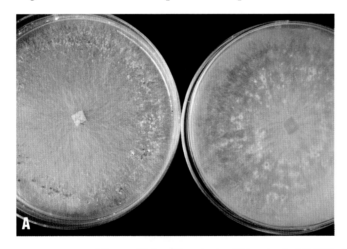 

Photo 43-1. Binucleate *Rhizoctonia* AG-D(I): (syn. *Rhizoctonia cerealis*) - the causal pathogen of Rhizoctonia spring dead spot and yellow patch.
A: isolate from a patch of Rhizoctonia spring dead spot.
B: isolate from a patch of yellow patch.
The growth rates of mycelium are different for each isolate.

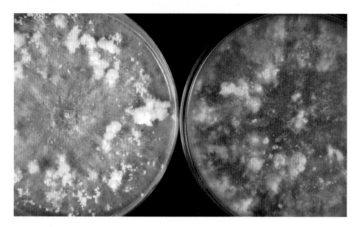

Photo 43-2. Binucleate *Rhizoctonia* AG-D(II): (syn. *Rhizoctonia cerealis*) -the causal pathogen of zoysia Rhizoctonia patch (elephant footprint).

   The surface behavior of the mycelial mat is different from that of photos 43-1A and B, while A and B in photo 43-1 are quite similar to each other. This is one of the indications that AG-D(II) is different from AG-D(I).

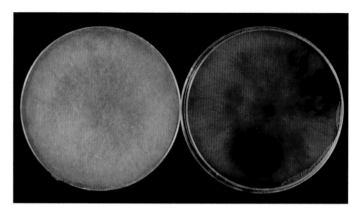

Photo 43-3. *Rhizoctonia solani* AG-2-2 (LP) - causal pathogen of large patch.

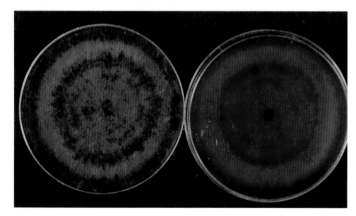

Photo 43-4. *Rhizoctonia solani* AG-2-2 (III B) - causal pathogen of Rhizoctonia brown patch.

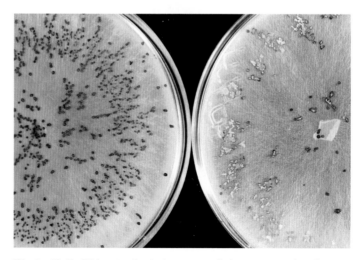

Photo 43-5. *Rhizoctonia circinata* var. *circinata* - causal pathogen of pseudo-Rhizoctonia brown patch: young (left) and mature (right) sclerotia.

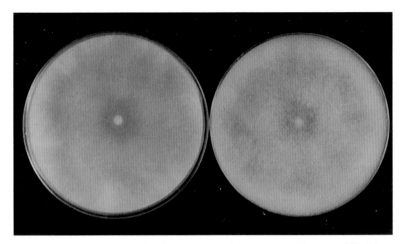

Photo 43-6. *Pythium aphanidermatum* - the causal pathogen of Pythium red blight.

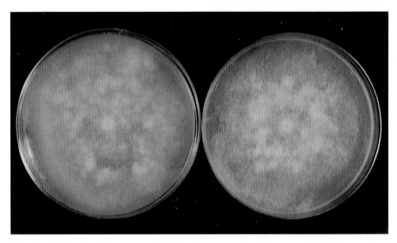

Photo 43-7. *Pythium graminicola* - the causal pathogen of Pythium spring dead spot and Pythium blight.

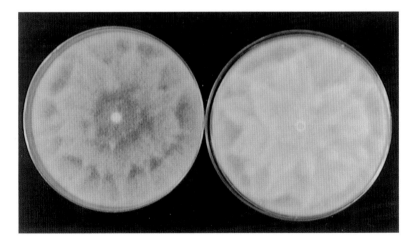

Photo 43-8. *Pythium vanterpoolii* - the causal pathogen of Pythium spring dead spot and Pythium blight.

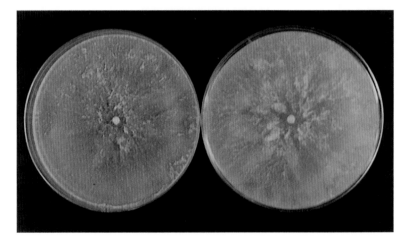

Photo 43-9. *Pythium periplocum* - the causal pathogen of zoysia Pythium blight.

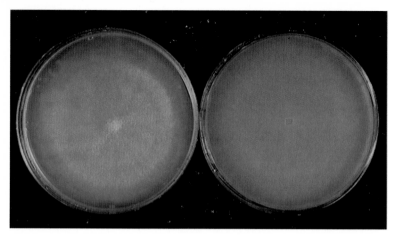

Photo 43-10. *Microdochium nivale* - causal pathogen of Pythium spring dead spot on zoysiagrass, winter Fusarium blight, and Microdochium patch.

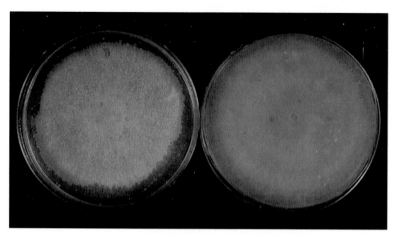

Photo 43-11. *Fusarium acuminatum* - the causal pathogen of Pythium spring dead spot and Fusarium blight of manila zoysiagrass.

Photo 43-12. *Gaeumannomyces graminis* var. *graminis* - the causal pathogen of zoysia decline.

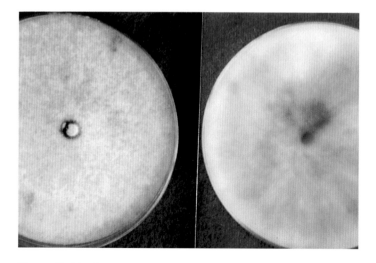

Photo 43-13. *Gaeumannomyces graminis* - isolated from take-all patch in Japan. *(Courtesy of Dr. Takayuki Hatta.)*

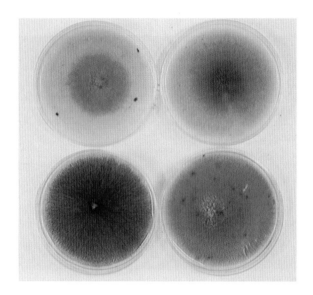

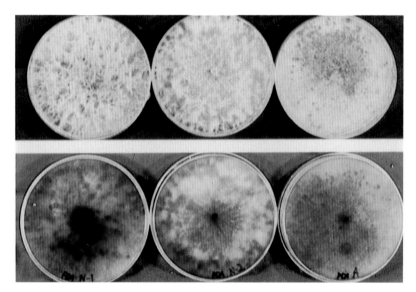

Photo 43-14. *Curvularia* species - the causal pathogen of Curvularia leaf blight:

        upper: geniculata type.
        lower: lunata type.

Note: mycelial mats of the genus vary to a large extent depending on the isolates.

Photo 43-15. The causal pathogen of dollar spot:

        upper: mycelial mat on the surface of the medium .
        lower: view from the bottom of the plate.

Note: above surface views of the mycelial mats on the medium do not differ considerably among isolates, but the view of the underside of mycelial mats vary to a large extent.

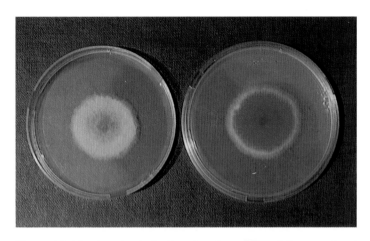

Photo 43-16. *Laetisaria fuciformis* - the causal pathogen of red thread.

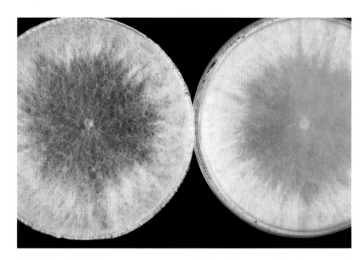

Photo 43-17. *Limonomyces roseipellis* - the causal pathogen of pink patch.

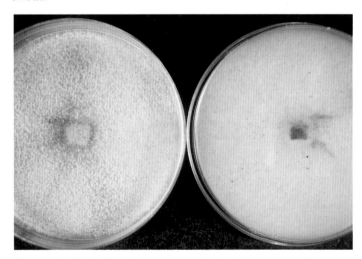

Photo 43-18. *Colletotrichum graminicola* - the causal pathogen of anthracnose.

Photo 43-19. *Typhula incarnata* - the causal pathogen of Typhula blight.

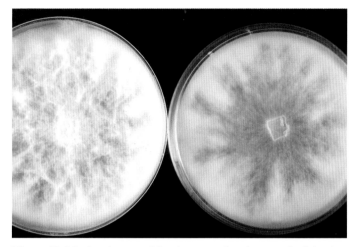

Photo 43-20. *Lepista sordida* - the causal pathogen of a fairy ring symptom.

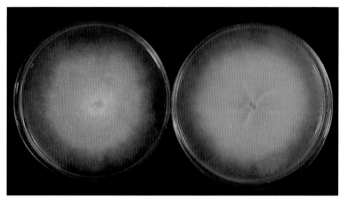

Photo 43-21. *Lycoperdon perlatum* - the causal pathogen of a fairy ring symptom.

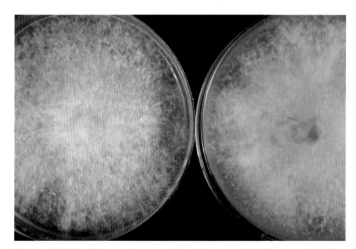

Photo 43-22. *Marasmius oreades* - the causal pathogen of a fairy ring symptom.

APPENDIX TABLE 1
NOMENCLATURE SUMMARY FOR THE TURFGRASS DISEASES AND THEIR CAUSAL PATHOGENS

Scientific Name	Common Name	Scientific Name	Common Name
Agaricus campestris	fairy ring	*Gaeumannomyces graminis* var. *avenae*	take-all patch
binucleate *Rhizoctonia* AG-D (I)	Rhizoctonia spring dead spot	*Gaeumannomyces graminis* var. *graminis*	bermudagrass decline
binucleate *Rhizoctonia* AG-D (I)	yellow patch (winter patch)	*Gaeumannomyces graminis* var. *graminis*	zoysia decline
binucleate *Rhizoctonia* AG-D (II)	Rhizoctonia patch (elephant footprint)	*Laetisaria fuciformis*	red thread
Bipolaris cynodontis	Bipolaris leaf blotch	*Lepista sordida*	fairy ring
Bipolaris sorokiniana	Bipolaris leaf spot	*Leptosphaeria korrae*	necrotic ring spot
Chlorophyllum molybdites	fairy ring	*Leptosphaeria korrae* & *Leptosphaeria narmari*	Leptosphaeria spring dead spot
Colletotrichum graminicola	anthracnose	*Leptosphaerulina australis* & *Leptosphaerulina trifolii*	Leptosphaerulina leaf blight
Coprinus kubickae	superficial fairy ring	*Limonomyces roseipellis*	pink patch
Curvularia geniculata *Curvularia lunata* *Curvularia lunata* var. *aeria,* & *Curvularia verruculosa*	Curvularia leaf blight (dog footprint)	*Lycoperdon perlatum*	fairy ring
Drechslera dictyoides	net blotch	*Magnaporthe poae*	summer patch
Drechslera erythrospila	red leaf spot	*Marasmius oreades*	fairy ring
Drechslera gigantea	zonate leaf spot	*Melanotus phillipsii*	white blight
Drechslera poae	melting-out	*Microdochium nivale*	Microdochium patch (pink snow mold)
Drechslera siccans	brown blight	*Mucilago spongiosa*	slime mold
Erysiphe graminis	powdery mildew	mycoplasma-like organism(MLO) or phytoplasma	white leaf yellow dwarf
Fusarium acuminatum *Fusarium avenaceum* *Fusarium oxysporum* & *Fusarium tricinctum*	Fusarium blight	*Myriosclerotinia borealis*	snow scald

Scientific Name	Common Name	Scientific Name	Common Name
Panicum mosaic virus strain group CMMV	St. Augustine decline (SAD)	*Pythium periplocum*	zoysia Pythium blight
Physarum cinereum	slime mold	*Pythium torulosum*	Pythium yellow spot
Uromyces dactylidis	leaf rust	*Rhizoctonia circinata* var. *circinata*	pseudo-Rhizoctonia brown patch
Puccinia coronata	crown rust	*Rhizoctonia solani* AG-2-2(LP)	large patch
Puccinia graminis	stem rust	*Rhizoctonia solani* AG-2-2(III B) & AG(1)	Rhizoctonia brown patch
Puccinia striiformis	stripe rust		
Puccinia zoysiae	zoysia rust	*Sclerophthora macrospora*	downy mildew (yellow tuft)
Pyricularia grisea	gray leaf spot		
Pythium aphanidermatum	Pythium red blight	*Trechispora alnicola*	yellow ring
Pythium graminicola & *Pythium vanterpoolii*	irregular Pythium patch	*Trechispora cohaerens*	superficial fairy ring
		Trechispora farinacea	superficial fairy ring
Pythium graminicola or *Pythium vanterpoolii* and *Microdochium nivale* & *Fusarium acuminatum* complex	Pythium spring dead spot	*Tricholoma sordidum*	fairy ring
		Typhula incarnata & *Typhula ishikariensis*	Typhula blights (gray snow mold)
Pythium graminicola *Pythium vanterpoolii* *Pythium ultimum,* & *Pythium aristosporum*	Pythium blight (I)	*Urocystis agropyri*	flag smut
		Ustilago striiformis	stripe smut
		Wheat mottle dwarf virus (WMDV)	zoysia dwarf virus
Pythium graminicola	Pythium blight (II)	pathovar of *Xanthomonas campestris*	bacterial wilt
Pythium iwayamani & *Pythium paddicum*	Pythium snow blight	Zoysia mosaic virus (ZMV)	zoysia mosaic virus
		(not clarified - will continue to use *Sclerotinia homoeocarpa*)	dollar spot

APPENDIX TABLE 2

NOMENCLATURE SUMMARY FOR THE COOL-SEASON TURFGRASSES By Scientific Names

U.S. Common Name	Scientific Name	Other Common Name
alkaligrass, weeping	*Puccinellia distans* (L.) Parl.	reflexed salt marshgrass
beachgrass, American	*Ammophila breviligulata* Fern.	
beachgrass, European	*Ammophila arenaria* (L.) Link	marramgrass
bentgrass, colonial	*Agrostis capillaris* L.	browntop bentgrass
bentgrass, creeping	*Agrostis stolonifera* L. var. *stolonifera*	
bentgrass, velvet	*Agrostis canina* L.	
bluegrass, annual	*Poa annua* var. *annua* L.	annual meadowgrass
bluegrass, Canada	*Poa compressa* L.	flattened meadowgrass
bluegrass, creeping annual	*Poa annua* var. *reptans* (Hausskn.) Timm.	
bluegrass, Kentucky	*Poa pratensis* L.	smooth meadowgrass
bluegrass, rough	*Poa trivialis* L.	rough meadowgrass
bluegrass, Texas	*Poa arachnifera* Torrey	
bluestem, little	*Schizachyrium scoparium* (Michaux) Nash	
crested dog's tail	*Cynosurus cristatus* L.	
fescue, Chewing's	*Festuca rubra* L. subsp. *commutata* Gaudin	
fescue, hard	*Festuca longifolia* Thuill.	
fescue, meadow	*Festuca pratensis* Hudson	
fescue, sheep	*Festuca ovina* L. var. *ovina*	
fescue, slender creeping red	*Festuca rubra* L. subsp. *littoralis*	
fescue, strong creeping red	*Festuca rubra* L. subsp. *rubra*	
fescue, tall	*Festuca arundinacea* Schreber	
redtop	*Agrostis gigantea* Roth	black bentgrass
rye	*Secale cereale* L.	cereal rye
ryegrass, annual	*Lolium multiflorum* Lam.	Italian ryegrass
ryegrass, perennial	*Lolium perenne* L.	English ryegrass
sea-oats	*Uniola paniculata* L.	
timothy, turf	*Phleum bertolonii* DC.	
wheatgrass, fairway crested	*Agropyron cristatum* (L.) Gaertner	

APPENDIX TABLE 3
NOMENCLATURE SUMMARY FOR THE COOL-SEASON TURFGRASSES By Scientific Names

Scientific Name	U.S. Common Name	Scientific Name	U.S. Common Name
Agropyron cristatum (L.) Gaertner	wheatgrass, fairway crested	*Lolium multiflorum* Lam.	ryegrass, annual
		Lolium perenne L.	ryegrass, perennial
Agrostis canina L.	bentgrass, velvet	*Phleum bertolonii* DC.	timothy, turf
Agrostis capillaris L.	bentgrass, colonial		
Agrostis gigantea Roth	redtop		
Agrostis stolonifera L. var. *stolonifera*	bentgrass, creeping	*Poa annua* var. *annua* L.	bluegrass, annual
		Poa annua var. *reptans* (Hauuskn.) Timm.	bluegrass, creeping annual
Ammophila arenaria (L.) Link	beachgrass, European	*Poa arachnifera* Torrey	bluegrass, Texas
Ammophila breviligulata Fern.	beachgrass, American	*Poa compressa* L.	bluegrass, Canada
		Poa pratensis L.	bluegrass, Kentucky
		Poa trivialis L.	bluegrass, rough
Cynosurus cristatus L.	crested dog's tail		
		Pucccinellia distans (L.) Parl.	alkaligrass, weeping
Festuca arundinacea Schreber	fescue, tall		
Festuca longifolia Thuill.	fescue, hard	*Schizachyrium scoparium* (Michaux) Nash	bluestem, little
Festuca ovina L. var. *ovina*	fescue, sheep		
Festuca pratensis Hudson	fescue, meadow		
Festuca rubra L. subsp. *commutata* Gaudin	fescue, Chewing's	*Secale cereale* L.	rye
Festuca rubra subsp. L. *litoralis*	fescue, slender creeping red		
Festuca rubra L. subsp. *rubra*	fescue, strong creeping red	*Uniola paniculata* L.	sea-oats

APPENDIX TABLE 4
NOMENCLATURE SUMMARY FOR THE WARM-SEASON TURFGRASSES By Common Names

U.S. Common Name	Scientific Name	Other Common Name
bahiagrass	*Paspalum notatum* Fluegge	
bermudagrass, African	*Cynodon transvaalensis* Burtt Davy	
bermudagrass, dactylon	*Cynodon dactylon* (L). Pers. var. *C. dactylon*	couchgrass
bermudagrass, hybrid	*Cynodon dactylon* x *C. transvaalensis*	
buffalograss, American	*Buchloë dactyloides* (Nutt.) Engelm.	
buffelgrass	*Cenchrus ciliaris* L.	
carpetgrass, common	*Axonopus affinis* Chase	narrow-leaf carpetgrass
carpetgrass, tropical	*Axonopus compressus* (Sw.) P. Beau.	cowgrass
centipedegrass	*Eremochloa ophiuroides* (Munro) Hackel	
grama, blue	*Bouteloua gracilis* (Willd. ex Kunth) Lagasca ex Griffiths	
grama, side-oats	*Bouteloua curtipendula* (Michaux) Torrey	
kikuyugrass	*Pennisetum clandestinum* Hochst. ex Chiov.	
lovegrass, weeping	*Eragrostis curvula* (Schrader) Nees	
mesquite, curly	*Hilaria belangeri* (Steudel) Nash	
St. Augustinegrass	*Stenotaphrum secundatum* (Walter) Kuntze	buffalograss
seashore paspalum	*Paspalum vaginatum* Swartz	
serangoongrass	*Digitaria didactyla* Willd.	blue couchgrass
zoysiagrass, Japanese	*Zoysia japonica* Steudel	noshiba
zoysiagrass, manila	*Zoysia matrella* (L.) Merr.	korishiba, manilagrass
zoysiagrass, mascarene	*Zoysia tenuifolia* Willd. ex. Thiele	mascarenegrass

APPENDIX TABLE 5

NOMENCLATURE SUMMARY FOR THE WARM-SEASON TURFGRASSES By Scientific Names

Scientific Name	U.S. Common Name
Axonopus affinis Chase	carpetgrass, common
Axonopus compressus (Sw.) P. Beau.	carpetgrass, tropical
Bouteloua curtipendula (Michaux) Torrey	grama, side oats
Bouteloua gracilis (Willd. ex Kunth) Lagasca ex Griffiths	grama, blue
Buchloë dactyloides (Nutt.) Engelm.	buffalograss, American
Cenchrus ciliaris L.	buffelgrass
Cynodon dactylon (L). Pers. var. *C. dactylon*	bermudagrass, dactylon
Cynodon transvaalensis Burtt Davy	bermudagrass, African
Cynodon dactylon x *C. transvaalensis*	bermudagrass, hybrid
Digitaria didactyla Willd.	serangoongrass
Eragrostis curvula (Schrader) Nees	lovegrass, weeping
Eremochloa ophiuroides (Munro) Hackel	centipedegrass
Hilaria belangeri (Steudel) Nash	mesquite, curly
Paspalum notatum Fluegge	bahiagrass
Paspalum vaginatum Swartz	seashore paspalum
Pennisetum clandestinum Hochst. ex Chiov.	kikuyugrass
Stenotaphrum secundatum (Walter) Kuntze	St. Augustinegrass
Zoysia japonica Steudel	zoysiagrass, Japanese
Zoysia matrella (L.) Merr.	zoysiagrass, manila
Zoysia tenuifolia Willd. ex. Thiele	zoysiagrass, mascarene

APPENDIX TABLE 6
NOMENCLATURE SUMMARY FOR SOME FUNGICIDES USED ON TURFGRASS DISEASES IN SOME PARTS OF THE WORLD

Generic Name	Some Trade Name(s)	Chemical Name	Action	Toxicity Class	Signal Word
benomyl	Benlate	benzimidazole	systemic-foliar penetrant	IV	caution
captan	Captan	dicarboximide	contact	I	danger
chloroneb	Proturf Fungicide V, Teremec SP, Terraneb SP, Tersan SP	substituted aromatic hydrocarbon	contact/local systemic- foliar/seed	IV	caution
chlorothalonil	Daconil 2787, Manicure, Thalonil	substituted aromatic hydrocarbon	contact-foliar	I	danger
cyproconazole	Sentinel	triazole	systemic-foliar penetrant (DMI)	III	caution
etridiazole	Koban, Terrazole	thiadiazole	contact-soil	II - WP III - G	warning caution
fenarimol	Rubigan	pyrimidine	systemic-foliar penetrant (DMI)	II - EC III - WP	warning caution
flutolanil	Moncut, ProStar	benzanilide	systemic-foliar penetrant/seed	IV	caution
fosetyl-aluminum	Aliette, Prodigy	organophoshate	systemic-foliar penetrant	III	caution
guazatine	Kaskiman, Kenopel	aminated amine	contact-foliar/seed	II	warning
hymexazol	Tachigaren	hydroxy isoxazole	systemic-soil	III	caution
iprodione	Chipco 26019, Rovral, Scotts Fungicide X	dicarboximide	contact/local systemic-foliar	IV	caution
isoprothiolane	Fuji-One	dithiolan	systemic-foliar	III	caution

APPENDIX TABLE 6 (Continued)
NOMENCLATURE SUMMARY FOR SOME FUNGICIDES USED ON TURFGRASS DISEASES IN SOME PARTS OF THE WORLD

Generic Name	Some Trade Name(s)	Chemical Name	Action	Toxicity	Signal
mancozeb	Dithane M-45, FORE, Formec 80, Mancozeb, Manzate,	dithiocarbamate	contact-foliar	IV	caution
mepronil	Basitac, Cleangrass	toluanilide	systemic-foliar/seed/soil	IV	caution
metalaxyl	Proturf Pythium Control, Ridomil, Subdue	phenylamide	systemic-foliar, penetrant	III	warning
myclobutanil	Eagle, Rally	triazole	systemic-foliar penetrant (DMI)	I - 20E II - tech III - 40W	danger warning caution
oxytetracycline	Terramycin	antibiotic	systemic, foliar		
pencycuron	Monceren	phenylurea	contact-foliar	IV	caution
polyoxin	Polyoxin D	antibiotic	systemic-foliar	IV	caution
procymidone	Sumilex	dicarboximide	systemic-foliar	IV	caution
propamocarb hydrochloride	Banol, Previcur N	dithiocarbamate	local systemic-foliar/ seed/soil	IV	caution
propiconazole	Banner	triazole	contact/systemic -foliar penetrant (DMI)	III	caution
quintozene	PCNB, Penstar, Revere, Terraclor, Turfcide	substituted aromatic hydrocarbon	contact-soil	III	caution
terbuconazole	Lynx	triazole	systemic-seed	III	caution
thiophanate-ethyl	Cleary's 3336	benzimidazole	systemic- foliar penetrant	IV	caution

APPENDIX TABLE 6 (Continued)
NOMENCLATURE SUMMARY FOR SOME FUNGICIDES USED ON TURFGRASS DISEASES IN SOME PARTS OF THE WORLD

Generic Name	Some Trade Name(s)	Chemical Name	Action	Toxicity	Signal
thiophanate-methyl	Fungo 50, Proturf Systemic Fungicide, Topsin M	benzimidazole	systemic-foliar penetrant	IV	caution
thiram	Spotrete, Thiramad	dithiocarbamate	contact-foliar/soil	III	caution
tolclofos-methyl	Rizolex, Grancer	phosphorathiolate	contact-seed/soil	III	caution
triadimefon	Bayleton, Scotts Fungicide VII	triazole	contact/systemic-foliar penetrant (DMI)	III	caution
triflumizole	Trifmine	imidazole	systemic-foliar	I	danger
validamycin A	Validacin	antibiotic	systemic-foliar	IV	caution
vinclozolin	Curalan, Touché, Vorlan	dicarboximide	contact-foliar penetrant	IV	caution

Contact - or nonsystemic; is only active on leaf and sheath surfaces.

Systemic - is absorbed and can provide activity outside and inside of plant tissues.

DMI - demethylation (sterol) inhibitor group.

APPENDIX TABLE 7
HUMAN TOXICITY HAZARD SUMMARY

Toxicity Category	Signal Word	Oral LD$_{50}$ (mg/kg)	Probable Oral Lethal Dose for a 150 lb (68 kg) person	
I	Danger	up to 50	few drops to 1 tsp	0.03 to 0.6 ml
II	Warning	50 to 500	1 tsp to 1 oz	0.6 to 29.6 ml
III	Caution	500 to 5,000	1 oz to 1 pt (1 lb)	29.6 to 473 ml
IV	Caution	> 5,000	1 pt to 1 qt (2 lb)	473 to 946 ml

Glossary of Terms

acervulus—an erumpent, saucer-shaped, cushion-like fruiting body of a fungus bearing conidiophores, conidia, and sometimes setae.

agar—gelatin made from seaweed, used as a growth medium for fungi.

alternate host—one of two species of plants some fungi (e.g., rusts) need to complete their life cycle; host of lesser economic importance.

anamorph—the asexual or imperfect stage in the life cycle of a fungus.

antheridium—a male sexual organ found in some fungi.

antibiotic—a chemical usually of microbial origin, that inhibits or kills other organisms.

arthroconidium—a jointed conidium that is composed of more than one cell and that can become separated.

ascocarp—a sexual fruiting body of an ascomycetous fungus.

ascomycete—a fungus that produces sexual spores, termed ascospores, within an ascus.

ascospore—a spore produced within an ascus.

ascus—a sac-like structure within an ascocarp in which ascospores are borne.

aseptate—without cross walls.

asexual—vegetative; without sex organs, gametes, or sexual spores; imperfect.

avirulent—unable to cause disease; nonpathogenic.

basidiocarp—a sexual fruiting body of a basidiomycetous fungus.

basidiomycete—a fungus that forms sexual spores, termed basidiospores, on a basidium.

biological control—controlling a pest by its natural or introduced enemies.

blade, leaf—the expanded portion of a leaf; the flat portion of a grass leaf above the sheath.

bleached—white to straw-colored; used to describe areas of necrotic tissue.

blight—the general and rapid killing of leaves and stems from a single point of infection.

blotch—a large, irregularly shaped, superficial, straw-colored to brown discolored lesion.

bulbil—a sclerotium-like structure lacking a distinct rind layer.

chlamydospore—a thick-walled, asexual spore formed by modification of a hyphal or conidial cell.

chlorosis—the fading of green plant color to light green or yellow.

clamp connections—bridges around the septa of a hypha; taken as evidence that the fungus is related to the basidiomycetes.

clippings—the leaves and, in some cases, stems cut off by mowing.

conidiophore—hypha that are differentiated to bear conidia.

conidium—any asexual spore, except for sporangiospores or chlamydospores.

cool-season turfgrass—turfgrass species best adapted to growth during cool, moist periods of the year; commonly having temperature optimums of 60 to 75°F (15 to 24°C).

crown—that portion of the grass plant which includes the stem apex, the unelongated internodes, and the lower nodes from which adventitious roots are initiated.

culm—a jointed, usually hollow stem, not including the leaves; the jointed stem of grasses.

cultivar—a plant of a single species that differs from another in specific characteristics such as leaf width and disease resistance.

cultivation, turf—working of the soil without destruction of the turf; e.g., coring, slicing, grooving, forking, spiking, shattering and water injection.

cutting height—of a mower, the distance between the plane of travel (base of wheel, roller, or skid) and the parallel plane of cut.

damping off—the rapid, lethal decline of germinating seed or seedlings before or after emergence.

decline—the reduced vigor of perennial plantings as a result of chronic symptoms of disease or environmental stress.

dieback—the progressive death of leaves, stems, or roots, from the tips back.

disease complex—a disease resulting from combined or sequential actions of two or more biotic or abiotic agents.

disease cycle—the chain of events involved in disease development.

dissemination—the transfer of inoculum from one area or source to another.

dormant—resting; living in a state of reduced physiological activity.

echinulate—having spines or other sharp projections.

ectoparasite—a parasitic organism that lives outside its host.

ectotrophic—describing a fungus that makes substantial growth along the surface of roots.

endogenous—coming or developing from within.

endoparasite—a parasitic organism that lives within its host.

endophyte—a plant growing within another plant; as a fungus in a higher plant.

erumpent—bursting or erupting through the surface.

exudate—that which is excreted or discharged.

facultative parasite—an organism that is normally self-dependent, but that is adaptable to a parasitic mode of life.

facultative saprophyte—an organism that is normally a parasite, but that is adaptable to a saprophytic mode.

filamentous—threadlike.

fleck—a minute spot.

flock—a cotton-like tuft.

foliar—pertaining to leaves.

fruiting body—a complex sporulating fungal structure.

fumigant—a vapor-active chemical used against microorganisms and other pests.

gene—the smallest functional unit of genetic material on a chromosome; a unit of inheritance.

genus—the taxonomic category ranking above species and below family; the generic name of an organism is the first word of the binomial.

germinate—to begin growth, as for a seed or spore.

germ tube—hypha resulting from an outgrowth of the spore wall and/or cytoplasm.

guttation—the exudation of water from stomates or hydathodes.

haustorium—a specialized hypha of a fungus within penetrated host cells that probably functions in food absorption.

host—a plant that is invaded by a parasite, from which the parasite obtains its nutrients and on which it reproduces.

hyaline—clear, translucent.

hybrid—the progeny resulting from a cross of individuals that differ in one or more heritable characters.

hydathode—an epidermal structure specialized for secretion or exudation of water, nutrients, and organic compounds.

hymenium—the spore-bearing, sporogenous layer of a fungal fruiting body.

hypha—the tubular filament of a fungal thallus or mycelium.

hyphopodium—the hypha of an epiphytic fungus that is specialized, usually flattened, for host attachment or penetration.

immune—not affected by or responsive to disease.

imperfect—the asexual portion of a fungal life cycle; *see* anamorph.

infect—to invade or penetrate as an initial phase of disease development.

infection court—the site in or on a host plant where infection can occur.

infection peg—a small, hyphal protrusion that penetrates the host cell wall.

infest—to contaminate, as with organisms.

inflorescence—the flowering part of a plant.

injury—damage to a plant by a biotic, physical, or chemical agent.

inoculate—to place inoculum in or on an infection court of a host plant.

inoculum—a pathogen or its parts that is brought into contact with a host.

isolate—a separated or confined spore or microbial culture.

lateral shoot—shoots originating from vegetative buds in the axils of leaves or from the nodes of stems, rhizomes, or stolons.

leaf—one of the lateral outgrowths of a stem; produced in definite succession from the stem apex.

leaf spot—a self-limiting lesion on a leaf.

lesion—a wound or delimited diseased area.

life cycle—stages in the growth and development of an organism that occur until the reappearance of the first stage.

mat—thatch intermixed with mineral matter that develops between the zone of green vegetation and the original soil surface; commonly associated with greens that have been topdressed.

medulla—the central part of an organ or tissue, as in a sclerotium.

meristem—plant tissue that functions principally in cell division and differentiation.

microflora—a composite of microscopic plants.

MLO—mycoplasma-like organism.

mold—any profuse fungal growth.

monoclinous—having gametangium and oogonium originating from the same hypha.

monocotyledon—a plant whose embryo has one cotyledon; e.g., grasses.

morphology—the study of form and structure.

mosaic—a disease symptom comprised of mixed green, light-green, and yellow patches.

mottle—a disease symptom comprised of light and dark areas in an irregular pattern.

multiple infection—to be invaded by more than one parasite.

multiseptate—having many septa.

mycelium—a mass of hyphae that comprises the thallus or body of a fungus.

mycoplasma—a procaryotic organism, smaller than conventional bacteria, without rigid cell walls, and variable in shape.

mycorrhiza—the association or resting structure of a symbiotic or nonpathogenic fungus in the roots of higher plants.

myxomycete—a fungus characterized by a multinucleate, motile mass of protoplasm.

necrosis—death, which is usually accompanied by darkening or discoloration.

node—a joint or enlarged area where leaves, roots, or branches of stems arise.

nonpersistent—dissipating; said of viruses that are infectious within insect vectors for short periods and are transmissible without a latent period and without prior multiplication and translocation within the vector.

nonseptate—without cross-walls.

obligate parasite—an organism that can survive only on or in living tissues.

obligate saprophyte—an organism that is limited to a saprophytic mode of life.

oogonium—a female gametangium of some oomycetes, containing one or more gametes.

oomycete—a fungus that produces oospores.

oospore—a thick-walled, sexually or asexually derived resting spore of oomycetous fungi.

oral toxicity—the degree of toxicity of a compound when it is ingested.

ostiole—pore; opening of a perithecium or pycnidium.

overwinter—to survive over the winter period.

parasite—an organism that lives with, in, or on another organism for its own advantage.

parts per million (ppm)—the number of parts by weight or volume of a given compound in one million parts of the final mixture.

patch—a distinctly delimited, somewhat circular area of plants in which most or all are affected by disease.

pathogen—an agent that causes disease.

pathogenesis—the sequence of processes in disease development from the initial contact between a pathogen and its host to completion of the syndrome.

pathogenicity—the ability to cause disease.

perfect—sexual; fungi capable of sexual reproduction; *see* teleomorph.

perithecium—a flask-like ascocarp with an ostiole-like opening.

persistent—pertaining to viruses that are infectious within insect vectors for long periods.

phycomycete—one of a group of fungi whose mycelium has no cross walls.

phytotoxic—harmful to plants.

plasmodium—a motile multinucleate mass of protoplasm resulting from the fusion of uninucleate amoeboid cells.

primary inoculum—inoculum that initiates, rather than spreads or magnifies, disease.

propagule—any part of an organism capable of independent growth.

protectant—an agent, usually a chemical, that prevents or inhibits infection.

pseudothecium—a perithecium-like ascocarp with a dispersed rather than an organized hymenium.

pustule—blister-like, usually erumpent, spot or sorus.

race—a group of individuals within a species distinguished by behavior, but not by morphology.

reestablishment, turf—a procedure involving (a) complete turf removal, (b) soil tillage, and (c) seeding or vegetative establishment of new turf; does not encompass rebuilding.

renovation, turf—improvement usually involving weed control and replanting into existing live and/or dead vegetation; does not encompass reestablishment.

resistance—the property of hosts that prevents or impedes disease development.

resting spore—a temporarily dormant, usually thick-walled spore.

rhizome—a jointed, underground stem that can produce roots and shoots at each node; may originate from the main stem or from tillers.

rhizosphere—the microenvironment in soil influenced by plant roots.

rind—outer layer.

rot—the softening and disintegration of succulent plant tissue as a result of fungal or bacterial infection.

runner hyphae—thickened hyphal strands.

saprophyte—an organism that uses nonliving organic matter as food.

scald, turf—injury to shoots standing in relatively shallow water; which collapse and turn brown if sun heats the water to lethal temperatures.

sclerotium—a hard, usually darkened and rounded mass of dormant hyphae with differentiated rind and medulla.

secondary inoculum—inoculum resulting from primary infections.

septum—cross-wall.

seta—a stiff, hair-like appendage.

sheath, leaf—the basal tubular portion of a leaf surrounding the stem.

shoot density—the number of grass shoots per unit area.

sign—the indication of disease from direct visibility of the pathogen or its parts.

sod—plugs or strips of turfgrass with adhering soil used in vegetative planting.

soil fumigant—a compound that kills most organisms in the soil by vapor action, usually permitting replanting soon after, e.g., metam-sodium or methyl bromide.

soil modification—the alteration of soil characteristics by the addition of physical amendments; commonly used to improve physical conditions of turf soils.

sorus—a compact fruiting structure of rust and smut fungi.

species (sp.)—a group of individuals similar in structure and physiology, and capable of interbreeding to produce fertile offspring which are like the parents.

sporangium—a flask-like fungal structure whose contents differentiate into asexual spores.

spore—a one to many-celled reproductive body in fungi and lower plants.

sporulate—to produce spores.

spot—a limited, chlorotic or necrotic, circular to oval area on leaves or other plant parts.

sprig—a stolon, rhizome, tiller, or combination used to establish turf.

sterile—infertile; free from contaminant organisms.

stippling—an abundance of specks.

stolon—a jointed, aboveground, creeping stem that can produce roots and shoots at each node and may originate extravaginally from the main stem of tillers.

stoma or stomate—a regulated opening in the plant epidermis for passage of gases and water vapor.

strain—the descendants of an isolated organism; biotype; race.

streak—a necrosis along vascular bundles in leaves or stems of grasses.

striated—marked with lines, grooves, or ridges.

stripe—the necrosis of tissue between vascular bundles in leaves or stems of grasses.

stroma—a compact mass of mycelium, with or without host tissue, that supports fruiting bodies.

substrate—a substance on which organisms grow.

susceptible—not immune; lacking resistance; prone to infection.

symptom—an indication of disease by the reaction of the host.

syn.—synonym(s).

synergistic—pertaining to a host response to concurrent pathogens that exceeds the sum of the separate responses to each pathogen.

systemic—pertaining to chemicals or pathogens that spread throughout plants, as opposed to remaining localized.

teleomorph—the sexual or perfect stage in the life of a fungus.

teliospore—a thick-walled resting spore of rust fungi that germinates to form a basidium.

thallus—a fungus body.

thatch—an intermingled organic layer of dead and living shoots, stems, and roots that develops between the zone of green vegetation and the soil surface.

tiller—the shoot of a grass plant originating intravaginally in the axis of a leaf in the unelongated portion of a stem.

tolerant—sustaining disease without serious damage.

topdressing—a prepared soil mix added to a turf surface and usually physically worked-in by matting, raking, and/or irrigating to smooth a surface.

transmission—the spread of virus or other pathogens from plant to plant.

turf—a covering of mowed vegetation, usually a turfgrass, growing intimately with an upper soil stratum of intermingled roots and stems.

turfgrass—a species or cultivar of grass, usually of spreading habit, which is maintained as a mowed turf.

turfgrass culture—the composite cultural practices involved in growing turfgrasses for purposes such as lawns, greens, sports facilities, and roadsides.

turfgrass management—the development of turf standards and goals which are achieved by planning and directing labor, capital, and equipment with the objective of manipulating cultural practices to achieve those standards and goals.

turfgrass quality—the degree to which a turf conforms to an agreed standard of uniformity, density, texture, growth habit, smoothness, and color, as judged by subjective visual assessment.

urediniospore—a binucleate, dikaryotic, asexual rust spore.

uredinium—the fruiting body, or sorus, of rust fungi that produce urediniospores.

variety—a division of species.

vector—an agent that transmits inoculum.

vertical cutting—involves a mechanical device having vertically rotating blades that cut into the face of a turf for the purpose of controlling thatch or grain.

virulence—the degree of pathogenicity; capacity to cause disease.

warm-season turfgrass—turfgrass species best adapted to growth during the warmer part of the year; usually dormant during cold weather or injured by it; commonly having temperature optimum of 80 to 95°F (27 to 35°C).

water-soaked—pertaining to plants or lesions that appear wet, dark, and usually sunken and translucent.

wear—the collective direct injurious effects of traffic on a turf; is distinct from the indirect effects of traffic caused by soil compaction.

wilt—the loss of turgidity and dropping of plant parts caused by a water deficit in the plant.

winter desiccation—the death of leaves or plants by drying during winter dormancy.

winter overseeding—the seeding of cool-season turfgrasses onto warm-season turfgrasses at or near their start of winter dormancy; used in mild climates to provide green, growing turf during the winter period when the warm-season species are brown and dormant.

yellows—a disease symptom characterized by yellowing and stunting of the host plant.

zonate—target-like; appearing in concentric rings.

zoospore—a flagellated fungal spore capable of locomotion in water.

Index

A

Agaricus campestris, 173–180
anthracnose, 147–149

B

bacterial wilt, 189–190
bermudagrass decline, 64–65
binucleate *Rhizoctonia* AG-D (I), 27–29, 87–89, 219
binucleate *Rhizoctonia* AG-D (II), 41–44, 220
Bipolaris cynodontis, 77–79
Bipolaris leaf blotch, 77–79
Bipolaris leaf spot, 152–153
Bipolaris sorokiniana, 152–153
brown blight, 151

C

Chlorophyllum molybdites, 173–181
Clavaria species, 183–186
Clitocybe species, 183–186
Colletotrichum graminicola, 147–149, 214, 224
Collybia species, 173–182
contact fungicide, 17
Coprinus kubickae, 183–186
crown rust, 159–161
Curvularia geniculata, 68–71
Curvularia leaf blight, 68–71, 212, 213, 223
Curvularia lunata, 68–71
Curvularia lunata var. *aeria,* 68–71
Curvularia verruculosa, 68–71

D

disease diagnosis, 198–225
dog footprint, 68–71
dollar spot, 22, 72–74, 141–146, 200, 205
downy mildew, 168–169
Drechslera diseases, 150
Drechslera dictyoides, 155–156
Drechslera erythrospila, 150
Drechslera gigantea, 150
Drechslera poae, 154–155, 213
Drechslera siccans, 155

E

elephant footprint, 41–44
Erysiphe graminis, 157–158, 214

F

facultative parasite, 10–11
facultative saprophyte, 10
fairy ring, 173–182
flag smut, 162
foliar attacking pathogens, 198
Fusarium acuminatum, 58–60, 111–114, 212, 222
Fusarium avenaceum, 111–114
Fusarium blight, 58–60, 111–114, 205
Fusarium culmorum, 112
Fusarium oxysporum, 111–114
Fusarium poae, 112
Fusarium tricinctum, 111–114

G

Gaeumannomyces graminis var. *avenae,* 115–118, 215
Gaeumannomyces graminis var. *graminis,* 61–66, 215, 222
gray leaf spot, 170–172
gray snow mold, 128–131

Pythium ultimum, 99–103
Pythium vanterpoolii, 21, 46–52, 91–103, 200, 211, 221
Pythium yellow spot, 109–111

R

red leaf spot , 150, 200
red thread, 135–138
Rhizoctonia brown patch, 16, 83-86, 200
Rhizoctonia circinata var. *circinata*, 90–91, 220
Rhizoctonia diseases, 26, 82, 209
Rhizoctonia patch, 41–44
Rhizoctonia solani AG-2-2(LP) 30–40, 220
Rhizoctonia solani AG(I), 16, 83–86, 200,
Rhizoctonia solani AG-2-2(IIIB), 16, 83–86, 200, 220
Rhizoctonia spring dead spot, 27–29
root attacking pathogens, 198
rust diseases, 159, 216

S

SAD, 194–195
Scleroderma species, 173–182
Sclerophthora macrospora, 168–169
Sclerotinia homoeocarpa, 22, 72–74, 141–146, 200, 205, 223
slime mold, 187–188
smuts, 162–163
snow molds, 187–188
snow scald, 133–134
St. Augustine decline, 194–195
stem rust, 159–161
stripe leaf roll, 194–196
stripe rust, 159–161
stripe smut, 162–163
summer patch, 119–121
superficial fairy ring, 183–186

T

take-all patch, 115–118
Trechispora alnicola, 183–186
Trechispora cohaerens, 183–186

Trechispora farinacea, 183–186
Tricholoma sordidum, 173–182
Typhula blights, 128–131
Typhula incarnata, 128–131, 224
Typhula ishikariensis, 128–131

U

Urocystis agropyri, 162
Uromyces dactylidis, 159–161
Ustilago striiformis, 162–163

W

Wheat mottle dwarf virus, 194–196, 218
white blight, 183–186
white leaf, 191–193
white patch, 87–89
WMDV, 194–196, 218

X

Xanthomonas campestris pathovar, 189–190. 217

Y

yellow dwarf , 191–193
yellow patch, 87–89
yellow ring, 183–186
yellow tuft, 168–169

Z

ZMV, 194–196
zonate leaf spot, 150
zoysia decline, 61–63
zoysia dwarf virus, 194–196
zoysia mosaic virus, 194–196
zoysia Pythium blight, 56–57
zoysia rust, 75–76